INTERPROFESSIONAL COLLABORATION IN SCHOOLS

Mark P. Mostert
Moorhead State University

Allyn and Bacon
Boston • London • Toronto • Sydney • Tokyo • Singapore

Senior Editor: Ray Short
Marketing Manager: Kathy Hunter
Production Coordinator: Holly Crawford
Editorial-Production Service: Connie Leavitt, Bookwrights
Composition Buyer: Linda Cox
Manufacturing Buyer: Suzanne Lareau
Cover Administrator: Jenny Hart

Library of Congress Cataloging-in-Publication Data

Mostert, Mark P.
    Interprofessional collaboration in schools / Mark P. Mostert.
        p. cm.
    Includes bibliographical references and index.
    ISBN 0-205-16689-X
    1. Handicapped students—Education—United States—Case studies.
2. Interpersonal relations—United States—Case studies. 3. Home
and school—United States—Case studies. 4. Community and school—
United States—Case studies. 5. Special education teachers—
Training of—United States. I. Title.
LC4031.M68 1998
371.9′0973—dc21   97-36026
                                                                                  CIP

Printed in the United States of America
10 9 8 7 6 5 4 3 2 1   02 01 00 99 98 97

Contents

Preface

Teacher educators are acutely aware of the difficulties preservice professionals sometimes encounter in translating their university coursework into practical teaching behavior in the schools. Not surprisingly, student teachers commonly attach high regard to their field experiences where they perceive they learn much more of what it's like "in the real world" than they were taught in the university classroom. Indeed, field experiences provide a context in which teaching decisions are complex, public, situationally dependent, and, in many instances, quite uncertain—that is, field experiences allow learning *in situ*. These experiences subject preservice and novice teachers to circumstances that, by their very nature, stimulate both failure and success, ultimately allowing for the construction of referential cognitive frameworks, which enable more effective future teaching performance.

For a host of very legitimate reasons, many college textbooks tend to be more theoretical than practical and may be partially responsible for student teachers' feeling somewhat unprepared for the many pitfalls of field experiences. Equally, it is quite common to find university instructors who teach their students without the benefit of having been teachers themselves, thereby exacerbating the divide between intellectually theoretical notions of education and the often commonsense applications of that theory which, to most teachers, at least in their initial experience, are more valuable.

While collaborative skill with colleagues, parents, and families is imperative in today's schools, only recently have some preservice teacher education programs begun to address this area through formal coursework. This book is an attempt to provide a practical reference for interprofessional collaboration for preservice teachers. The brief chapters provide an overview of the general background that influences interprofessional collaboration, the broad nature of collaboration, how collaboration occurs in the context of teaching, a summary of the advantages and disadvantages of collaborative approaches, and a host of practical hints related to professional behavior in collaborative settings. This book emphasizes the necessity of learning, practicing, automatizing, and constantly reflecting on and improving inter-professional collaborative skill. To enhance readability and to emphasize the practical nature of the content, the writing style of the text is informal. Thus, a representative reference list is provided at the end of each chapter rather than in-text. Reflection questions at the end of each chapter challenge students to react not only to the content of the chapter, but also to how the content might usefully translate into their own attitudes and approaches to teaching.

The chapters also serve as a backdrop for discussion of the fifteen teaching cases. The cases present a variety of common problematic situations, many of which teachers are likely to encounter early in their careers. The cases were constructed from interviews with classroom teachers willing to share their collaborative experiences. Each case, by definition multidimensional and inherently either simple or complex, depending on the instructor's teaching objectives, can be presented from a variety of perspectives and in more or less detail. The Instructor's Manual provides a discussion of case-based teaching, a list of references related to teaching with cases, and instructor aids to teaching each individual case.

Many people have willingly given of their time and effort to produce this book. My deep appreciation is, first and foremost, to the teachers who told me their stories: Linda, Carol, Eva, Alana, Janice, Karl, Martha, and Kent. In addition, my sincere thanks to Mary Sudzina, University of Dayton, who practices her professional life in the truest spirit of collaboration and whose support of my work is deeply appreciated. I also gratefully acknowledge the help of those who reviewed the book for Allyn and Bacon: Linda Hargrove, Ball State University; Sandra Lloyd, University of Texas–El Paso; and Ellen Williams, Bowling Green State University.

Finally, a debt of appreciation to Jude Hall of Allyn and Bacon who first suggested this project, to Ray Short, my Allyn and Bacon editor, and to Christine Svitila, also of Allyn and Bacon, without whose guidance and patience this task would have been quite impossible.

M.P.M.

1

Introduction to Interprofessional Collaboration

Overview of Interprofessional Collaboration

Working with other people to achieve a common professional goal is difficult work—difficult, but not impossible. While independent professional decision making is still viewed as important and necessary, many professions have simultaneously come to value the process and results of collaboration for professional action. Outside the helping professions, from giant corporations

1

with vast bureaucracies to small businesses and local nonprofit organizations, the trend toward communal decision making through teamwork and consensus for professional action is now commonly accepted as desirable professional behavior.

Teachers make hundreds of decisions alone in their classrooms each day, and have historically been trained to act autonomously. The autonomous nature of professional work in schools has traditionally resulted in teachers and other school professionals being somewhat isolated from each other for much of their time at work. Equally, while competent interprofessional collaboration has always been a distinguishing characteristic of effective teachers, collaborative skill has not generally been the centerpiece of teacher training. More recently, however, the stereotypical image of individual teachers as the ultimate and only authority for decisions about the children they teach has given way to increased awareness for shared decision making. More than ever before, the need for collaboration has increased the need for all teachers and other professionals, whatever their level of experience or expertise, to acquire group decision-making skills.

Many forces have shaped, and continue to shape, this fundamental shift. The renewed emphasis on professional teamwork in education, especially interprofessional collaboration, arose out of a complex set of factors that have radically changed the expectations of teacher performance. A working knowledge of these factors will increase your professional effectiveness as you work with parents and families, many of whom cannot be expected to possess the knowledge of this historic context.

Major Influences on Interprofessional Collaboration in Education

For most general purposes, collaboration can be defined as a mutual effort among and between professionals, parents, and families to deliver appropriately effective interventions to children for each child's increased physical, emotional, and academic well-being. Among a host of historically influential factors leading to increased interprofessional collaboration are several major aspects, which are discussed next. In considering your professional role as collaborator with colleagues, parents, and families, you should understand some basic historical aspects of how collaboration became a central theme in school life through three streams of influence: social change, legal precedent, and educational change.

Historical Aspects

In the 1950s, mental health services to schoolchildren shifted into schools, and school psychologists began to fill an effective consultative function. As school psychology and counseling became a frequently accepted, functional part of education, the need for effective collaborative relationships among other helping professions, teachers, administrators, and other educational staff became clear. By the mid-1960s, many schools had informal collaborative networks among various professionals and school service personnel. Beginning in the 1970s, collaboration became more formalized as the need for a wide range of professional services for meeting students' needs became more apparent. Simultaneously, a host of factors in education and special education modified not only the manner of service delivery to children and adolescents, but also dictated a change in the way professionals worked together. Factors influencing this change can generally be classified as social, legal, and educational.

Social Changes

The vast societal upheaval of the 1960s culminated in significant debates about the purpose of public education and other services provided for children in public schools. These changes in social perception redefined both educational methods and teacher training. These changes also emphasized the need for more effective educational services for all students, especially for students perceived as historically underserved, such as students who are poor and students with disabilities.

A major outcome of this social attitudinal change was an increase in federal and state funding and in mandates for educational compensatory services to give all students in public schools maximum advantage for academic success. Compensatory programs have continued to grow in size and influence over the past two decades as professionals have emphasized the importance of a wide variety of services not only to address the diverse needs of the individual child in school, but also the needs of the family and the community, generally perceived as the most important support systems for children outside of school. This consistent expansion of services has gradually required a growing circle of interrelated helping professionals who, by force of circumstance, if for no other reason, have been required to work more closely together to provide comprehensive federally and state-mandated services to children in public schools.

In addition, public education has reflected a marked demographic shift in the last twenty years to a much more diversified public school population.

Minority populations have increased significantly as a proportion of school-going children, as have the numbers of students with special needs. Furthermore, school populations in most large urban areas and many rural areas now face educational and service impediments not experienced by previous generations. For example, many indicators of social change such as teen pregnancy, illiteracy, and behavioral problems are on the increase in almost all sectors of the school population.

Socioeconomically, the configuration of the family has also changed drastically in the last twenty years. Many more two-parent households have both parents fully employed and with the sharp increase in the number of single-parent families, children are much more likely to be unsupervised and have a lower standard of living than in the recent past. These societal changes have also resulted in an increased number of students being designated as at risk for school failure and other social problems. As the population of public school children has grown over the last thirty years, so has the proportion of children needing special educational, psychological, and other forms of assistance. These and other social changes have influenced both legal and educational shifts which, in turn, have shaped educators' perceptions of interprofessional collaboration.

Legal Precedent

A major influence shaping the ideas and professional behavior we know today as collaboration has been legislation and litigation determining the types of services available to students in public schools. A significant goal of this legislation and litigation was to assure education for those who had previously been excluded from educational and other helping services. This legislation also described, in broad terms, professional roles and functions that encouraged increased coordination of educational services to ensure appropriate educational interventions with students. While a detailed discussion of legal precedent and practice is beyond the scope of this book, it is important to note that effective professionals understand and practice under the major legal mandates that affect their field.

Professional collaboration in education is most heavily influenced by several mandates including the initial landmark legislation of PL 93–112, *The Rehabilitation Act*—section 504 (1973), which required that institutions receiving federal funding not discriminate against persons with disabilities. Other significant federal laws, ratified in spirit and intent by the states, included PL 94–142, *The Education for All Handicapped Children Act*—EHA (1975), which indicated some explicit expectations that professionals work together as a team to decide on effective interventions for students with special needs from five to eighteen years of age. Among EHA's most important provisions were stipulations that schools were to provide a full range of services to special needs children, that helping professionals were to preserve the spirit and intent of due process—especially by ensuring that parents or guardians participated in and were informed about educational decisions—that clear procedures were followed demonstrating the student's placement in the least restrictive environment, and that all professionals involved in service delivery of effective interventions develop and monitor Individual Education Plans (IEPs) based on nondiscriminatory testing procedures.

PL 99–457, *Amendments to EHA (1986),* followed EHA and included several provisions that strengthened professional collaboration by focusing on services to younger children. These services were mandated for three to five year olds. PL 99–457 also provided incentives for states to provide services for children from birth to three years. Another major provision of this amendment was stipulation for an early childhood version of the IEP, known as the Individualized Family Services Plan (IFSP).

Two important laws were passed in 1990. The first was PL 101–476, *The Individuals with Disabilities Education Act*—IDEA (1990), which renamed and expanded PL 94–142. IDEA stipulated increased collaboration among related services personnel especially for transition services for students in secondary school who were preparing for the move from school to work. The amendment further stipulated two new categories of special needs individuals (traumatic brain injury and autism) and expanded the definition of related services to include rehabilitation counseling and social work services. The second mandate was PL 101–336, *The Americans with Disabilities Act*—ADA (1990), which extended protection for people with disabilities into the private sector through civil rights statutes and stipulating, for example, that businesses employing fifteen or more people, public transportation, and all newly constructed facilities be made accessible for persons with disabilities.

Generally, federal and state legislation has highlighted several key aspects of services to persons with special needs, including *the right to education,* whereby all children, irrespective of their disability, have a right to public education; *a zero reject philosophy,* whereby public schools cannot turn away students because of any special needs they might have; *a least restrictive environment,* specifying education in a setting as close as possible to a general education class setting and simultaneously as far from a general education class as necessary for effective education; *parental involvement* in any and all education decisions for referral, evaluation and assessment, placement, and instruction in special settings; *due process* whereby students' parents or guardians or the school are bound by rules regarding placement decisions, information sharing, and the right of appeal; *protection from discriminatory evaluation or assessment practices* for placement in any special education setting; and *Individual Education Plans,* which detail, among other provisions, these important instructional safeguards: the extent of students' participation in general education, modifications to the general education program, the role and function of all professionals involved in service delivery, comprehensive details of intervention implementation, a timeline for the delivery of services, and a plan of accountability. Clearly, given these legal stipulations, competent professionals are required to work together with other service providers for the good of each student. Social and legal influences have, predictably, led to making changes in education.

Educational Changes

Given the far-reaching dimensions of the above mentioned social and legal events, the 1970s and 1980s produced a sharp focus on the mission and functions of public education. For example, several national reports on the status of schools and teaching appeared in short order, beginning with an assessment of the shortfalls of public education known as *A Nation at Risk: The Imperative for Educational Reform* (1983). Other reports followed, such as *Making the Grade: Educating Americans for the 21st Century* (1983), which highlighted the country's apparent inability to educate students for responsible citizenry and the workplace. *Making the Grade* clearly reflected the need to prepare students for a workplace revolutionized by advances in technology. These reports, in turn, provoked responses, such as the report by the U.S. Department of Education (*The Nation Responds: Recent Efforts to Improve Education,* 1984) and replies from various educational think tanks such as *Reaching for Excellence: An Effective Schools Sourcebook* (1985).

The overall aim of these policy reports was to evaluate the current state of public education and to stimulate national debate on how to improve it. Efforts were initiated at the national, state, and local levels to strengthen educational standards through revised curricula; more rigorous promotion and graduation requirements; increased accountability at the state, district, and individual school levels; and other similar initiatives to strengthen standards for teacher performance.

These reports spurred renewed debate about the role and responsibilities of all helping professionals in the schools and were precipitated by a growing awareness among professionals at all levels that student needs appeared to be more complex and severe than at any time in the nation's educational past. Simultaneously, the national debate was fueled by the public's demand for increased educational accountability to taxpayers and by media coverage of supposed educational failure in public school systems across the country. The calls for reform were heightened by a decreasing tax base for education and by the political and social imperative that education do more with the money allocated, or, preferably, do a better job for less. Generally, the public at large seemed unsupportive of teachers' complex jobs or teachers' concerns for a public education system that appeared to be substandard. Other issues added to the "do more with less" mentality. In special education, teacher shortages existed in most exceptionalities, especially the mild handicapping categories of mental retardation, learning disabilities, and emotional and behavioral disturbances. Most often, the shortages were seen as the result of poor working conditions, overwhelming workloads, and the demands of meeting students' special needs.

Other powerful factors were also at work, all of which would increase the potential, opportunity, and necessity of interprofessional collaboration as educators attempted to respond to the various critiques of their mission and its effectiveness. For example, teacher educators responded by examining and increasing standards of professional behavior and accountability for both collaboration and independent decision making. They also emphasized the need for more teacher reflection for effective action, especially as it related to classroom management, problem solving, and increased contact with other professionals and parents. The teacher preparation programs at many universities and colleges examined innovative ways of allowing teachers to be more autonomous and creative in teaching the curriculum.

Growing awareness of the need for more collaboration was not isolated in teacher training institutions, however. School districts also became more aware of their place in the community and renewed outreach efforts to parents and local organizations and agencies. Changes were also visible at the level of the individual school where states and school districts allowed building principals more leeway and authority for on-site decision making. Borrowing principles from management and industry, schools began to emphasize shared ownership and collective decision making and responsibility over the more traditional image of the teacher as the isolated, classroom-bound professional, an image still very familiar to the public. In many instances, educators examined the collaborative practices of the business world and sought to adapt some industrial collaborative strategies to school settings. In addition, a renewed emphasis was placed on participatory and site-based management as well as increased attention to teacher empowerment for on-site decision making without unnecessary bureaucratic constraints. These and other changes heralded a distinct decentralization of power, authority, and decision making to individual districts and schools rather than maintaining such authority at the federal or state levels.

In terms of public schools' responses to the students they served, research on teaching has continued to raise and address issues of instruction, service delivery, and collaboration in the context of social change, legal precedent, and educational considerations. Innovative forms of instruction—such as peer tutoring, direct instruction, and cooperative learning—coupled with a renewed emphasis on teaching across the curriculum, all impacted by significant increases in the use of computer technology, have made increased demands on teachers' skills and creativity.

Other changes impacting schools have also indicated the need for increased professional collaboration. As schools have recognized the need to attend to educational problems earlier in students' lives, formalized efforts to identify students at risk for school failure have increased. Educators have come to realize that waiting to attempt to reach students until after they have entered school meant that, for many students, problems were already well established and therefore more difficult to solve. To remedy this situation, the continuum of services—through federal legislation and funding—was increased downward to birth. In addition, early childhood education received priority in research and program funding over the last several years in the hopes of establishing more effective intervention programs. Such programs generally require a wider range of professional specialties and expertise to address the complex problems these students present.

Another important influence for increased collaboration involved significant advances in medical research and technology as well as behavioral and management techniques. These have allowed more infants and young children who previously would not have lived long enough to be enrolled in educational programs. More children with complex medical problems—such as HIV, Fragile X Syndrome, Fetal Alcohol Syndrome, and other better known conditions, such as severe cerebral palsy, mental retardation, and autism—are now enrolled in public schools than ever before. Addressing the needs of these children in the classroom has meant incorporating an even wider group of specialists for effective schooling.

On the opposite end of the developmental continuum, it became clear that many students, even after the best efforts of the education system, were ill prepared for their lives after school in terms of living, job, and social skills that would help them become productive members of their communities. These students needed a completely different set of professional supports in making their transition from school to work. As in the case of early childhood education, the variety of professionals needed for these services increased and became a much more familiar part of the services offered by public education.

Along with the general increase of attention to students' needs, a major justification for increased professional collaboration was precipitated by a shift to include students with disabilities, previously placed in special education classrooms, in general education settings. Special educators, well aware of the rhetoric accompanying reform debates in regular education, became embroiled in controversial reform issues such as the efficacy of their professional practices, the dilemmas of mainstreaming, and the legitimacy of special education as a viable alternative for educating students with mild, moderate, and even severe handicaps. This last issue quickly became embodied in the umbrella debate known as the Regular Education Initiative (REI). Essentially, most REI advocates called for a radical restructuring of the special education system, including some who advocated for a complete dismantling of special education. The REI is undergirded by assumptions which generally hold, for example, that children with special needs can be accommodated and taught effectively in regular classes, that effective teaching strategies work irrespective of specific educational problems students may exhibit, and that different teacher training for special and regular educators is artificial, unnecessary, and costly.

Retreating from twenty years of mandated special services, and the historical failure of general education to meet the needs of students with disabilities, the momentum of the REI (later to be foundational to the inclusion movement) contended that special education settings for most or all students with disabilities were discriminatory and ineffective. The inclusion movement has succeeded, largely without empirical support and by aggressively placing many special education students in general education, in creating an immediate need for greatly increased collaboration between general and special education teachers.

Generally, therefore, public education has seen an increased focus on the growing needs of students across all grades and the resulting mobilization of a much wider span of professionals to meet these needs. Not only have these trends meant use of a greater variety of specialties across the helping professions, but they have also increased the need for *coordination* of professional efforts to ensure appropriate, effective, and unwasted intervention for maximum effectiveness. Such meticulous execution of professional energy requires exceptional collaborative skill of all professionals involved and especially of teachers, who, in their classrooms, are likely to be responsible for students with a much wider range of educational, intellectual, behavioral, psychological, and social strengths and weaknesses.

These factors have led educators to make interprofessional collaboration a primary focus of teacher preparation and practical behavior. In order for such preparation to be effective, however, it is necessary to define interprofessional collaboration and its underlying tenets. A working definition of interprofessional collaboration with colleagues, parents, and families is discussed in Chapter 2.

Summary

Interprofessional collaboration has a distinct developmental history as a style of serving students in schools. Originating in psychological services to students in public schools in the 1950s, and influenced by social changes, legal precedent, and educational reform efforts, interprofessional collaboration is today commonly assumed to be a critical element of teachers' work as a primary way of delivering effective educational and support services adapted to the unique and varied needs of children who display academic, psychological, or behavioral difficulties.

Questions for Reflection

1. What evidence of social changes, legal precedent, and educational changes do you see in the schools in your community?

2. How will interprofessional collaboration be uniquely influenced by the geographical, political, and social characteristics of your community?

3. How can schools increase interprofessional collaboration given that they often assume the standards and ideals of the local community?

4. Given the historical influences of interprofessional collaboration, what problems do you foresee in working collaboratively within any particular school and community setting?

5. How would you use the geographical, political, and social context of the school and community in which you work to increase interprofessional collaboration with parents and families?

References

Americans with Disabilities Act of 1990, PL 101–336, 42 U.S.C. at 12101 *et seq.*

Carnegie Forum on Education and the Economy, Task Force on Teaching as a Profession. (1986). *A nation prepared: Teachers for the 21st Century.* New York: Author.

Cuban, L. (1990). Reforming again, and again, and again. *Educational Researcher* 19(1), 3–13.

Dettmer, P., Thurston, L. P., & Dyck, N. (1996). *Consultation, collaboration, and teamwork: For students with special needs.* (2nd Ed.). Boston: Allyn & Bacon.

Dryfoos, J. G. (1996). Full service schools. *Educational Leadership, 53*(7), 18–23.

Education for all Handicapped Children's Act of 1976, PL 94–142 at 1401, U.S.C. Title 20, *et seq.*

Education for all Handicapped Children's Act Amendments of 1986, PL 99–457 at 1145 *et seq.*

Friend, M. (1988). Putting consultation into context: Historical and contemporary perspectives. *Remedial and Special Education, 9*(6), 7–13.

Friend, M., & Cook, L. (1996). *Interactions: Collaboration skills for school professionals* (2nd Ed.). New York: Longman.

Fuchs, D., & Fuchs, L. S. (1991). Framing the REI debate: Abolitionists versus conservationists. In J. W. Lloyd, N. N. Singh, & A. C. Repp (Eds.), *The regular education initiative: Alternative perspectives on concepts, issues, and methods* (pp. 241–255). De Kalb, IL: Sycamore.

Gartner A., & Lipsky, D. K. (1987). Beyond special education: Toward a quality system for all students. *Harvard Educational Review, 57,* 367–395.

Gartner A., & Lipsky, D. K. (1989). *The yoke of special education: How to break it.* Rochester, NY: National Center on Education and the Economy.

Geske, T. G., & Hoke, G. A. (1985). The national commission reports: Do states have the fiscal capacity to respond? *Education and Urban Society 17,* 171–185.

Good, T. L., & Brophy, J. E. (1991). Looking in classrooms (5th Ed.). New York: Harper Collins.

Helge, D. (1992). Solving special education problems in rural areas. *Preventing School Failure 36*(4), 11–15.

Holmes Group. (1986). *Tomorrow's teachers.* East Lansing, MI: Author.

Idol, L., Nevin, A., & Paolucci-Whitcomb, P. (1994). *Collaborative consultation* (2nd Ed.). Austin, TX: PRO-ED.

Individuals with Disabilities Education Act of 1993, Part B, PL 101–476, 20 U.S.C. at 1411–1420.

Jenkins, J. R., Pious, C. G., & Jewell, M. (1992). Special education and the Regular Education Initiative: Basic assumptions. *Exceptional Children, 56*(6), 479–491.

Kauffman, J. M. (1989). The regular education initiative as Reagan-Bush education policy: A trickle-down theory of the hard-to-teach. *Journal of Special Education, 23,* 256–278.

Kauffman, J. M. (1991). Restructuring in sociopolitical context: Reservations about the effects of current reform proposals on students with disabilities. In J. W. Lloyd, N. N. Singh, & A. C. Repp (Eds.), *The regular education initiative: Alternative perspectives on concepts, issues, and methods* (pp. 57–66). De Kalb, IL: Sycamore.

Kauffman, J. M., & Hallahan, D. P. (1990). What we want for our children: A rejoinder to REI proponents. *Journal of Special Education, 24,* 340–345.

Kauffman, J. M., & Hallahan, D. P. (1995). *The illusion of full inclusion: A comprehensive critique of a current special education bandwagon.* Austin, TX: PRO-ED.

Kauffman, J. M., & Pullen, P. L. (1989). An historical perspective: A personal perspective on our history of service to mildly handicapped and at-risk students. *Remedial and Special Education, 10*(6), 12–14.

Kyle, R.M.J. (Ed.). *Reaching for excellence: An effective schools source book.* Washington, DC: U.S. Government Printing Office.

Lipsky, D. K., & Gartner A. (1991). Restructuring for quality. In J. W. Lloyd, N. N. Singh, & A. C. Repp (Eds.), *The regular education initiative: Alternative perspectives on concepts, issues, and methods* (pp. 43–56). De Kalb, IL: Sycamore.

Lloyd, J. W., Singh, N. N., & Repp A. C. (Eds.). (1991). *The regular education initiative: Alternative perspectives on concepts, issues, and methods.* De Kalb, IL: Sycamore.

McCarthy, M. M., & Sorenson, G. P. (1993). School counselors and consultants: Legal duties and liabilities. *Journal of Counseling and Development, 72,* 159–167.

Mostert, M. P. (1991). The regular education initiative: Strategy for denial of handicap and the perpetuation of difference. *Disability, Handicap and Society, 6*(2), 91–101.

National Commission on Excellence in Education. (1983). *A nation at risk: The imperative for education reform.* Washington, DC: U.S. Government Printing Office.

National Science Foundation. (1983). *Educating Americans for the 21st century: A report to the American people and the National Science Board.* Washington, DC: Author.

Peterson, P. E. (1988). Economic and political trends affecting education. In E. Haskins & D. McRae (Eds.), *Policies for America's public schools: Teachers, equity, and indicators.* (pp. 25–54). Norwood, NJ: Ablex.

Polsgrove, L., & McNeil, M. (1989). The consultation process: Research and practice. *Remedial and Special Education, 10*(1), 6–20.

Pugach, M. C., & Johnson, L. J. (1995). *Collaborative practitioners collaborative schools.* Denver, CO: Love Publishing.

Rehabilitation Act of 1973, PL 93–112, Sec. 504, 87 U.S. Statutes at Large, at 394 *et seq.*

Reynolds, M. C. (1989). An historical perspective: The delivery of special education to mildly handicapped and at-risk students. *Remedial and Special Education, 10*(6), 7–11.

Sikula, J. (1990). National commission reports of the 1980s. In W. R. Houston, (Ed.), *Handbook of research on teacher education* (pp. 72–82). New York: Macmillan.

Skrtic, T. M. (1991). *Behind special education: A critical analysis of professional culture and school organization.* Denver, CO: Love Publishing.

Thomas, C. C., Correa, V. I. & Morsink, C. V. (1991). *Interactive teaming: Consultation and collaboration in special education* (2nd Ed.). New York: Macmillan.

Thurend, M. (1988). Putting consultation into context: Historical and contemporary perspectives. *Remedial and Special Education, 9*(6), 7–13.

Wang, M. C. (1988). Four fallacies of segregationism. *Exceptional Children, 55,* 128–137.

Wang, M. C., Reynolds. M. C., & Walberg, H. J. (1988). Integrating the children of the second system. *Phi Delta Kappan, 70,* 248–251.

2

Definition and Characteristics of Interprofessional Collaboration

Introduction

Definition
    A Style of Professional Interaction
    Collaboration Occurs between and among Professionals,
         Parents and Families, and, Where Appropriate, Students
         Themselves
       Professionals
       Parents and Families
       Students Themselves
    Share Information
    Engage in Effective Decision Making
    Develop Effective Interventions
    Commonly Agreed upon Goal
    In the Best Interests of the Student

Collaborative Foundations
    Reflection
    Boundaries

Characteristics of Interprofessional Collaboration
    Voluntary
    Indirect Service Delivery
    Professional Relationships
    Communal Trust

Introduction

While the formal emphasis on collaboration in education is relatively new, human beings are often collaborative by nature. A cursory examination of any social or work setting reveals an astonishing array of collaborative configurations for many purposes. Most societies and organizations operate on the understanding that, at least for part of the time, it is necessary for members to collaborate for the good of a common goal—a goal that most or all members agree is worth attaining. The necessity of collaboration should not eliminate the need for competition or individualism, but should rather be viewed as one tool for achieving certain goals that may be untenable in any other way. For example, collaborative efforts in certain circumstances may often achieve much more than any individual effort: many positive benefits are derived from working with others, and collective ownership and responsibility in professional work are often seen as preferable to individual risk-taking. Whatever definition of interprofessional collaboration you use, it is important that you develop a professional *collaborative orientation* through your general knowledge of what collaboration means to you, why collaborative skills are necessary, and the impact collaborative work has on your colleagues, your students, and their families.

Developing a collaborative orientation will also help you avoid common misperceptions about collaboration: for example, collaboration is *not* unfocused general discussion devoid of clear goals, it does *not* involve casual conversation in generalities too unspecific for problem solving, it is *not* some form of generic professional support, and it should *not* be confused with popular notions of psychotherapy or seen as a way of controlling other professionals' behavior. Defining more clearly what collaboration is, therefore, will support any collaborative behavior you choose to undertake.

Definition

For the purposes of this book, collaboration is a *style of professional interaction between and among professionals, parents and families, and, where appropriate, students themselves to share information, to engage in collective decision making, and to develop effective interventions for a commonly agreed upon goal that is in the best interests of the student.*

Such a general definition involves multiple important elements. Each element is fully described individually in the following sections.

A Style of Professional Interaction

Attaining proficient collaborative skills is only the beginning of making interprofessional collaboration a *style,* or habit, of working with others. If collaboration is going to address effectively students' often difficult and chronic problems, competent teachers understand that collaborative skills and competencies must become internalized and routinized to the point of becoming reflexive professional behavior. Generally, it is to your benefit to practice repeatedly and reflect critically on your collaborative skills until they are almost second nature. However, it is equally true that you should also develop a heightened sense of awareness of your collaborative behavior as a way of improving any shortcomings such awareness may uncover. In addition, collaboration is essentially *interactive,* implying a reciprocal, communicative exchange for effective professional work. Collaboration, by definition, implies cooperation and mutual consent for problem identification, decision making, intervention implementation, and evaluation, all undergirded by a common agreement of what is best for the student.

Given the increased pressures of educational reform and social change discussed in Chapter 1, it is unlikely that attempting to meet your professional responsibility without highly developed collaborative skills will be successful. Most competent professionals demonstrate collaborative skills easily, appropriately, and effectively.

Collaboration Occurs between and among Professionals, Parents and Families, and, Where Appropriate, Students Themselves

Because interprofessional collaboration is characteristically reciprocal, it is most effective when it involves active participation by everyone who can contribute to defining the problem, deciding on an intervention, implementing that intervention, and measuring the intervention's effects. Generally, three groups of people should, where appropriate, be involved in this interactive process: professionals, parents and families, and students themselves.

Professionals

In order to solve any pressing educational problem, it is likely that more than one professional, and usually in more than one discipline, will be involved. Given the complex nature of most educational problems, no one professional, no matter how effective, is likely to possess all possible knowledge or skill to solve a presenting difficulty. Engaging several professionals for effective intervention will ensure a broad range of approaches whereby information, experience, and expertise can be shared by all involved to provide a detailed and coherent response to the student's problem. For example, if a student is experiencing learning problems, some or all of the following might be involved: general and special education teacher, school psychologist, administrator, speech pathologist, school counselor, and physician.

Considering your collaborative skill with other professionals is important for a number of reasons. First, the participants will reflect different professional orientations and training, highlighting the need for collaboration to assure a common and relevant professional language and purpose. This will allow you and your colleagues to interact more easily and with more focus. Second, using your collaborative skills with other professionals will facilitate the development of a common professional goal unhampered by unnecessary misunderstanding, disagreement, or misperception. In this way collaborative skill ensures the quickest effective path to a common educational goal by common consensus. Third, being collaboratively skilled will allow you to present yourself as competent to your colleagues, thereby building your professional integrity and reliability. Finally, exercising such collaborative skill will help build professional relationships and trust that will be a distinct advantage in working with these and other professionals in the future.

As a novice teacher, it is important that you not only develop interprofessional collaborative skills, but also that you know enough about other related professional fields to ascertain who should be involved in addressing any particular educational problem. Maintaining a high level of collaborative skill will provide you the best chance of enhancing your professional standing, to forge new relationships and reinforce established work alliances, and to allow you to become an effective change agent for your students and their families.

Parents and Families

Another important aspect of collaboration for effective problem solving involves working with the student's parents and family. While caregivers are most often biological, step-, or adoptive parents, you may encounter other adults who are responsible for the student's welfare, such as grandparents, extended family members, other court-appointed guardians, or even social service agencies. In the past, parents, other caregivers, and families have been far less involved in solving students' problems than they are today. Historically, each professional, or even several professionals working collaboratively with a student, were seen as the experts possessing all the knowledge necessary to solve a given problem. Once the problem had been defined and a solution devised, the interventions were executed with only cursory attention to parents and families who were usually viewed as being peripheral to the professionals.

Today, however, teachers understand that parents and families play a pivotal role in any collaborative effort. First, parents spend much more time with their children than teachers do, so they generally possess a great deal of relevant knowledge that, unless explicitly uncovered and used, can negate any educational remedial action. Second, including parents and families as collaborators also increases the chances that they will support any proposed intervention. Parents are much more likely to follow up on professional suggestions, report the results of interventions, and provide feedback for modifying those interventions if they have been included in the problem-solving process and have been valued as collaborators who possess distinct expertise. Third, in a very real sense, including parents as part of the decision-making process allows them to become extensions of the professional team, ensuring that the interventions are carried out beyond the school setting.

Students Themselves

In addition to including parents and other family members as active collaborative contributors, experienced teachers also understand that, where possible and appropriate, including students themselves can benefit and strengthen any proposed intervention. First, as with parents, students possess a knowledge of themselves that may well contribute to the success of any professional plan. Understanding the problem from the student's point of view may increase the chances of the student's cooperation. Second, uncovering such knowledge will explicate the student's individual preferences, needs, and perceptions, all of which can easily influence the efficacy of any educational program. Third, including the student in the collaborative process increases the likelihood that the student will be motivated to change out of a sense of ownership and personal responsibility.

It is important, therefore, for all teachers to learn as much as they can about their students. Aside from any information that can be supplied by colleagues and parents, get to know students individually both in school, and, where possible, in less familiar settings outside of school.

Share Information

The primary purpose for optimum collaboration between and among professionals, caregivers, and, where appropriate, students themselves is to uncover as much relevant information as possible. The more information available to all parties, the more likely that, in considering any proposed intervention, (1) important information will not be overlooked or omitted, (2) unimportant information will be ignored, (3) all parties involved in the collaboration will share the same information, (4) such sharing will enhance collaborative understanding and reduce misunderstanding, (5) the broadest initial approaches to the problem will be fostered, (6) duplicate efforts will be reduced, (7) everyone involved will understand the function of all other collaborators, and (8) information will flow more freely among all participants.

Gaining access to and sharing of information are two of the most important aspects of interprofessional collaboration. In other words, a major advantage of habitual, extended collaborative activity is that it provides the potential for access to a great amount of knowledge that might otherwise not be available. It cannot be emphasized too strongly that the effectiveness of any educational intervention is directly correlated to the amount of information gathered prior to any implementation decision.

However, even though more information for decision making is usually better than less information, it is equally true that effective teachers develop an acute awareness of knowing when they have enough information for action. Remember that spending all your energy and time needlessly seeking out irrelevant or marginal information may distract you from taking appropriate action.

As an inexperienced teacher, therefore, you should probably gather as much information as you can in the time you have. As you gain experience, you will develop a feel for what is important and what is irrelevant. A good rule of thumb is to pay more attention to information that is directly related to the student's problem and less attention to information that is further removed from the immediate problem. Still, do not completely ignore periph-eral information as it may become more important in the future. Try to glean this information from as many different sources as possible, ignoring duplicate information and adding previously uncovered information as you proceed. It will also help if you develop dependable memory skills and if you document and organize the information you receive.

Engage in Effective Decision Making

A primary focus of interprofessional collaboration is to share information gleaned from other professionals, parents and families, and students them-selves in order to make appropriate and effective educational decisions. Remember, however, that you will rarely engage in interprofessional collabo-ration where a single isolated decision will immediately solve a problem. In any collaborative problem solving, there will be many smaller decisions which, at some point, will cumulatively result in some kind of professional action.

Several other aspects of information sharing are also important. First, shared information is the foundation for discussion and debate that will later define the problem, lead to the most appropriate intervention from among competing alternatives, and dictate how to implement, execute, and evaluate the chosen intervention. Second, shared information allows all involved par-ties to focus on a common set of facts that provides a basis for problem solving. This common knowledge tends to develop a mutual sense of ownership, responsibility, and commitment among the participants while simultaneously lessening the possibility of conflict or misunderstanding. A third aspect of shared information is that it allows all participants to examine the common problem from their own point of view. This allows a greater diversity for brainstorming ideas, increased interaction among the participants, and a broad-based approach to the problem using different combinations of ideas and orientations.

Develop Effective Interventions

The purpose of any interprofessional collaboration is to share information as a precursor to effective intervention. It is difficult, and may not be possible, to devise an optimally effective intervention without a great deal of relevant information. There is also little point in attempting interventions that are less than optimal given the information available. Such attempts waste precious time and energy and engage all participants in needless effort that would be better spent in other ways. The selected intervention is the nexus between prior gathering, sharing, and discussing of information on the one hand, and implementation, execution, and evaluation of the intervention on the other.

Commonly Agreed upon Goal

A major advantage of interprofessional collaboration is that the perceptions, ideas, and expertise of many people are all brought to bear on a common problem. The decision to implement an intervention can only be made once the participants have agreed on (1) the nature and extent of the problem and (2) the goal of the intervention. It is important that all participants agree, at least in part, on what needs to be achieved. Agreement is much more likely if every participant is able to contribute, however tangentially, to solving the problem.

A major characteristic of interprofessional collaboration, therefore, is an emphasis on consensual decision making. First, consensus for decision making ensures that each participant has had the opportunity to express their point of view and to have their suggestions considered. This aspect of collaboration is crucial to foster a sense of common understanding in the decision-making process. Members of the team are much more likely to be motivated for the common good if they feel they have been listened to and included in all phases of the collaborative process. Second, participation by all participants increases everyone's sense of ownership of the problem and responsibility in executing the problem-solving intervention. Third, consensus allows the burden for success or failure of any intervention to be shared among all the participants. Sharing this burden when interventions fail helps avoid blaming any one particular participant and renews the sense of future common problem solving. Less often noted, but probably even more important, is the advantage of sharing the responsibility when interventions are successful. When collaborative efforts are successful, every member can then claim some of the credit for a job well done, which in turn leads to an increased sense of professional efficacy and self-worth as well as a higher level of collaborative morale for future endeavors.

In the Best Interests of the Student

Any collaborative effort should be permeated with an overarching sense of whether decisions and interventions will, in both the long and the short term, be in the best interests of the student. While such a goal seems obvious, experienced teachers understand that in any collaborative process there are many factors that can detract from this important focus. For instance, inexperienced teachers often assume that all parties naturally work in the best interests of the student and are sometimes surprised and disappointed when this is not the case. It is unlikely that professionals who seem to ignore the best interests of the student do so deliberately or with malice. It is much more likely that a complicated set of factors common to most schools, including workload, working relationships, interprofessional conflicts, school or district policies, and so on, interfere with many aspects of collaborative work and can easily derail the most sincere efforts. Furthermore, the best interests of the student must be considered as a primary criterion in deciding on appropriate interventions because quite often, as effective and reliable as an intervention might be, it may not be feasible or ethical, and may in fact harm the child in the long run.

Collaborative Foundations

Given the many skills and combinations of skills necessary for effective inter-professional collaboration, two broad undergirding concepts will help you make the best use of your collaborative knowledge. Developing acute reflective skills and knowing the boundaries of your expertise will facilitate effective intercollaborative behavior with colleagues, students, and their families.

Reflection

All of your professional behavior should be supported by attention to what is arguably your greatest potential asset in becoming a competent teacher: your ability to *reflect* on what you do by carefully and critically examining the reasons for your professional actions and what they teach you. While it is true that many teachers lead "unexamined lives," it is unlikely that these teachers are among the most effective colleagues you will encounter. Developing a sure skill in self-evaluation and contemplation of your professional self should be an ongoing career venture. Effective teachers are likely to be people who constantly contemplate their professional behavior to seek ways of improving their performance.

There are two primary ways of developing reflective skill. First, it is essential that you develop reflection introspectively, that is, that you reflect on and examine your professional actions from your own point of view. Introspective reflection is psychological and emotional work to help you learn from your experience for more effective future performance. Effective teachers work very hard at making professional introspection a matter of habit. This task can be accomplished in many ways. For example, some professionals find it effective to spend time mulling over a particular problem, writing down what they see as advantages and disadvantages of their dilemma, and then trying to fashion a solution. Others choose to keep a journal or diary of important professional events and then, in retrospect, reflect on their writing to gain new insights about what they could do differently in the future. However, while it is critical for you to think about your own professional actions, your introspection will always be subject to your own biases and feelings, which might be more or less accurate.

Second, it is imperative that you balance your personal introspection by engaging in reflection on your professional behavior with a trusted colleague or mentor. Discussing your professional behavior with a mentor often provides support for new insights into problems that may at first seem intractable. A trusted mentor may or may not be able to validate your views, but their outlook will, at the very least, provide you with an alternative slant on your professional behavior. If you engage in such reflection, it is vital to understand, and to ensure that *they* understand, that whatever they may share can only be provided from their perspective, which is itself subject to their own personal and professional biases. In addition, it is important to remember that in the final analysis, *you* must make your professional decisions and take responsibility for those decisions irrespective of any others' points of view.

In addition to self-reflection and reflection with others, many experienced teachers understand that any professional self-examination is inextricably intertwined with who they are as human beings outside their professional roles. A common mistake made by novice teachers is to assume that their professional roles are, or should be, completely divorced from who they are as people. While in some very obvious ways this is, of course, appropriate, this is less clear when reflecting on your professional actions. It is appropriate, therefore, that as part of your reflection on your professional practice, you spend time working on understanding yourself better as a person, especially in identifying your unique individual strengths and weaknesses. Work, too, on the understanding that all your personal strengths, weaknesses, and perceptions will have a significant, if often unseen, influence on your professional actions.

Boundaries

Given that interprofessional collaboration is a style or work habit, it is important to remember that a number of limits, by circumstance, will restrict your collaborative efforts. Two major boundary considerations are most likely to influence your collaborative ability: limitations on your time and energy, and the limitations of inexperience.

While many inexperienced teachers understand that their time is finite, fewer are aware that energy and motivation are also limited. If you are unaware of your energy limits, and assuming, like most new teachers, that you are fervently enthusiastic about your work and are trying to make a favorable impression on your colleagues, you may underestimate the amount of effort required for effective collaboration. Such circumstances lead quite easily to discouragement and burnout. In addition to developing a sense of priority in your professional activities, try to pace yourself with the understanding that part of being an effective teacher is to develop a good sense of what your limits are and to work within them. If you are successful in this endeavor, you will stand a much better chance of doing a good job.

Equally, experienced teachers will tell you that there will inevitably be times when you will work at or beyond the limits of your capacity and that in doing so you will develop a useful set of coping skills, such as a sense of how long and how hard you can work before overwork becomes detrimental. Furthermore, obviously, you will be seen as less than competent if you use the admonitions discussed here as an excuse to shirk any of your professional responsibilities. Generally, however, discovering your limits is to your advantage.

Inexperience can be a major limiting factor in several ways. For example, it may result in a limitation of your collaborative perspectives. Also, your collaborative skill, knowledge of resources, and so on, are likely to be less developed than those of many of your more experienced peers. Inexperience requires that you maintain a careful awareness of what you know and what you do not know and that you operate within those limits. If you are able to collaborate using what skills you have while simultaneously working hard to broaden your experience—while also refraining from working in areas where you are clearly incompetent or uncertain—you will enhance your professional integrity and broaden your experience.

Characteristics of Interprofessional Collaboration

Collaboration is marked by a set of characteristics that separate it from other ways of working. Understanding these characteristics and being aware of them as you go about your professional responsibilities will help ensure your ability to collaborate effectively.

Voluntary

Collaboration is, perhaps most importantly, a voluntary professional activity, mainly because it is only one of many working styles, and other teachers may choose other modes of professional behavior. Also, it would be pointless to force teachers and other school professionals to collaborate, as collaboration relies heavily on motivation and a conscious commitment to choose this mode over other, more isolated ways of working.

The voluntary nature of collaboration has several major advantages. First, professionals, parents and families, and students who volunteer to work to-gether generally indicate by volunteering that they are motivated and willing to engage in mutual work to solve a problem. Such motivation is vital as it increases the chances that participants will not only address the current problem, but also that their commitment and energy will keep them engaged long enough to reach resolution. Attempting to solve *any* problem when participants are unmotivated and disinterested is usually difficult and often impossible. Second, the voluntary nature of collaboration tends to increase the morale and positiveness of the participants much more quickly and deeply than when professionals work in isolation. Because participants *want* to col-laborate, group cohesion and a mutual sense of common purpose are often evident. Third, voluntary behavior is quite often contagious. That is, people who are not initially convinced that collaboration is important or effective often come to such a conclusion after watching others involved in the process and by seeing the effective results of such collaboration. It is this aspect of collaboration, rather than any attempt manipulatively to coerce reluctant colleagues, that has the best chance of winning over others who remain unconvinced of its appropriateness. Fourth, engaging in collaboration volun-tarily will increase your sense of self-efficacy and professional self-worth. Choosing to engage voluntarily in professional action is self-motivating and will increase your knowledge of working with others, an important path to quicker, enhanced professional development. Finally, the voluntary nature of collaboration ensures that educational problems will likely be more speedily addressed than if professionals, parents and families, and students wait for some mandate or directive that forces action. Generally, then, the charac-teristic voluntariness of collaboration is a highly effective way of creating professional energy and focus.

There are also distinct disadvantages related to the voluntary nature of collaboration. A major drawback is that some highly competent people who could add immeasurably to collaborative effectiveness may not participate. Competent teachers who choose not to collaborate do so for many reasons, and it is unwise to rush to negative conclusions. If people whose expertise you highly value choose not to participate, you have several options. Whatever option you choose, let your decisions be influenced by the understanding that you will have to work with these colleagues in the future. First, you can simply accept their nonparticipation, which might be appropriate if you can easily find substitutes. On the other hand, such disengagement might be inappropriate if no substitutes are available, or if you suspect that, with further negotiation, these people might change their minds. In most instances, it is appropriate to tactfully inquire as to the reason for nonparticipation. Second, you may elect to manipulate or coerce someone into participating, but experienced teachers will tell you that such efforts are usually unproductive and may lead to negative consequences in the long run. Essentially, most people resent being manipulated or forced to do something they have the right to refuse.

A second problem related to the voluntary nature of collaboration is that volunteers often are left to shoulder more than their fair share of the work. You should be aware that there are two distinct aspects to this problem. On the one hand, volunteers are usually motivated and hardworking—even willing to work disproportionately hard. On the other hand, many people who are reluctant to volunteer are quite prepared to allow volunteers to shoulder more than their fair share. Indeed, in some instances, the nonparticipants may actually volunteer to pass on work to the volunteers!

A third disadvantage of almost all voluntary activity is that the rewards, at least any tangible rewards, are not commensurate with the amount of effort expended. Many people, therefore, might be reluctant to engage in any professional behavior that does not offer very clear benefits. It is often difficult to convince these people of the more intrinsic rewards that are often part of collaboration, such as an increased sense of efficacy and professional self-esteem, positive camaraderie, gains in new knowledge, and so on.

A fourth drawback is that anyone involved in the collaborative process may discontinue their participation whenever they choose. Persons who initially engage in collaboration and then withdraw at some later time are particularly problematic for at least three reasons: (1) Their withdrawal is likely to be disruptive. It will necessitate a restructuring of collaborative responsibilities to fill the workload gap. (2) Such a departure is likely to reconfigure the professional and personal relationships of the remaining collaborative participants. (3) Colleagues may be reluctant to collaborate with this person in the future because the person's withdrawal may be seen as a sign of unreliability.

A fifth disadvantage of collaborative voluntariness arises when people who are not needed or who do not possess relevant knowledge or expertise volunteer to be part of the collaborative process. Such circumstances can be particularly vexing because while you do not want to offend people who offer their effort and energy, it is often equally true that adding unnecessary or unqualified persons to the process creates the potential for distraction, conflict, or unnecessary delays.

A sixth problem arises when, due to outside influences or pressures, people are directed or mandated to "volunteer." Such clumsy attempts at forcing collaboration are usually counterproductive as they engender, at best, negative reactions and, at worst, may precipitate openly rebellious or extreme passive-aggressive avoidant behavior, none of which are in the best interests of either the professionals involved or the students they serve.

Overall, the voluntary nature of collaboration is probably both its largest asset and its largest drawback. Problems tend to arise more often around nonparticipation than overparticipation. Some professionals advocate strategies for dealing with professionals who choose not to participate, insisting that such "resistance" must be overcome. Effective teachers, however, are wary of such attempts to manipulate others into collaborating. These efforts will have, at best, temporary success and run the distinct long-term risk of alienating nonparticipants for a very long time. Instead, effective teachers understand that it is important to work positively with those who choose to participate while simultaneously respecting the wishes of those who choose not to in the hopes that by modeling effective collaboration and by demonstrating its many positive outcomes, nonparticipants will choose, sometime in the future, to become involved.

Indirect Service Delivery

Interprofessional collaboration is usually seen as an indirect form of educational service delivery to students because, while many people are involved in devising an intervention, the intervention itself is usually carried out by only one or two professionals. Generally, the major advantage of indirect service delivery is that it allows many people to be part of the problem-solving and decision-making process, thereby increasing the potential for novel or more comprehensive solutions. On the other hand, indirect service delivery systems often take longer to reach consensus for intervention implementation and actual intervention delivery.

Professional Relationships

Perhaps more than any other working style in education, collaboration, an imminently social activity, encourages exploration of professional relationships not only for service delivery to students, but also for professional growth and career advancement for participants. It is difficult to work collaboratively and not forge professional relationships at many levels of intensity—relationships that might, on the one hand, be extremely beneficial and rewarding, and, on the other, perhaps frustrating or destructive. Clearly, work relationships are a crucial part of building your professional support network, of gaining knowledge and experience, for increasing your expertise, and as a significant way of doing what is best for your students.

While experienced teachers often say that interprofessional relationships must be learned through trial and error, this is not entirely true. As an inexperienced teacher, for example, you can practice interpersonal communication skills, reflect on your own professional practices and those of your colleagues, gauge your limitations and work to improve them, assess the efficacy of your professional strengths, and acknowledge that while you have a great deal to learn, you can also, even very early in your career, contribute to both your students' and your colleagues' well-being. Paying attention to these issues while simultaneously approaching your tasks with enthusiasm, honesty, and tact will serve you well in establishing your professional relationships.

As you gain collaborative experience you will discover that, essentially, your working relationships will develop along a spectrum from very negative to very positive. By and large, most of your relationships will be positive. Positive interprofessional relationships are characterized by warm personal interactions, a mutual desire to get the job done, and a consistent deepening of your relationships with your colleagues. Working in these relationships will be nurturing and motivating, providing you with many advantages for learning and improving your skills.

Positive working relationships will also vary in their intensity. Your most positive relationships are likely to come from colleagues with whom you collaborate frequently and intensely. Such close contact will shape secure, deeply rewarding connections, some of which will last your entire career. In addition, you may have extremely cordial relationships with some colleagues but only work with them infrequently or for very short periods of time. In such circumstances, you will come to rely on these colleagues as predictably competent even if you do not collaborate with them regularly.

Infrequently, for any number of valid, invalid, or unknown reasons, you may encounter professional relationships that are quite negative and strained. Such relationships may be quite aversive, engender high levels of frustration, conflict, and, in rare instances, outright hostility. These relations are detrimental not only to your professional life but also to the students you serve. Inexperienced teachers often spend a great deal of precious time and energy, unnecessarily, on negative relationships. Given the myriad variables affecting all relationships, however, the expectation of equally cordial interactions with everyone you work with is quite unrealistic. It is important that you gauge the extent to which negative interactions are sapping your energy and that you attempt to redefine such negative situations more positively.

If you encounter negative relationships, a number of options are open to you, all of which have their own advantages and disadvantages. First, you may choose to spend time on repairing and improving the relationship. This course of action may be important if you will work closely with this colleague in the future or if current collaborative efforts are being derailed by the relationship problem. A second course of action might be to simply do nothing and see if the problem resolves itself. This may be your course of action if the negativity is minor or if you feel that the problem is fleeting and unlikely to recur. A third, much more radical action might be to sever professional ties with a colleague, although this is an extreme reaction and may have serious consequences for everyone involved. Such an option should not be considered except for extreme circumstances and only after extended efforts to repair the relationship and careful reflection of what such a decision might mean to you, your colleagues, and your students.

Generally, active work on your professional relationships should be given high priority, especially if you are new to teaching or if you are in a new work setting. It is in your best interests to constantly consider the state of your interprofessional relationships and to spend adequate time and effort building positive, productive connections while simultaneously dealing effectively with any relational problems that might arise. The characteristic emphasis on interprofessional relationships in collaborative work, therefore, strongly implies that all participants conduct their business with friendliness where possible, cordiality where necessary, and always with a palpable sense of mutual respect and careful consideration for others' points of view.

Communal Trust

Competent teachers observe that interprofessional collaboration requires, and can build, as well as easily damage, communal trust in working with parents and families and students. Positive interprofessional interactions coupled with effective problem solving and conflict resolution can lead to a heightened sense of honesty, empathy, and willingness to engage in further collaboration. Repeated collaborative experiences that are generally positive and helpful to the student will result in increased professional and personal integrity and a pervasive sense of accomplishment for all involved as well as engendering a level of trust that will accelerate the efficacy of future collaborative efforts. It is in your best interest and the interests of those you serve, therefore, that you strive for the most positive and productive collaborative experiences possible.

Alternately, if collaborative experiences, for whatever reason, turn out to be unduly negative, frustrating, or antagonistic, the potential for mistrust and a general sense of failure are increased, creating an ineffective foundation for further accomplishment. While establishing professional trust with colleagues, parents and families, and students only develops over time and with a great deal of concerted energy, it is imperative to your professional success and the success of your students.

Collective Involvement

Unlike many other styles of professional work that do not place a high priority on collective involvement, collaboration is characterized by the interaction of many different professionals, parents and families, and, where appropriate, students. It is this collective involvement that fosters flexibility and creativity for problem solving and intervention implementation. Collective involvement also allows adaptable configurations of participants to directly address unique problems while simultaneously developing more positive working relationships. Without collective involvement toward a common goal and without the willingness to share collective responsibility based on collective decisions for action, educational collaboration is likely to be unfocused and meaningless.

Shared Goals and Collective Responsibility

Professionals, parents and families, and students engage in collaboration as a specific means (defining a problem and a potentially successful intervention) to a well-defined end (implementing the intervention and evaluating its efficacy). Such work is impossible without a clear, consensual, well-defined goal.

A key element in collaborative shared goals involves collective responsibility. When teachers work in isolation, they are often compelled to make independent decisions with only the information they themselves possess. Individual noncollaborative decisions are often unavoidable and necessary. Competent teachers are appropriately trained and socialized to make many of their decisions in this way. Individual decision making has many advantages, including the swiftness with which decisions can be made and implemented and the lack of necessity to consult with, or be accountable to, other professionals. Another major advantage of individual action is that the individual receives all of the praise and enjoys all of the success. On the other hand, individual decision making also implies that if a professional decision turns out to be ineffective, inappropriate, or negative, the same rule generally applies—that the individual will have to take all the responsibility for failure—a heavy burden indeed.

The same advantages and disadvantages apply to working collaboratively, except the outcomes of positive or negative decisions have different effects. If a collaborative decision results in positive outcomes, then all of the collaborating participants share in the success. Sharing success in a collaborative group after a great deal of hard work is not only gratifying for each individual, but also collectively increases morale and motivation for future endeavors. Alternately, if the collaborative decision is negative or inappropriate, the resulting failure is spread across all members of the group. Collective failure lessens the trauma for each individual and often generates energy for attempting further more successful interventions.

Action for Problem Solving

Interprofessional collaboration emphasizes action for solving education problems through collective effort. Characteristically, effective collaborative participants maintain a tight focus on keeping their interactions geared to implementing effective interventions rather than on establishing prescribed aspects of planning, record keeping, and evaluation, although all of these are necessary to some degree. Generally, action for resolution is viewed as much more important than formality or structure, which could detract from or delay effective problem resolution. The use of a logical, goal-directed problem-solving process, therefore, is a hallmark of interprofessional collaboration.

Collaborative Resources

A primary advantage of interprofessional collaboration involves a pooling of resources for more effective action. In addition, sharing resources is a way of encouraging others to engage in collaborative endeavors.

It is important to remember that such shared resources take many different forms. Experienced professionals understand that the more aware they are of the extent of available resources, the more flexibility they have in addressing any issues for intervention. One crucial resource, for example, is the diverse specialized expertise each participant brings to interprofessional contact.

A second resource involves the knowledge each participant possesses of other extended and indirect forms of support that might be brought to bear on any particular educational problem. Because of each individual's training, professional orientation, or experience, the group will be aware of increasingly more agencies, other individuals, support networks, and so on—many more than any one individual is likely to know. Such knowledge allows participants to address issues from a resource-rich perspective. Remember, however, that a resource-rich setting holds the potential for derailing intervention decisions if the group focuses more on the novelty of the resources than the problem or if excessive resources are brought to bear. However, it is generally preferable to have more than less knowledge about resources that might assist all participants in solving the problem at hand.

A third resource is the advantage of including in the collaborative process people who are highly experienced. For example, participants with high levels of experience are much more likely to have encountered similar problems in the past, are usually more adept at focusing on significant aspects of the problem, possess extended knowledge of resources, and tend to be more seasoned in the collaborative process. In addition, highly experienced professionals will be more likely to model collaborative and other professional skills and be more adept at facilitating collaborative efforts among all participants. However, experience does not always equal competence. Many experienced teachers will tell you that they have worked with colleagues who, while highly experienced, are ineffective. They may also tell you that they have worked with colleagues who, while relatively inexperienced, were extremely competent. Clearly, however, experience, when coupled with competence, is an important factor for interprofessional collaboration.

A fourth resource, perhaps less often considered, but in many instances quite relevant, is related to the logistical aspects of collaboration. Often inexperienced teachers assume that everything about collaboration involves interprofessional relationships and technical knowledge. However, this is not always the case. For example, having a quiet, undisturbed place to conduct professional business can sometimes make or break an important collaborative interaction. Decisions related to meeting times and places are usually important but sometimes overlooked. Coordinating schedules for meetings and decisions related to record keeping, a formal procedure for decision making, and many other similar details are crucial logistical aspects of ensuring that collaborative time is not wasted. Effective teachers spend some time thinking through these more mundane aspects of collaboration with the understanding that ignoring them can result in significant disorganization and disruption.

A fifth resource, which is less relevant but sometimes related to logistical resources, involves financial support of the collaborative endeavor. In most collaborative instances you are likely to encounter, there will be little to no need for financial considerations. However, at some point, you may become involved in or be asked to organize a sizeable collaborative venture where financial considerations are necessary. For example, if a collaborative venture involves many professionals who have to meet on a regular basis, there may be a need to provide refreshments, purchase office supplies, and so on. If this is the case, these details should be taken care of *in advance* so that the collaborative process can proceed without any distractions due to lack of funds.

Finally, it is important to consider political resources available to you. Effective teachers understand that most of their colleagues, to a greater or lesser extent, have personal issues and agendas that they wish to see furthered through their daily professional interactions. For example, some of your associates might seek out and obtain political power to further their careers, some might seek power for the good of their students, while others might be highly skilled at circumventing various aspects of educational authority and school policy for their own or others' benefit. In addition, there is likely to be a history of past positive, neutral, or negative relationships that have affected working alliances. This collaborative history is inherently political because individuals have taken sides, engaged in conflict from time to time, and generally developed strong opinions, often covert, that will have an exceptional influence on the current collaborative process. Experienced teachers know, and take into account, that every collaborative participant comes to the process with such political intent. Generally, political agendas have the capacity for great professional (and personal) good or evil, depending on the composition and collaborative goal of the group. It is to your advantage, therefore, to know as much as possible about the political agendas of your colleagues, take them into account, and learn to work with them while simultaneously making sure that their political influence, as far as possible, is to your advantage rather than to your detriment.

Confidentiality

Effective professionals understand the paramount importance of confidentiality as one of the most important safeguards of students' and families' rights to privacy. While confidentiality is not exclusively a characteristic of interprofessional collaboration, it takes on special significance in collaborative settings because many individuals are likely to be privy to confidential information. As the number of individuals involved in the collaborative effort increases, so, too, does the potential for confidentiality to be compromised.

Effective professionals maintain confidentiality in a number of ways. First, it is important to remember that a great deal of information available to professionals might be damaging in many ways if it is passed on to others who are less professionally inclined or who might use it negatively. Second, competent teachers cultivate good confidentiality skills in terms of record keeping and maintenance. For example, they may only share sensitive information on a need-to-know basis, take great care of confidential records, and ensure that all information relating to their current work is protected from accidental or deliberate compromise. Third, effective teachers place a high premium on demonstrating their serious commitment to maintaining confidentiality to their colleagues, parents and families, and the students themselves. Fourth, competent teachers should remain vigilant for any possible breaches of confidentiality and take appropriate action. Finally, it is in your best interest to be familiar with school, district, and state policies that govern the extent and limitations of confidentiality in your particular workplace.

The Student as Priority

All of the above characteristics of collaboration meet in a single central consideration: that any interaction among professionals, parents and families, and the students themselves in any educationally problematic situation be governed by *attending to the needs of the student* as the first and overriding priority. Once you have spent any time in a classroom at all, it will become obvious that there are many competing variables that can easily force you to lose your priority of attending to your students' needs and that preventing these competing priorities from interfering with your work with students is easier said than done. You will also come to realize that one of the most effective and economical ways to keep the student as your top priority is to habitually engage in interprofessional collaboration.

Given these characteristics of interprofessional collaboration, it is important to remember that while you should always take your work seriously and do your best at all times, hard work taken seriously does not necessarily imply drudgery. There are many positive benefits and joys related to collaborative professional work. For example, you will establish many significant working relationships, which will provide considerable support in your current work and many of your future endeavors. In addition, collaboration will greatly increase the potential for you to explore other areas of interest in your field but less directly connected to your day-to-day work. Finally, interprofessional collaboration will provide you with opportunities for leadership and, in general, an excellent opportunity for professional and personal growth.

Summary

Effective teachers understand and use a working definition of collaboration that is practical and easily applicable to their everyday work. They understand that their collaborative style is undergirded by the essential elements of intra- and interpersonal reflection and a recognition of their own limitations within the collaborative context. Developing a useful collaborative style also depends on a number of important collaborative characteristics, which should be taken into account in any collaborative action.

Questions for Reflection

1. Consider the ways in which you might increase your ability to reflect on your teaching practice. How can you possibly practice such reflection within yourself and in sharing your reflections with a trusted colleague or mentor?

2. How do the collaborative characteristics mentioned in this chapter interact with each other, and what does their interaction mean for your professional behavior?

3. Will all characteristics of collaboration always be present in every inter-collaborative setting? What are the ramifications of their presence or absence for your collaborative behavior?

4. How do you deal with colleagues who do not understand the collaborative process or who are unaware of the important characteristics of collaboration?

5. What potential problems do you foresee in using a collaborative style in settings where such a style is either undervalued or absent? How could you change this situation?

References

Brill, N. (1978). *Working with people: The helping process* (2nd Ed.). Philadelphia, PA: J. B. Lippincott.

Brown, D. (1993). Training consultants: A call to action. *Journal of Counseling and Development, 72,* 139–143.

Brown, D., Pryzwansky, W. B., & Schulte, A. C. (1995). *Psychological consultation: Introduction to theory and practice* (3rd Ed.). Boston: Allyn & Bacon.

Conoley, J. C., & Conoley, C. W. (1988). Useful theories in school-based consultation. *Remedial and Special Education, 9*(6), 14–20.

Dettmer, P., Thurston, L. P., & Dyck, N. (1996). *Consultation, collaboration, and teamwork: For students with special needs* (2nd Ed.). Boston: Allyn & Bacon.

Friend, M., & Cook, L. (1996). *Interactions: Collaboration skills for school profes-sionals* (2nd Ed.). New York: Longman.

Fuqua, D. R., & Kurpius, D. J. (1993). Conceptual models in organizational consultation. *Journal of Counseling and Development, 71,* 607–618.

Heron, T. E., & Harris, K. (1987). *The educational consultant: Helping profession-als, parents, and mainstreamed students.* Austin, TX: Pro-Ed.

Idol, L. (1989). The resource/consulting teacher: An integrated model of service delivery. *Remedial and Special Education, 10*(6), 38–48.

Idol, L. (1993). *Special educator's consultation handbook* (2nd Ed.). Austin, TX: Pro-Ed.

Kurpius, D. J., & Fuqua, D. (1993). Fundamental issues in defining consult-ation. *Journal of Counseling and Development, 71,* 598–600.

Kurpius, D. J., Fuqua, D. R., & Rozecki, T. (1993). The consulting process: A multidimensional approach. *Journal of Counseling and Development, 71,* 601–606.

Meyers, J., Gelzheiser, L. M., & Yelich, G. (1991). Do pull-in programs foster teacher collaboration? *Remedial and Special Education, 12*(2), 7–15.

Quinn, K., & Cumblad, C. (1994). Service providers' perceptions of interagency collaboration in their communities. *Journal of Emotional and Behavioral Disorders, (2),* 109–115.

Sugai, G. M., & Tindal, G. A. (1993). *Effective school consultation: An interactive approach.* Belmont, CA: Wadsworth.

3

The Context of Interprofessional Collaboration
Effective Teamwork

Introduction

Collaborative Group Characteristics

Collaborative Supporting Skills
Positiveness
Sense of Humor
Enthusiasm
Patience
Willingness to Learn
Awareness
Helpfulness
Flexibility
Commitment to Hard Work
Honesty
Uncertainty and Hesitancy
Self-Determination and Integrity

Practical Supporting Behaviors for Collaboration
Personal Health
Personal Life
Balance
Prioritizing

Introduction

Interprofessional collaboration occurs most often in the context of teamwork with other professionals, parents and families, and your students. Experienced teachers understand that an intricate balance of technical, personal, and collaborative skill is required for teamwork to effectively address and solve educational problems. Teamwork is successful only to the extent that team members are willing to engage in constant learning, reflection on professional behavior, and prioritizing the needs of the student. The complexities of teamwork are, to some extent, only learned through practice. As a new teacher, you will find that trial and error will account for some of what you learn irrespective of your level of expertise. It is unwise, however, to assume that the only way to acquire collaborative skill is through haphazard and unpredictable events after you begin your first job. There are many ways to prepare yourself ahead of time. One way of gaining a great deal of foreknowledge about your profession is to learn about the complex context in which intercollaborative work occurs.

Given the human proclivity to social behavior, working in groups is a part of our personal and professional lives. In our personal lives we may belong to many different groups, such as the family, civic organizations, and so on. Similar group membership exists in professional interactions with one distinguishing factor: Professional group or team configurations are usually not focused on social interactions—although these play an important role—but instead are created, shaped, function, and disbanded around the accomplishment of some professional task. Collaborative groups, therefore, are distinguished by a number of group characteristics that influence their behavior.

Collaborative Group Characteristics

Groups created specifically to address professional problems comprise a highly socialized intact system where specific goals and tasks are defined, implemented, and evaluated for a clear professional purpose. This collaborative system comprises several undergirding characteristics.

First, collaborative groups are characterized by specific functions. They usually articulate specific short- and long-term goals that will define the team's actions and purpose while simultaneously clarifying the tasks that will execute and evaluate these goals. These functions will be more or less complicated depending on, among other factors, the nature of the individual problems, the number of professionals involved, and the practical contextual limitations within which the problem and the proposed remedial actions occur. Other team functions, such as how decisions will be made, how consensus will be achieved, and how any collaborative problems will be addressed, tend to be much more formal than in loosely defined social groups.

Second, collaborative groups vary in size. Some groups may be small, consisting of perhaps two or three participants, while other groups may consist of many more. The size of the collaborative group depends on a number of factors, including the availability of interested or necessary participants, the nature and extent of the problem under consideration, the individual needs of the student, and the complexity of any proposed interventions. It is important to remember that the size of the group should be no bigger, and certainly no smaller, than the number of people necessary to complete the task. Experienced teachers know that it is possible to have a collaborative team of too many members, thereby running the risk of duplicating both effort and tasks or potentially creating a context for confusion. However, it is much more likely that collaborative teams may be too small and constitute fewer professionals than necessary to accomplish effective intervention.

Third, experienced teachers understand that as team members work together over time, relationships develop and find their own level of intensity. Individually, team members will have different levels of intimacy and social distance with their colleagues. Both personal and team levels of interactive intensity will differ from team to team and be strongly influenced not only by the size of the team, but by factors such as the professional background and experience of each team member, the complexity of the team task, the personal perspectives and biases of each participant, and the life span of the team. In addition, the team as a whole will tend to settle at some collective level of agreed upon collaborative behavior; that is, it is likely that each team will have a distinctive "feel" in terms of levels of compatibility, the nature of the decision-making process, and how general consensus is reached.

Fourth, collaborative groups are characterized by a pattern of group decision making. Patterns of group decision making will be different from group to group depending on many of the variables just mentioned. Collaborative groups will also establish ways of negotiating individual views and agree on a method of resolving misunderstandings. Such patterns should lead to improved group performance in terms of the quality of the group's decisions, its overall effectiveness, and the extent to which it fosters critical thinking and creative problem solving. This pattern of decision making is also likely to be a significant influence in how the group establishes its collaborative norms and how it deals with group members who deviate from these norms.

Fifth, because collaborative teams are constituted for very specific purposes, their functional life span will vary. In some cases a team may work on a problem over months or even years, while in other situations a few meetings over a few weeks may solve the problem. Experienced teachers will tell you that considering the collaborative team's life span is important for a number of reasons. For example, if the life span of the collaborative team is too short, it is likely that the problem for which the team was assembled will not be solved or will be only partially addressed. In addition, a short team life span lessens the likelihood of team members developing effective collaborative relationships, which take time to build. On the other hand, if the team life span is much longer than what it needs to be and the team spends unnecessary energy on a problem that has already been effectively addressed, then the likelihood of boredom, lowered morale, conflict, deteriorating professional relationships, and an aversion for working together in the future are all distinct possibilities. Perhaps the best way of avoiding either of these pitfalls, aside from sheer experience, is for the team to develop consensual methods of evaluating when the team's tasks have been satisfactorily accomplished. Having a clear idea of what the end product of the team should be will help define the *productive* length of the team life span.

Finally, given these characteristics of team functioning, the nature of professional communication will differ from team to team. In some teams, for example, there may be more written communication than in others. Alternately, some collaborative teams might demonstrate less overt overall communication than others because all the team members have worked with each other before and have established secure, effective working relationships.

As a novice teacher, you need to be aware of these characteristics so that your entry to any team setting is as smooth as possible. Being aware of the factors that influence team functioning will allow you to immediately be an effective team member, to contribute your expertise to all aspects of the collaborative work, and to build your professional integrity for future professional endeavors.

In addition to the functional characteristics of groups, several supporting skills will determine how effectively interprofessional collaboration proceeds.

Collaborative Supporting Skills

Collaborative work requires much effort, reflection, and skill. As a new teacher, there are many supporting skills that will help you establish yourself as a competent professional. Not only will these skills enhance your professional integrity, but also they can assist you in learning as much as possible from any collaborative experience. It is also important to understand that these supporting skills assume that you are technically competent in your job and that you are skilled at communicating effectively.

Positiveness

We generally prefer to associate with positive people, so it is important to develop a consistently hopeful outlook about your collaborative relationships. Obviously, not everyone is completely positive all the time, but an overall attitude that focuses on constructive interprofessional behavior is important. In some cases, a positive attitude may be all that stands between you and a very complex problem. Nurturing a positive attitude also has many other advantages. For example, a positive outlook increases the chances of building healthy professional relationships by making you more collaboratively attractive. Demonstrating a positive outlook will also instill a sense of hope and promise in any collaborative effort and will model positive outlooks for your colleagues, parents, and your students.

As with many other collaborative skills, developing a positive attitude can be demanding, especially if you are not inherently optimistic. There is little point, however, in not cultivating a positive outlook because negativity, aside from being unproductive and energy sapping, does not usually enhance your working relationships and can convey to others a very real sense of unapproachability.

There are many ways to develop a positive outlook to enhance your professional collaboration. For example, be sure that you are technically adept and able to perform the duties you have been trained for. Your competence will bring you a sense of satisfaction that increases your professional self-image. You should also engage in reflection on your professional activities and behavior as a way of learning from your mistakes and for celebrating your successes. This will help you develop a realistic sense of your strengths and weaknesses, a sense that is important because many negative attitudes arise from unrealistic expectations or demands you might place on yourself or on others.

In addition, spend time carefully delineating your work responsibilities from those responsibilities that belong to others or over which you have no control. This will prevent unnecessary discouragement by trying to solve problems that are either not your responsibility or which might be insoluble at your level of experience or expertise. You may also wish to surround yourself, as far as possible, with colleagues who are positive and supportive. They not only will enhance your own sense of professional self-worth, but also will be a source of encouragement if you become despondent. Finally, as an inexperienced teacher, it is crucial that you understand that negative feelings are part of any job and that learning how to deal with negativity is much more important than pretending that it does not exist. It is equally important that you not dwell on feelings of negativity for extended periods of time without taking some remedial action. It is professionally stifling to either ignore negativity or obsess about it. Experienced teachers understand that the most effective middle ground is to acknowledge any negativity, take action to remediate it effectively, and then reengage in positive collaborative activity.

Sense of Humor

Professional collaboration is work that is both labor intensive and serious. The complex set of collaborative factors addressed in this book make it clear that as a novice teacher, you certainly have much hard work ahead of you. However, many effective professionals understand that serious undertakings must be balanced by an appropriate lighter perspective. An excellent way not only to nurture a positive attitude, but also to extract as much joy from your work as possible, is to develop your sense of humor. You will have many experiences throughout your career that, on the one hand, appear to be quite weighty. Yet, many of those same situations are likely to have a humorous or even comical streak that can make even the most mundane task quite delightful. Do your best, where appropriate, to see the funny side of your collaborative tasks. Appropriate humor can often change the course of an overly serious discussion and is underused as a way of brainstorming novel ideas and solutions. Using humor appropriately can also break down communicative barriers and enhance others' willingness to collaborate. Shared humor can also often help create a strong sense of community and common cause as well as providing an appropriate outlet for frustration or excess energy.

While an astute sense of humor can be a positive way of helping you balance your professional perspectives, it is also necessary to develop an acute sense of timing and tact. Humor can sometimes be quite inappropriate and insensitive in serious collaborative circumstances. An occasional inappropriate attempt at humor can damage collaborative relationships, be distracting, and possibly lead to unnecessary conflict. Intermittent inappropriate humor can lower your professional integrity while consistently inappropriate attempts at humor may create the perception that your personal and professional judgments are unsound. In general, however, many professionals value a sense of humor and welcome its appropriate use in collaborative interaction.

Enthusiasm

Most novice teachers bring to their first job a deep sense of enthusiasm and energy. New teachers convey a great deal of excitement at their arrival in "the real world." As you enter your first teaching position, you will be privy to complex settings and events quite different from any prior student teaching experience. You will be bombarded by a bewildering array of exciting challenges. Initially, many aspects of your work will appear to be novel and somewhat mysterious, generating a deep sense of curiosity and a healthy compulsion to learn.

Aside from the energy generated by a new job and setting, most novice teachers also understand that they are expected to be zealous and available to assume their share of the professional load. Indeed, experienced teachers understand that such enthusiasm among novices is an important motivator and support during the first few years of teaching, when the stress of adjusting to the job and learning from experience are highest. Being enthusiastic will generate a great deal of positiveness in your outlook and accelerate your learning.

It is equally true that being less than enthusiastic can be problematic for a number of reasons. First, your colleagues will hold a strong expectation that you will enter your new profession enthusiastically. If you appear unmotivated, your professional integrity might be compromised from the start. Novices who lack enthusiasm are quickly discovered, often isolated, and may even be completely ignored by their more experienced or highly motivated colleagues. Second, a lack of enthusiasm usually results from other underlying factors, such as job dissatisfaction, personal or professional conflicts, or incompetence. Whatever the cause, a lack of enthusiasm will negatively impact the growth of your professional integrity and is likely to compromise your status among your colleagues. Third, it is much more difficult to maintain a positive professional outlook unsupported by energetic application to your work. A lack of enthusiasm may well turn any positive professional attitudes you may have into negativity and an overly critical attitude to all aspects of your job. Fourth, the longer any teacher remains unenthusiastic without attempting to become enthusiastic, the more difficult it will become to change.

It is also possible to be at a disadvantage by being too enthusiastic. For example, as a novice teacher it is important to temper your enthusiasm so as not to appear overbearing. Excessive enthusiasm can sometimes be perceived, at best, as irritating or distracting and, at worst, dictatorial or arrogant. Clearly, such perceptions, whether accurate or not, are unlikely to enhance your collaborative relationships or to increase your professional standing. In addition, excessive, unfocused enthusiasm can engender the perception that you possess little professional substance. Being inappropriately enthusiastic will use up a great deal of your energy that would be better spent on other more important aspects of your work.

Overall, it is important, therefore, that you maintain an appropriate sense of enthusiasm for your work. Simultaneously, you should harness your energy to avoid being inappropriately enthusiastic and to conserve your energy for the many tasks collaboration will require you to perform.

Patience

Most teachers understand that exercising patience is very important to their collaborative work. Being patient can sometimes be the difference between achieving desirable results and professional failure. Interprofessional collaboration, for example, often requires that team members be patient as they try to reach consensus, to communicate effectively, or to establish effective working relationships. Many novice teachers, largely due to enthusiasm and the drive to enhance their professional standing among their colleagues, fail to use patience to its greatest advantage.

Patience is rightfully prized as a social attribute because it tends to encourage understanding and communication while simultaneously reducing the likelihood of conflict. There is little point, therefore, in cultivating impatience as a routine professional behavior. You will discover that colleagues who are constantly impatient increase the potential for negativity, misunderstanding, and deteriorating interprofessional relationships. Impatience can also lead to professional isolation or even ostracism. Impatience can, too, often have a disastrous effect in working with students and their families. Patience should not be confused with professional incompetence, however. There is a great deal of difference between a well-considered exercise of patience and inaction due to incompetence.

Many factors will influence your decision to exercise patience and it is crucial that you learn to make judgments about when to exercise patience prudently or whether being patient can actually be detrimental. On the one hand, exercising patience can allow you time for effective decision making as you gather more important information, consult with others, or reflect on your professional options. Patience can also enhance your collaborative relationships by allowing others some time to consolidate their collaborative responsibilities or perhaps to give collaborative relationships time to develop. On the other hand, in some circumstances exercising patience is quite inappropriate and may, in some extremes, even be harmful. For example, it may be inappropriate to be too patient with a colleague or subordinate who is engaging in unprofessional or unethical behavior. Work hard to develop a sense of perspective that will allow you to extend or shorten your patience depending on your professional circumstances.

Generally, effective teachers understand that patience is a very positive personal and professional quality that is far more likely to help than to hinder. However, they also understand that the extent of their patience is based on numerous extenuating professional circumstances and, in the final analysis, is a finite and precious resource.

Willingness to Learn

One of the characteristics of competent and exceptional professionals in most fields, including teaching, is a distinct sense of curiosity and a willingness to learn. You are likely to have already encountered persons both personally and professionally whose reluctance to learn is characterized by arrogance or deception. A willingness to learn will help you, as a novice teacher, to grasp the many details of your new profession.

If you nurture high levels of motivation to learn, you will assimilate what you need to know more quickly, enhance your credibility more deeply, and extend your professional influence more widely. Effective teachers understand that over time your willingness to learn and explore the many aspects of teaching will make you a better teacher than many of your peers whose willingness to learn has declined or vanished. Furthermore, if you establish a deep willingness to learn early in your career, it is much more likely that you will remain a curious professional for your entire professional life. Being willing to learn also helps establish a positive attitude toward your collaborative work and will give you added credibility with families and students.

Awareness

A basic skill that will support many aspects of your professional behavior is a general sense of awareness and sensitivity to events, people, and the diverse circumstances of your job. The old adage of keeping your ears and eyes open and your mouth firmly shut is still, in some professional instances, sound advice. Discerning sensitivity also communicates your competence, empathy, and overall professional maturity. Cultivate the habit of observing your professional surroundings and colleagues closely as a way of gauging the collaborative atmosphere. Close observation will provide you with considerable information that, had you remained unaware of it, might have had awkward or even undesirable results. Such sensitivity is especially important in collaborative relationships with families and students.

It is equally important that, along with your sense of awareness, you develop an evaluative notion of the significance of what you observe. Being overly sensitive or disproportionately pensive can easily distort a simple reality into a full-blown crisis with a concomitant overreaction that can diminish your professional integrity. Evaluate what you observe by carefully avoiding wild speculation, by dealing with situational facts as you know them, by acting only on verifiable particulars, and, where possible, by consulting with trusted peers or a mentor.

Helpfulness

Being helpful and supportive of your colleagues and students and their families is one of the surest ways to enhance your professional integrity. Helpfulness is especially valuable in collaborative endeavors because it communicates your willingness to extend your efforts on behalf of others and tends to engender very positive working relationships. Often novice teachers feel that they are too inexperienced to be of much help to anyone. In some circumstances this is undoubtedly true, but there are many unique ways of being helpful in your profession that do not rely on years of experience or advanced expertise.

Flexibility

Flexibility, essentially, is the ability to adapt your professional behavior and decision making quickly, appropriately, and effectively to the unique circumstances of any particular problematic situation. It is important that as a novice teacher you begin to develop ways of dealing with your work creatively. All teachers make hundreds of decisions daily and routinely encounter difficult circumstances that require some ingenuity to surmount. Spend time cultivating an attitude that seeks different ways of approaching, defining, and solving problems in your work. Flexibility is especially important during collaboration. Remember that there is rarely only one way to solve a problem. Remind yourself that, generally, the more energy you devote to problem solving, the more knowledge and collaborative skill you will possess and the more flexible you are likely to be. Flexibility is a key element in adjusting to your new career and is a major asset in dealing with professional situations that at first glance seem intractable or baffling.

Commitment to Hard Work

It will be to your benefit to develop a professional habit of commitment to hard work. This may seem obvious, but a conscious awareness to develop a disciplined, conscientious attitude will enhance your collaborative relationships immensely. Hard workers are generally respected for their devotion to duty, and collaborative situations require, at least, that you shoulder your fair share of the workload. However, some professionals take their commitment to hard work to unhealthy extremes—overwork is a common hallmark of diligent novice teachers. While you should work hard, and even do a little more than what is required, you should also develop a sense of perspective that will allow you to gauge and respect the limits of your work capacity.

Honesty

A key ingredient of professional integrity is honesty. In all of your professional relationships, honesty will play an important role in others' perceptions of your professional integrity. If you demonstrate honesty as a matter of course to those with whom you are professionally involved, you will be well on the way to developing a deep sense of trust and professional reliability that will make it easier to resolve conflict and communicate your professional needs and concerns. Very few professionals are deliberately dishonest, but such people exist in every profession. If you encounter such a person, it is best to deal with them cautiously, especially if their dishonesty interferes with your collaborative relationships or services to your students. However, it is much more likely that some teachers demonstrate a benign form of dishonesty by default. For example, it is not unusual for novice teachers to take on more than they are able to handle because they fail to disclose that they cannot, or should not, attempt tasks beyond their level of experience or expertise. Many novice teachers take on tasks that are somewhat unreasonable for their abilities, thereby creating the potential for failure or inadequate performance. If you find yourself in similar circumstances, rethink your job responsibilities, the limits of your current professional abilities, the reality of the circumstances involved, and then make a decision as to whether to proceed or attempt to redefine or renegotiate the task.

Generally, blatant dishonesty is sure to cause a great deal of conflict and will more than likely lead to seriously damaged collaborative relationships. Lesser, more subtle forms of dishonesty are much more likely to occur, often in spite of your best intentions; they may, however, have no less effect than outright deception.

Uncertainty and Hesitancy

Uncertainty is a fact of professional life that is not always detrimental to the collaborative process. Experienced teachers are well aware that in some cases uncertainty and subsequent hesitancy to take professional action is appropriate and even necessary. They also know that uncertainty can be lessened by collaborative experience, by professional expertise, and by obtaining as much information as possible around any given professional dilemma. Generally, however, novice teachers are uncertain of how to act in new professional situations, including collaborative interactions. Uncertainty is most often the result of a lack of knowledge—knowledge, for example, about policy and procedures, modes of professional behavior, technical aspects of the work, and so on. All of the skills discussed in this book will help you overcome uncertainty and allow you effective decision making for professional action.

Self-Determination and Integrity

The responsibility for who you become as a teacher is, by and large, your responsibility. Cultivate an astute awareness, as you work, of always striving to be more effective and competent. If you take responsibility for your own professional development, you are much more likely to be responsible, hard working, and competent. Strive to learn as much as you can about your work through reflection, in-service training, collaboration with your colleagues, involvement in professional organizations, and immersion in your career. Emulate experienced, competent professionals you admire, and if at all possible, make at least one of them a mentor. Seek out opportunities for leadership that match your abilities and work diligently to establish a deep sense of professional integrity. Maintain a balanced, realistic, yet positive perspective of your work and exercise patience. Be appropriately tolerant, forgiving, and sensitive while simultaneously avoiding taking on responsibilities or problems that are rightfully the responsibility of others. Ensure that you are organized, that you learn quickly and appropriately from your mistakes, be supportive of others' earnest endeavors, and develop a keen sense of judgment for professional survival.

Practical Supporting Behaviors for Collaboration

Clearly, interprofessional collaboration involves hard work and a long-term commitment. To maximize your effectiveness in collaboration, and also to enhance your professional ability and stamina overall, there are many actions that, when made a regular part of your approach to your work, will support your efforts and help you maintain a high energy level for effective professional performance.

Personal Health

Perhaps nothing is more detrimental to effective professional performance than ill health. Health problems siphon off a tremendous amount of energy and time from your professional duties. Certainly, many short-term and chronic illnesses are not the result of any individual actions or neglect. On the other hand, some forms of ill health are directly related to individuals' refusal to take good care of themselves. Novice teachers are probably more vulnerable than their more experienced peers in this regard. As novices become aware of the many pressures of their new job, they tend to neglect health maintenance in favor of unnecessary and unrealistic overwork. Realize that you have finite levels of energy and monitor your disposition closely so that extreme overwork does not lead to illness. Develop a sense of pacing, and when you become ill, take immediate corrective action. Generally, the idea is to engage in preventive action that will result in your approaching your work with energy by reducing the potential for avoidable illness. In addition, pay attention to your living habits and, if necessary, modify them to provide maximum support for your professional endeavors.

Personal Life

This book makes clear that your professional and personal selves are inextricably intertwined and reflected in your professional behavior. It is therefore crucial that you take personal experiences and circumstances into account when making any decisions for professional action. With experience you will benefit from acknowledging that your personal circumstances, feelings, and relationships are an integral part of what you bring to teaching and that consciously working to lessen their effects in your work is to your benefit. Your personal life circumstances will ebb and flow. You will sometimes teach when you are happy and contented. At other times, you will be responsible for your work even if you are angry, resentful, frustrated, or depressed. Recognize that such cycles are a normal part of being human. Importantly, also realize that if you deny any personal conflict states, you are much more likely to have these states interfere subtly with your work. Take time to gauge your emotional and psychological disposition and then decide on how best to keep it in check so that it does not detract from your professional performance. If you find that this is impossible, it is important that you seek the help of therapeutic professionals or the counsel of a colleague, friend, or mentor.

Balance

Many enthusiastic professionals, especially novices, attack their new job responsibilities by working long hours, deeply immersing themselves in every aspect of their work, and by generally viewing their professional lives as their top priority. Highly effective professionals understand that they need to go the extra mile in their work and that, at times, they must put job responsibilities ahead of almost everything else. They also understand, however, that a careful balance between work and other life activities is the best way to maintain professional enthusiasm, curiosity, and motivation.

If you do not strive for such a balance, you run at least two significant risks, which can detract from your professional effectiveness. On the one hand, being overly involved in your work may lead to a loss of perspective about your professional actions and decisions. Excessive overinvolvement increases the potential for burnout, risks interprofessional conflict, and may be detrimental to your personal relationships and private life. On the other hand, underinvolvement may lead to disinterest in your work, may lower your motivation, and may create the perception among your colleagues that you are doing less than your best.

Over- and underinvolvement in your work, therefore, both have significant personal and professional drawbacks. Certainly, if you must choose, being overinvolved may have more positive consequences than being underinvolved, but there is a very real price to pay. Effective, experienced teachers strive to balance their professional involvement by prioritizing their work demands; paying attention to their emotional, physical, and spiritual needs; exercising effective assertiveness skills; and using their time efficiently.

Prioritizing

All professionals come to understand that their work is never completely done. There is always another project, another meeting, or another issue that has to be resolved. Try your best to develop a sense of priority in what you should attend to given that not all demands are equally important and that you must use your finite energy and expertise for maximum effect. Many ineffective teachers spend inordinate amounts of time and energy on relatively unimportant tasks.

On the other hand, you may also encounter a few professionals who appear to be capable not only of doing everything that comes their way, but also of doing it well. These extraordinary people are the stars of the profession who seem to possess boundless energy, creativity, efficiency, and grace. They are almost never inexperienced. Should you wish to emulate such professional behavior, you should consider the ramifications carefully and with the full understanding that such professional behavior takes a great deal of time to develop and has powerful advantages *and* disadvantages. If you wish to elevate yourself to this level of productivity, do it slowly over a long period of time without, as far as possible, exceeding your ability level.

Realistic Achievement

Most novice teachers have a deep desire to do well and to perform effectively in their new profession in order to receive positive collegial attention and to build professional self-esteem. Consequently, most novice teachers set high professional expectations for themselves. Setting such goals is appropriate and necessary to make the most of your professional opportunities and to develop understanding of the many complex professional roles you are expected to fulfill. However, that enthusiasm and a driving desire to do well can sometimes lead to unrealistic goal setting and unreasonable achievement standards. On one hand, setting realistic goals is difficult given that you will initially be unfamiliar with the demands of your teaching and other professional duties. On the other, setting goals will help define the limits of your responsibilities and assist you in better managing your time, energy, and professional interactions. For professional achievement to be realistic, goals must be matched to your level of teaching experience, expertise, motivation, and the many other limits found in any job. When you set professional goals, carefully assess how much you know about the task at hand and what has to be done. Spend time judging whether you have the necessary competence and the extent to which you can reasonably extend your knowledge, skill, and energy. Establish whether, in your opinion, you are able to at least attempt the task. Also examine how much time the task is likely to take and what other responsibilities and work priorities will be affected by your decision. Make sure that the task is, in fact, your responsibility and, above all, try not to take on more work than you know you can successfully accomplish. If you are still unsure after these steps, you may gain some added insight by consulting with other experienced teachers or a trusted mentor.

Time and Energy Management

Time and energy are finite resources. Consequently, you should develop a habit of using what time you have effectively. Cultivate a habit of using every work moment productively and develop the understanding that the more time you waste, the less time you have to accomplish what you need to do. Do not be seduced by the idea that leaving important projects until the last minute will force you to work more effectively or creatively. Few people who operate in this way are able to sustain acceptable, let alone superior, performance. Furthermore, working under self-imposed pressure increases the chances of making mistakes, missing deadlines, and wasting energy. Develop a habit of planning how to spend your work time and be alert for needless distractions while simultaneously developing a habit of attending to unexpected, legitimate problems that may arise. It is also helpful, from time to time, to engage in reflecting on how you spend your time in your job so that you can establish ways of improving your time management and your productivity.

In addition, be alert to colleagues who have elevated wasting time to the level of an art form. Effective teachers understand that a small minority of their peers waste a great deal of time engaging in casual conversation, daydreaming, and other nonproductive behavior. If you encounter such people, resist their attempts to socialize you to their low level of performance. Instead, model effective time management skills that will increase your effectiveness, productivity, and integrity on the job.

Collaborative Maintenance Work on Relationships

Interprofessional collaborative relationships are like any other social relationship: They will need to be maintained and nurtured if they are to grow and mature. Novice teachers commonly neglect this aspect of their collaboration, either by assuming that such maintenance is unnecessary or, more likely, that somehow collaborative relationships simply "happen." It is often too late to begin work on a collaborative relationship when the need for collaborative action arises. There are many ways to actively maintain collaborative relationships, and such efforts should be undertaken with the understanding that your efforts will not always be immediately effective, that your efforts will have different levels of effectiveness in relationships of different intensity, and that, in a few instances, your efforts might have no effect at all. It is unrealistic to expect that in your first few months as a teacher you will be able to develop deep working relationships with almost all of your peers and your students. You are much more likely to develop these relationships if you apply sustained effort over time rather than erratic, intense spurts of effort. Use your communication skills to the best of your ability and ensure that you pay attention to your colleagues both as professionals and as human beings. Try, where possible and appropriate, to learn a little about your colleagues' personal interests and lives to convey a sense of caring and the perception that you see each of them as individuals. Do not confine your interactions with them strictly around professional issues, but, on the other hand, do not get so involved with them outside of professional commitments that your interprofessional collaboration suffers. Strive to be positive, helpful, and encouraging while simultaneously taking care not to be overbearing. Refrain from gossip and comments about colleagues, parents, or students. Instead, confine your opinions to the professional task at hand, model exemplary leadership skills such as innovation and consensus building, and consistently seek out the good in others. When conflicts arise, deal with them immediately and fully to avoid long-standing resentments. In addition, develop an acute sense of which parts of interprofessional problems are changeable and which are not.

Generally, maintaining and building collaborative relationships requires a great deal of work, caring, and, in some instances, sacrifice. If you take time to reflect on what is needed in such relationships and then implement your efforts with honesty, sincerity, and a willing flexibility, you will greatly increase the quality of your collaborative relationships.

Increased Collaboration

An important way of learning and maintaining collaborative skill is by increasing your availability for collaborative efforts. The more you collaborate, the more comfortable you will feel with this way of working and the more likely you will be to collaborate in the future.

As you seek out collaborative relationships, remember that not all of your colleagues will wish to engage in such alliances. Develop a habit of being consistently amenable to collaborative efforts tempered by the understanding that you will not have such relationships with all of your peers. In addition, remember that some colleagues' reluctance to engage in such relationships is

not necessarily negative. As a novice teacher, spend time learning to discriminate between colleagues who ignore collaboration, those who collaborate at
every opportunity, and those, who while reluctant or hesitant, might engage
in collaboration with some encouragement or change of circumstances.

Furthermore, consider that not every collaborative relationship is, or
should be, equally significant. Some working relationships will be more or less
superficial than others because the level of collaboration is directly related to
the nature of the collaborative task, prior history of the collaborative relationship, and the expertise of the participants. Develop a level of flexibility that
allows you to match the collaborative intensity level to the collaborative task.
Developing such flexibility is largely a trial-and-error endeavor. You will be
able to gauge the level of collaborative intensity as long as you understand that
such levels exist and that you should negotiate your collaborative relationships
accordingly.

Support Networks

Many novice teachers struggle to adjust to their new career on their own. Some
feel that this is their professional responsibility, while others do not know to
whom to turn for help. Experienced teachers understand the value of building
and maintaining a support network of friends, family, and colleagues to whom
they can turn for support. Spend time as a new teacher identifying such people
and establish a relationship level with them that will allow you to access their
goodwill when you feel frustrated or discouraged.

Interesting and Meaningful Projects

One way of maintaining your motivation and extending your expertise while
simultaneously building collaborative relationships is to embark, where possible, on projects in which you are interested or which for some reason are
personally or professionally meaningful. Such projects are infrequent, but
when the opportunity arises, they can be of great professional and personal
benefit. While it is true that effective teachers execute their routine duties to
the best of their ability, there is little doubt that even the most enthusiastic
teacher becomes fatigued and somewhat desensitized over time. One way of
renewing interest and replenishing a positive attitude is to seek out positive,
extraordinary professional experiences. Be alert to opportunities offered by
your school and district, such as inservice workshops, special training opportunities, or the chance to work with visiting specialists. Keep in close touch
with faculty and staff at local universities and colleges. You may also wish to
take an active role in professional organizations that sponsor interesting pro-

fessional ventures. These undertakings, while they often involve extra work over and above your routine duties, can give you a distinct advantage in collaborative work.

Assertiveness

Even many experienced teachers find themselves overwhelmed with extra work—possibly work that is not even their responsibility—because they have difficulty being assertive and find it almost impossible, even where appropriate, to say "no." Refusing demands or requests from fellow professionals is a difficult issue for most teachers and especially so for novice teachers. Essentially, refusing professional demands revolves around several issues. For example, many people have considerable difficulty deciding when refusal is appropriate. When you are asked, as a new teacher, to perform certain tasks over and above your regular duties, your inclination will be to agree to do them, as you will probably wish to appear cooperative. Agreeing to extraordinary tasks, especially when you are new, has many benefits. For example, it demonstrates your willingness to go above and beyond routine assignments. It also shows that you are responsive to the many extra demands of your job and demonstrates your understanding that, in teaching, extraordinary effort is often required. In addition, such willingness is evidence of high levels of motivation, enthusiasm, and a general can-do attitude. However, agreeing to extraordinary demands can also be detrimental. For example, if you agree to many demands over and above the requirements of your job, you may find yourself overextended beyond your current levels of ability and energy. In addition, agreeing to every request made of you might create the perception that others can relinquish their duties to you, a situation that can often overwhelm your resources and increase the possibility of collaborative confusion and conflict. Remember that undiscriminating acceptance of every possible task that comes your way does not necessarily place you in a favorable professional light. Alternately, refusing to participate or complete extraordinary tasks does not necessarily detract from your professional image.

There are several ways to develop a sense of discrimination about what is your responsibility and what is not. It is important to clearly understand your exact job responsibilities and those of the people around you. Seek guidance from trusted colleagues and mentors when you are not sure whether to take on extra tasks or not, and be vigilant of taking on too much before you realize it—extra tasks pile up quickly and many professionals realize this only after committing to far too much. Be sure, when considering extra professional tasks, that they will not interfere with more pressing priorities for which you are directly and involuntarily responsible.

Almost everyone has been in the frustrating position of having agreed to something that they truly felt they should have refused, and such experiences are common among novice teachers. The issue of whether to refuse an extraordinary demand or task depends largely on your ability to discriminate between legitimate and illegitimate demands. Many inexperienced teachers believe, mistakenly, that saying "no" to anything they are asked to do over and above their regular duties will be detrimental to their professional progress and will be taken personally by the colleagues they refuse. While in isolated instances this may well be the case, it is much more likely that careful consideration of a demand and a thoughtful decision to refuse will not only preserve your energy and time for more appropriate tasks, but also will communicate your professional sense of task priority and discrimination, a hallmark of leadership and professional maturity. Your saying "no" will also be influenced by the manner in which you refuse. You are much more likely to be understood if you refuse politely, and where appropriate, by providing the logical reason for your decision.

Overall, the most effective way to negotiate these obstacles is to develop an accurate sense of your professional priorities, responsibilities, expertise, and available energy. Also, spend time developing acute assertiveness skills, that is, the ability to communicate your professional needs and limitations firmly but without becoming aggressive or patronizing. Developing a good sense of your capabilities while still communicating your willingness to go the extra mile will enhance your professional and collaborative standing immensely.

Be Organized

A hallmark of effective teachers is their ability to organize their professional lives efficiently for maximum effort over extended periods of time. While it is true that some professionals pride themselves on being disorganized, as a novice you should strive to make ordered sense of your duties, always allowing time and energy for the many unexpected or underestimated tasks that teaching brings. Developing a sense of organization will help you to make better professional sense of the almost overwhelming volume of tasks demanded of you. The more you are organized, the less likely you will be to miss deadlines, forget required assignments or projects, or to misunderstand what is required of you.

Being organized will also allow the maximum amount of time possible to devote to teaching or collaboration with your colleagues. Spend time thinking of how you wish to organize and routinize many of your tasks *prior* to your first teaching day and regularly spend time reflecting on how to improve the organization of your professional tasks. Ask your colleagues for organizational hints and observe their organizational structure. Remain flexible enough to constantly modify your organizational system for increased efficiency. Over time you will discover that many teaching and collaborative tasks benefit from careful planning and established routines.

Summary

This chapter has described a number of personal and professional aspects that comprise the context of teamwork. These supporting skills are intertwined and mediate your collaborative performance. While these skills will undoubtedly be refined with experience over time, they may also be carefully considered ahead of time to allow you optimum potential for adjustment and effectiveness early in your career.

Questions for Reflection

1. Conduct a personal inventory of the skills discussed in this chapter. Evaluate which skills and dispositions you possess, which need more attention, and which skills you still need to acquire. How will you accomplish any necessary improvements?

2. Reflect on your personal qualities, abilities, and attitudes. Compare who you are as a person to who you wish to be as a teacher. Is who you are as a person correlated to who you wish to be as a professional? If so, how can you improve? If not, how can you reconcile these two issues?

3. Brainstorm ways that will help you improve your skills for collaboration.

4. How can you encourage these skills in your colleagues and professional peers?

5. How can you adjust your collaborative relationships with colleagues or peers who do not possess such high levels of skill as you do?

References

Dettmer, P., Thurston, L. P., & Dyck, N. (1996). *Consultation, collaboration, and teamwork: For students with special needs* (2nd Ed.). Boston: Allyn & Bacon.

Friend, M., & Cook, L. (1996). *Interactions: Collaboration skills for school professionals* (2nd Ed.). New York: Longman.

Idol, L. (1983). *Special educator's consultation handbook* (2nd Ed.). Austin, TX: PRO-ED.

Johnson, D. W. (1987). *Human relations and your career* (2nd Ed.). Englewood Cliffs, NJ: Prentice-Hall.

Larson, C. E., & le Fasto, F. M. J. (1989). *Teamwork: What must go right, what can go wrong.* Newbury Park, CA: Sage.

Pugach, M. C., & Johnson, L. J. (1995). *Collaborative practitioners, collaborative schools.* Denver, CO: Love Publishing.

Sugai, G. M., & Tindal, G. A. (1993). *Effective school consultation: An interactive approach.* Belmont, CA: Wadsworth.

4

Practical Aspects of Interprofessional Collaboration

Introduction

Collaborative groups or teams require an astute sense of interpersonal communication, social awareness, and goal-oriented professional behavior. A key aspect of interprofessional collaboration revolves around your awareness of group dynamics that may affect any professional behavior. Collaborative groups in educational settings are most often used as a way of solving problems through multifaceted personal and professional interaction. Most teams comprise a number of individuals from different professional backgrounds and levels of experience, which increases significantly the potential for considering a wider range of intervention options, blends team members' complementary strengths, and tends to balance out any individual negative influences.

When teamwork is the appropriate mode for solving an educational problem, your professional integrity will be enhanced and your collaborative performance improved by an acute understanding of the significant advantages and disadvantages of most intercollaborative work. It is important that you reflect on and promote the positive aspects of interprofessional collaboration while simultaneously acknowledging some potential disadvantages and seeking, wherever possible, to negate or at least lessen the effects of such problems.

Advantages of Teamwork

Seek at every opportunity to promote and model the positive effects of interprofessional collaboration as it relates to your setting. By emphasizing the advantages of collaboration and teamwork, you will not only improve your own professional practice but also model for others the very real effectiveness such collaboration can bring.

Shared Professional Competence and Experience

A major asset of teamwork is that individual members bring to the group a wide range of skills and specialized knowledge from their unique personal, professional, and experiential backgrounds. While some of these skills or experiences may overlap, much of what each individual's perspective will be is quite distinct from that of any one else in the group. All participants will therefore be able to increase the group's sense of professional and experiential diversity and to generate multifaceted approaches to problem solving and intervention implementation.

Diverse levels of competence and experience are a distinct advantage for both novice and expert teachers. Novices benefit from the wealth of knowledge shared by their more experienced colleagues, whereby they acquire professionally effective attributes more quickly than if they were working on their own. In addition, novices will also benefit from the modeled professional collaborative behavior of their more senior colleagues. On the other hand, highly experienced teachers can benefit from the characteristic energy, enthusiasm, and willingness to learn of most novice teachers. Less experienced colleagues also provide experienced teachers with important opportunities for mentoring and increased professional interaction.

Collective Responsibility

All teachers are trained, appropriately, to accept individual responsibility for their actions. Indeed, much professional decision making would not be possible or practical without isolated individual action. However, given the complex nature of many educational problems, individual responsibility, in some instances, holds the potential for professional debilitation. For example, if individual professional action results in resounding success, there is the possibility that the individual teacher might inappropriately seek further individual success in the future. Such actions might lead to devaluing team approaches or result in increased professional isolation. Should an individual teacher make a serious professional misjudgment, the resulting fallout can sometimes be inordinately severe.

Mutual responsibility, on the other hand, encourages all members of the team to agree to or at least consent to a team decision for which everybody takes collective responsibility. Both success and failure of the team's decision is then distributed across the team with resultant positive reinforcement or lessening of any negative effect.

Interprofessional Communication

Working in a group setting increases the opportunities for all teachers to communicate within their profession and across professional boundaries with members from other professions. Such communication tends to increase each participant's professional knowledge of their colleagues' ability and professional perspectives. This knowledge increases the chances of group members reaching consensus while simultaneously reducing unnecessary conflict that often arises when others' professional viewpoints are not understood. Also, interprofessional dialogue provides many opportunities for each member's views to be challenged and examined closely by his or her colleagues, a useful professional activity which, through responsible self-reflection, can lead each participant to a renewed understanding of their own professional assumptions and a refinement of their professional attitudes and judgment. Such communication, therefore, ensures that any collaboration for effective problem solving is a reciprocal, dynamic process that encourages increased focus and goal orientation.

Spread of Resources

Clearly, when several teachers, other helping professionals, and parents or family members agree to collaborate in the best interests of the student, a wider range of resources becomes available through the participants' pooled knowledge and experience. Again, the complexity of many educational problems makes it very difficult for one professional to be aware of all possible resources that might be available at any given time, while several team members, focusing on a common problem or goal, can often provide other relevant assets that might positively impact their work and the welfare of the student.

Disadvantages of Teamwork

While it is probably inappropriate to consistently emphasize the shortcomings inherent in most collaborative ventures, it is equally important that you remain aware of the potential disadvantages common to working with others. You should ensure that others are also aware of potential difficulties and spend time rectifying such problems as they arise or, at the very least, neutralizing such disadvantages as much as possible.

Communication Difficulties

Collaboration requires skilled communication. The intricacies of interprofessional communication tend to proliferate relative to the number of participants because of variations in individuals' communicative ability and style, diverse professional orientations, levels of experience, personal agendas, and prior communicative history with other team members. In addition, persons on the team who have not worked in team settings might have difficulty adjusting to the often complex communicative demands such settings routinely generate. Added into this rather volatile mix will be a complex educational problem with many unpredictable or unchangeable facets. Experienced teachers know that team efforts often fail or are only partially successful as a direct result of communication problems. For these reasons, it is very important to acquire and practice effective interprofessional communication skills throughout your career as a means of ensuring the well-being of your students, their parents, and your colleagues.

Time

A major problem in any collaborative approach is finding the time to meet and conduct business. While some work can be accomplished individually and in isolation before being shared with the team, it is equally true that there are many aspects of collaborative work that can only be conducted when all or most of the members meet as a group. Most teachers and helping professionals involved in services to students in schools are extremely busy, so demands on their time are great. Consequently, arranging a mutual time to meet is often extraordinarily difficult and the task usually becomes more laborious in proportion to the number of people involved.

Many experienced teachers lament the lack of time for collaboration but go to extraordinary lengths to arrange collaborative meetings. While some schools have recognized the time dilemma and have deliberately scheduled a formal time for collaborative teams to meet, this is generally the exception and not the rule. It is far more likely that meetings will be scheduled at awkward times, that they will often be conducted hurriedly, and, in many cases, with less than the full complement of team members present. Clearly, such constraints greatly increase the chances for collaborative problems.

Commitment

Teamwork, aside from being extraordinarily demanding of your energy and expertise, usually occurs over an extended period of time. Given the complexity of many educational problems and practical collaborative issues, teamwork requires an obvious sustained professional commitment. Such commitment, while usually desirable and appropriate, can be problematic for several reasons. For example, some team members who wish to obligate themselves to the team effort may, due to other legitimate commitments, be unable to do so. On the other hand, some other teachers, while they could potentially be an asset to the team, may not wish to commit their resources and energy over extended periods of time. A third problem arises when team members who initially commit to the collaborative effort fail to sustain their commitment. This is especially problematic as it inevitably means that other team members will need to bridge the gap until a replacement arrives and is adjusted to the workload and focus of the group effort.

Resistance

Another common problem in teamwork is resistance to serving on the team. Some believe that any resistance should be seen as a barrier that needs to be overcome by any means possible. Such a position assumes that some teachers resist collaborative work based on unstated selfish motivation—incompetence, disinterest, or plain opposition. While this might be the case with a few teachers, it is much more likely that there are legitimate reasons why teachers decline such requests.

Given the generally voluntary nature of collaboration, there is little point in attacking or manipulating colleagues who decline collaborative invitations. While initial efforts to coerce colleagues into collaborative endeavors might succeed, these tactics often cause more harm than good. For example, such coercion increases the possibility of damaging long-term professional relationships. Furthermore, any attempts at coercion or manipulation will tend to reflect poorly on your own professional integrity and increase the chances that your efficacy will suffer as a result.

Differing Professional Views

Ideally, team membership should reflect as much diversity as possible in terms of professional orientations and other views that potentially might contribute to solving the educational problem. However, diverse views are only helpful if all members of the team are prepared to consider others' points of view and are then prepared to modify their own understandings in light of others' opinions. However, most teachers have, by and large, been trained to make decisions from their own professional point of view and, in many cases, independent of others' input. Such standard professional socialization works against the collaborative give-and-take that characterizes most team efforts. Unless team members have been trained in collaborative undertakings or are prepared to devote significant energy to understanding others' points of view, different professional orientations pose a notable threat to team cohesion. Also, this aspect is particularly problematic if an unyielding team member happens to possess high levels of expertise that are valuable to any decision the team might make.

Lack of Collaborative Skills

While the idea of collaboration in teaching has often been implied, it is only recently that formal training in collaboration has appeared in preservice coursework. It is likely, therefore, that many teachers have not been trained in specific collaborative skills. A lack of training is often the reason why otherwise competent teachers and other helping professionals are reluctant to engage in teamwork. A lack of training may also mean that some teachers who engage in professional collaboration might not be as effective as their better trained counterparts. In addition, adequate in-service teacher training is often unavailable. Such a deficit may mean either that the resources of those lacking collaborative skills is lost to the team or that less skilled team members increase the chance of misunderstanding or conflict among team members.

Quality of Decisions

Generally, as mentioned above, a diverse group of teachers working together to solve a common problem means that important aspects of solutions that would otherwise be lost, are considered. However, a common problem related to this strength often appears when the team attempts to build consensus among different participants with very different views on the problem. In short, reaching a consensus for action can often be difficult. However, in order to obtain such a consensus, the quality of the decision might suffer, becoming watered down to ensure that all team members, even those with very different points of view, are accommodated in the final decision. The decision quality in the final consensus, therefore, depends on the individual and collective collaborative skill of all team members and their willingness to compromise.

Lack of Resources

Given the demands on team members, simple operating matters that remain unproblematic in other settings take on significantly important proportions in collaboration. Resources from a number of domains all converge in effective teamwork to produce optimum results and generally fall into three areas: each professional's personal and professional resources, resources of the team, and resources outside of, but supportive of, the team.

All professional work requires careful, effective, and efficient utilization of your own personal resources. Not paying careful attention to appropriate use of these resources can be quite problematic, especially among novice teachers. Personal strengths, energy, and effort should be used to your best advantage and to the best advantage of others. A capacity for hard work, positiveness, patience, creativity, and problem solving will impact your working relationship with the team as will your ability to communicate, your perceptions of why you are a teacher, and how you manage your weaknesses. Remember, too, that your personal resources are, in the long run, finite, so it is especially appropriate to develop a keen sense of pacing in your work.

Professional resources also have an important influence on collaborative efforts. For example, your level of teaching and collaborative experience, knowledge of resources in your school, and your capacity to uncover previously unknown sources of support will all make you a more effective team member. Other professional resources—such as your technical teaching expertise, your knowledge of your field and other related fields, and your skill in developing working relationships—will assist you in becoming a more skilled professional and increase your professional integrity.

A third set of factors, related to both personal and professional resources, are often more crucial in determining collaborative team outcomes than many inexperienced teachers think. These factors operate outside the direct collaborative efforts of the team but can often interfere, positively or negatively, with team outcomes. For example, experienced teachers will tell you that time is the chief resource most likely to be unavailable. Time is often discounted as a resource factor because it is less tangible than some other influential resources, but it has a profound effect on how the team operates. Other resources are also important here. A place to meet can become a major obstacle to team functioning if it is uncomfortable or unavailable; a lack of administrative support to complete documentation or maintain records can result in misunderstanding; or funds necessary to fulfill team goals might be negligible or nonexistent.

Experienced teachers understand that while the ideal availability of resources may be accessible only to a greater or lesser degree, the work of the team should remain a priority and team members should, where possible, work around resource problems. Novice teachers sometimes feel that unless optimal resources are immediately available, there is little that can be accomplished by collaborative teamwork. However, effective teachers know that ideal resources are seldom, if ever, available and that one of the more interesting challenges of interprofessional collaboration is to get the job done in spite of these disadvantages.

Role Ambiguity and Duplication of Effort

While professional diversity on a team is a distinct advantage, it may also, in some instances, become an equally significant disadvantage. Most team members will have been trained and socialized into clear professional roles with concomitant well-defined responsibilities and obligations. However, these very roles may well overlap with others' collaborative obligations. For example, school psychologists and special educators are both capable, within their professional responsibilities, of conducting achievement testing on students referred for special services.

When teachers work in isolation, overlapping roles can sometimes cause minor problems or misunderstandings, but in a team setting this can become a significant problem. Role ambiguity is usually problematic in two forms. First, different teachers sharing a common role might become inordinately distracted in deciding who will be responsible for any particular work role. Second, unless the role ambiguity is resolved, there is a very real chance that each professional, acting in good faith, might complete similar tasks and needlessly duplicate efforts.

Experienced teachers understand that the most effective way to avoid role ambiguity is to establish exactly what the work role of each team member will be at the outset of the collaborative work. It is also important to remind team members periodically of their roles and make adjustments where necessary.

Levels of Experience

Obviously, not all collaborative participants will possess the same level of experience at the outset of the collaborative task. While diverse experiences can enhance team functioning in many ways, experiential issues can also prove to be a distinct impediment to team functioning.

Generally, experienced teachers will possess considerably more professional knowledge than novices, although competent teachers understand that experience does not necessarily equate with increased levels of professional ability. Optimal utilization of professional growth and integrity requires reflection, self-evaluation, and active learning. On the other hand, many teachers *do* learn a great deal from their experience, and their contributions will enhance the functioning of any collaborative team.

The juxtaposition of more and less experience in collaborative work can be problematic. For example, if more experienced teachers do not allow for the inexperience of some of their colleagues, friction and even conflict can quickly appear. Alternately, if inexperienced teachers fail to recognize the limits of their expertise, they can compromise both their individual integrity and the functioning of the team.

Voluntary

The voluntary nature of teamwork is a distinct disadvantage in two ways. First, this may mean that some highly competent individuals who could provide valuable contributions to the team might not choose to join the team. These persons might decline membership for very legitimate reasons, but their loss is nevertheless significant. Second, and much less likely, is that an individual whose professional preparation or experience is unneeded or irrelevant joins the team. Given these two possibilities, the former is more damaging to team functioning.

Group Dynamics in Team Settings

Many aspects of this book illustrate that interprofessional work is influenced by a wide range of factors that may operate as collaborative participants endeavor to complete their assigned tasks. The more you understand the intricacies of how people interact in group situations, the more likely that you will be an effective professional and that your professional integrity will grow consistently. The following basic factors affect the group dynamics of inter-professional collaboration.

Types and Purposes of Collaborative Groups

An elementary aspect of how groups work is to remember that many different types of groups are constructed to serve different purposes. For example, group membership depends on the task or goals of the team and the availability of such persons for service on the team. Groups may also vary in their styles of interaction. Some might be formal, with meetings conducted strictly to a written agenda and according to the established rules of meeting protocol, while others might be quite informal or less structured.

The specific group configuration in which you work should be directly influenced by the purpose for which the group is formed. Early in the forma-tion of the group, therefore, some decision must be made as to the most effective level of formality given the understanding of what the problem is and how it is to be solved.

Group Operation

How effectively the collaborative group operates depends on a number of factors irrespective of the purpose for which the group is formed or its level of formality. First, the professional characteristics of the team have a direct bearing on how well it operates. If the team members are competent, experienced, enthusiastic, goal-directed, and skillful collaborators, then collaboration has a much better chance of succeeding. Second, the number of persons in the group is a crucial aspect of operation. If the group is too small, there can be very real disadvantages for team functioning. For example, too few team members can lead to excessive workloads, which quite often are detrimental to performance or might even create conflict. In addition, too few team members may also limit the pool of expertise and experience so important for quality team decision making and interaction. On the other hand, if the team is excessively large, the potential is raised for unwieldy organization, duplication of effort, and misunderstandings or conflict. Generally, defining the team's size for effective operation should be guided, at least initially, by who is available, their levels of skill relevant in the team setting, and how essential they are or might be to the problems the team aims to address.

Third, the general way in which the team conducts its business will tend to influence how effectively the team operates. Most teams operate under some set of explicit or implicit rules that govern the professional behavior and work of the participants. The more formal the modes of operation, the more likely it will be that these rules are explicit and understood by each team member, and vice versa for less formal team settings.

Fourth, and often ignored by even the most effective collaborative groups, is the influence of the physical setting in which business is conducted. Where possible, the team's meeting place should be free from distraction, relatively comfortable, and private in order to allow the best opportunity for remaining focused and productive. Finally, no matter how successful any collaborative group is, its functionality is always constrained, more or less, by the guidelines and rules of the larger organization within which it operates. Many inexperienced teachers and parents waste enormous amounts of energy straining needlessly against institutional limitations that detract from the focus of the immediate problem. Of course, this is not to say that many aspects of any organization cannot be improved, but it is important to realize that such change takes effort over time.

Team Members

Each member of the collaborative team brings a wealth of professional and personal knowledge to the problem-solving and decision-making process. In order for collaboration to be as effective as possible, you, your colleagues, and parents should be aware that each individual arrives in the group setting with certain expectations, personal and professional strengths and weaknesses, and a lifetime of experience, all of which have resulted in each individual's status on the team. These factors will play a subtle yet important part in all interprofessional group collaboration. The more you are aware of these factors in yourself and in others, the more likely it will be that the team can function effectively.

Personal Characteristics

Many inexperienced teachers assume that personal characteristics should not play any part in professional work. However, this perception is unrealistic for two reasons. First, it is likely that all persons on the team will have several very positive personal characteristics that can add immensely to the effectiveness of the group dynamic. For example, personal warmth, genuine empathy, and a sense of humor, among many others, are personal qualities that are generally considered to be desirable in any group. Second, it is unrealistic to expect that our perceptions of negative personal attributes in ourselves and others will be ignored in favor of purely "professional" interaction. Experienced teachers understand that, in most instances, it is very difficult to ignore others' negative characteristics. For example, team members who are aggressive, belligerent, lazy, or perpetually confused are likely to have profoundly negative effects on the team in a very short period of time. Therefore, rather than pretending that such characteristics do not exist or are unimportant, it is imperative that you acknowledge the potential influence of personal characteristics in the group process and use your collaborative and communicative skill accordingly.

Professional Characteristics

All team members will also bring a similar set of professional strengths and weaknesses to the group setting. As with personal characteristics, the professional characteristics of each group member will vary by factors such as professional orientation, level of experience, and collaborative expertise. Unlike personal characteristics, however, group members are much more likely to consider your professional behavior, as interprofessional expertise is expected as part of your collaborative work. Again, you and your colleagues will display individual professional strengths and weaknesses, which should be reinforced or limited as necessary and appropriate.

Formal and Informal Collaborative Roles

Personal and professional characteristics influence the nature of the roles members of the team assume during collaboration. The roles assumed by team members may be either formal or informal. Experienced interprofessional collaborators understand that both types of roles play an equally important part in the efficient functioning of the collaborative team. Formal roles are those assumed and accepted as professional behavior governed by members' professional training, ethics, and the behavioral norms of each individual team. Formal roles include your professional skill areas, your level of experience and expertise, and your behavior in formal settings, such as team meetings. However, informal roles—such as social interactions in your work, relationships outside of professional meetings, and so on—have an effect on your formal, clearly delineated professional obligations.

Behavioral Norms

As the collaborative group works to achieve a common goal, and as the members of the team learn each other's characteristics, roles, and functions, a set of interprofessional behavioral standards is likely to emerge. That is, the group will find its own level of professional intimacy and each individual's functions within the group will become more clearly defined. Once such a norm has developed, more attention can be paid to problem solving and intervention implementation rather than interprofessional issues of how members should work together. It is important that, as such norms are established, you and your colleagues evaluate whether they are enhancing or hampering the team's progress. You will need to keep behavioral norms that are supportive while discarding or modifying norms that are less helpful.

The dominant behavioral norm evident in most collaborative groups is its pattern of performance—that is, the pressure the team places on itself to perform consistently at a certain level of competence. Standards of professional and group performance are rarely addressed directly except in the most formal settings but are almost always an important implicit part of what the team does. Group standards can be influenced in a number of ways. First, each individual will bring to the group professional and personal performance standards that frame their collaborative behavior. While individual higher standards are usually preferable to lower standards of performance, it is important to remember that group members with unrealistically high performance standards can sometimes be more of a hindrance than a help. Ideally, standards should be challenging but realistic.

Second, as the collaborative group evolves, a common standard of performance will emerge. The collective press to achieve group goals will automatically set a performance level that mediates success. However, the team standard is significantly influenced, among many other factors, by the personal and professional collaborative skills of each participant, their motivation to achieve, and the appropriate match of each participant to individual and collective tasks. Third, factors beyond the group's control can influence the chances of success. Organizational limitations, unpredictable events, or legal considerations, for example, may enhance or detract from optimum perform-ance. Fourth, the consequences of the group's action may reinforce or modify its current performance standards. If the group is successful in reaching its designated goals, its performance standard is likely to remain unchanged than if measurable failure forces a reassessment of goal attainment. Finally, the power exerted on the group dynamic by strong or aggressive participants, especially if displayed by a group leader, can influence performance standards. Again, the use of power flowing from professional status within the group can be a major asset in goal attainment, but there is always the chance for misuse or abuse of authority, which can cripple performance.

Status
Every group member will bring to the collaborative effort a sense of status based on their personal, professional, and interprofessional characteristics. The status of various group members may or may not be known to you or your colleagues. Status, or others' perceptions of status, however, can have a pro-found influence on group functioning. For example, if a group member is highly regarded based on professional expertise or experience, such status can translate into a significant team strength. On the other hand, such high status may be intimidating to less experienced or ineffective group members and may prevent them from full participation. Conversely, group members who appear to have a much lower status might benefit from working with others who are more expert than themselves, although there is often equal potential that more aggressive members might intimidate members they see as being of lower status.

Issues surrounding teachers' status raise important matters of power in group settings. While a detailed discussion of power and empowerment is beyond the scope of this book, experienced teachers understand that status, irrespective of its source, usually correlates to power or a lack thereof.

Group Focus

Given the many variables affecting collaborative performance and interaction, it is imperative that the team remain as focused as possible on the problem it was created to address. It is each individual's responsibility to remain vigilant for distractions and contain them wherever possible. If you and your colleagues take the following into consideration, you are much more likely to be able to enhance the performance of your professional group.

Procedural Agreement

One way to maintain the focus of the group is to ensure that all members of the group agree on how the team should operate, at least on major issues of interaction, information gathering, and decision making. Another way to maintain collaborative focus is for everyone to define, agree to, and maintain the limits of their duties and the problems they attempt to solve. Failing to recognize and abide by the limits of the group's functions increases the potential for distraction. While abiding by such limits will be supportive of group functioning, it is equally important to remember that operational parameters should not be viewed as rigid and unchangeable. As the group develops its collaborative personality, and given that the group's problems might change over time, operational limits should be modified if there is a legitimate need to do so.

Common Goal. Any collaborative group runs a serious risk of becoming unfocused if it fails to agree on or loses sight of a common goal. For example, being distracted from team goals squanders resources that otherwise would have been spent more efficiently and effectively in addressing the original problem. Also, once the group loses sight of common goals, even more resources are squandered getting the team refocused. As a team member, therefore, it is important that you do your best to remain focused, model such collaborative behavior, and encourage such behavior in any of your colleagues who might be more distractable.

Collective Precedence. By definition, teams function best when working by consensus. Obviously, when collaborating on any team there will be areas of disagreement or conflict. However, effective team operation assumes that the collective team decisions far outweigh any individual opinions or professional wishes. This does not imply, however, that every team member will always agree with every last detail of a team decision but rather that the general thrust of any team decision is agreed to by all participants. Problems may arise in this area, however, if a team member disagrees strongly with collective team wishes or when any collective decision is of poor quality. It is in the best interests of the team, therefore, to maintain a balance between quality decisions and consensus for optimum team focus.

Communication. Obviously, a major element in maintaining team focus is the level of skilled communication that occurs between all members of the collaborative group. The more communicatively skilled team members are, the more likely it will be that the team focus will be on the problem at hand rather than on attempting to understand each other.

Interprofessional Skill. Many collaborative groups become or remain unfocused due to a low level of interprofessional collaborative skill among its members. There are many reasons for such an absence of skill, but they can generally be individually or collectively traced to inexperience, a lack of training, or a lack of motivation to engage meaningfully for the benefit of the team.

Forming the Group

Clearly, forming an interprofessional group is an intentional act that affects not only your colleagues and your students and their families, but also is likely to affect the organization around you. Characteristically, many human service organizations, including schools, react quite slowly, and sometimes negatively, to change. If, therefore, you wish to form an interprofessional team, there are a number of factors you should consider before proceeding. Remember that, especially in the initial stages of reflecting about forming a team, you should carefully weigh the *relevance* of collaborative work rather than assuming that it is equally effective in every professional situation. If a team approach is justifiable, there are several important issues you should bear in mind.

First, it is important that you are clear about *why* you or you and several of your colleagues wish to form a collaborative group. It is unlikely that any team, whatever its status, will be effective if there is not a pressing reason for such a team. Take time to formulate your professional rationale for wanting to engage yourself and others in collaborative teamwork and informally establish the level of support for such a team among potential team members. Second, consider how your school and other work might be affected by forming such a team and predict, as far as possible, the ramifications such a team might have. Third, once you have a fairly coherent understanding of what you wish to achieve, discuss your proposal with your administrator. Sharing your proposition with administrators is crucial because their willingness to endorse the formation of the team or their opposition to such a plan is key to any further team development. In addition, if an administrator sanctions your idea, you are more likely to receive more professional and logistical support than if you had attempted to conduct team business without such sanction.

Fourth, it is important to identify the types and amount of resources that will be needed in order for the team to function effectively. Again, the nature and range of such resources will vary greatly from team to team. For example, perhaps the single most important team resource is the team members themselves, including parents, and all that they bring professionally to their collaborative work. Without carefully constructing team membership for optimum performance, team functioning can be affected from the very beginning of the venture.

Fifth, once the team has been formed and sanctioned for service, it is important to establish the conditions and procedures under which the team will operate. Clear and appropriate operating procedures, such as how meetings will proceed, team members' responsibilities, how consensus will be reached, and so on, will help provide a sense of structure and purpose that promotes effect use of the team's time, resources, and energy.

Collaborative Life Cycle

The group and behavioral dynamics of any collaborative team progress through a developmental cycle, only a part of which is the actual performance of actions to achieve team goals. Over time the collaborative group tends to take on a life of its own. As with any other personal or professional relationship, collaborative relationships and competency do not immediately appear when a team is first formed. Only after several preliminary phases will the actual high-quality work of the team emerge.

The evolution of a collaborative team can best be described as a series of phases beginning with the initial formation of the team and ending when the team goals have been met and the team either disbands or redefines itself for a new task. While most teams generally follow this evolutionary process, each phase is not discrete and is rarely completely isolated from the other phases. However, if you observe most collaborative teams over time, you will be able to identify a definite progression from initial team formation to final dissolution.

Phase One: Initial Formulation.   Once all initial procedural issues have been cleared, and the formation of the team appears viable, the initial task is to assemble the designated group participants. This initial step is important for several reasons, including introductions among members who do not know each other, a preliminary discussion of team goals and objectives, consideration of any immediate or long-term problems that might affect team functioning, the team focus, and descriptions of and access to resources. This initial step allows team participants to gauge the general potential for the forthcoming collaborative venture and facilitates the establishment of interprofessional relationships. In this phase, actual work on the problem at hand is unlikely to occur. Instead, the group is occupied with a great deal of planning, goal formulation, and resource identification.

Phase Two: Conflict and Resolution.   As the initial stage of team formulation progresses, team members are likely to be accommodating, somewhat overly flexible, and eager to please. However, this "honeymoon" fades quickly as the team moves closer to making important decisions for collective action and when it becomes clear that the fervent professional wishes, orientations, and perceptions of each member cannot always be completely accommodated. While some may view all conflict as negative, experienced teachers understand that, in many instances, conflict can be a healthy precursor for effective action as it reveals members' willingness, based on familiarity with their colleagues, to make their points of view known. It is important to understand and accept that conflict will arise in any group setting, and that effective team effort results from *resolution* rather than avoidance of conflict. While conflict can certainly arise at any point in the entire team process, it tends to be more pronounced during this early stage.

Phase Three: Consensual Behavioral Norms. If team members are skilled in dealing with conflict, if the team can remain focused, and as participants become increasingly familiar with their own and others' interprofessional place in the group, instances of serious conflict should decrease, and a more settled way of operating emerges. Team members, by this time, have come to know each other and have the measure of their own and their colleagues' strengths and weaknesses. If conflict has been handled effectively and if the team members are relatively collaboratively skilled, they will have found a performance level accommodating most personal and professional differences and will be able to devote more attention to the executive task for which the team was created.

Phase Four: Optimum Performance. It is only after these three crucial phases that most collaborative teams can turn their full attention to the problem they were originally formed to address. If the first three phases have been satisfactorily negotiated, then unfamiliarity and conflict will not distract the team from their work. Here the team goes about its business for the benefit of the student.

Phase Five: Evaluation and Redirection. Once the team has addressed the problem to the best of its ability, the next phase involves evaluating the effectiveness of its intervention. Evaluation is a crucial step to gauge whether team goals have been achieved. If the evaluation reveals that the team has indeed met its goals successfully, it can then move to the final developmental phase, dissolution. However, in many instances, the team will discover that its goals have only been partially met. If this is the case, the participants will redefine their performance goals and implement further interventions as necessary. Also, many teams may achieve their original goals but be faced with new, unrelated problems that they may attempt to solve. When this is the case, the basic collaborative tools already in place can be applied immediately to new collaborative challenges.

Phase Six: Termination and Dissolution. This final phase of team or group functioning is often overlooked, even by very successful collaborative teams. Just as collaborative groups are usually constituted to address some specific problem, so they should be dissolved if there is no further work for them to do. Given that every team marshals and consumes significant personal and professional resources, effort should not be wasted on meaningless or directionless activity. All members of the team should be acutely aware of when the team task has been accomplished and act accordingly. Appropriate termination of the team activities and dissolution of the team itself will ensure that resources are conserved and that team members will be willing to work on the team in the future.

Summary

This chapter has examined the significant advantages and disadvantages that mediate effective teamwork with other teachers, students, and their families. Also, the chapter described the importance of in-depth knowledge of operational group dynamics, which appear at all developmental stages of teamwork from initiating the team structure through dissolution of the collaborative team.

Questions for Reflection

1. How can you use your knowledge of the advantages and disadvantages of working in team settings to improve the work performance of the collaborative team?

2. How would you educate less experienced team members to more realistic professional expectations of collaborative work?

3. How would the different developmental stages of team development affect interprofessional communication? How could you improve interprofessional communication at each developmental stage?

4. How would you develop team members' divergent points of view to a consensus for a common team goal?

5. Think of instances where teamwork might be inappropriate. In these instances, how should teachers proceed in making appropriate decisions for their colleagues as well as for students and their families?

References

Brill, N. I. (1976). *Teamwork: Working together in human services*. Philadelphia: J. B. Lippincott.

Brown, D., Kurpius, D. J., & Morris, J. R. (1988). *Handbook of consultation with individuals in small groups*. Alexandria, VA: American Association for Counseling and Development.

Dettmer, P., Thurston, L. P., & Dyck, N. (1996). *Consultation, collaboration, and teamwork: For students with special needs* (2nd Ed.). Boston: Allyn & Bacon.

Friend, M., & Cook, L. (1996). *Interactions: Collaboration skills for school professionals* (2nd Ed.). New York: Longman.

Giangreco, M. F., Edelman, S., & Dennis, R. (1991). Common professional practices that interfere with the integrated delivery of related services. *Remedial and Special Education, 12*(2), 16–24.

Johnson, L. J., Pugach, M. C., & Hammite, D. J. (1988). Barriers to effective special education consultation. *Remedial and Special Education, 9*(6), 41–47.

Katzenbach, J. R., & Smith, D. K. (1993). *The wisdom of teams: Creating the high performance organization* Boston: Harvard Business School Press.

Larson, C. E., & le Fasto, F. M. J. (1989). *Teamwork: What must go right, what can go wrong*. Newbury Park, CA: Sage.

Pfeiffer, S. I. (1980). The school-based interprofessional team: Recurring problems and some possible solutions. *Journal of School Psychology, 18,* 388–394.

Phillips, G. M. (1990). *Teaching how to work in groups*. Norwood, NJ: Ablex Publishing.

Rosen, N. (1989). *Teamwork and the bottom line*. Hillsdale, NJ: Lawrence Erlbaum.

Sugai, G. M., & Tindal, G. A. (1993). *Effective school consultation: An interactive approach*. Belmont, CA: Wadsworth.

Thomas, C. C., Correa, V. I., & Morsink, C. V. (1991). *Interactive teaming: Consultation and collaboration in special education* (2nd Ed.). New York: Macmillan.

5

Ethical Aspects of Interprofessional Collaboration

Introduction

Aside from the many technical skills and the content area expertise required in teaching, it is crucial that you pay attention to the ethical aspects of your work. Teaching is fraught with difficult decisions and fragile situations that will require you to make judgments, from a principled point of view, about students, parents, and colleagues. Ethical considerations and decisions are not always as easily resolved as more straightforward questions of curriculum and technique, especially seeing that personal perceptions are inextricably inter-woven into your professional decisions. Given the earnest nature of these issues, therefore, it is inestimably to your benefit to develop a solid set of professionally appropriate behavioral, reflective, and collaborative standards to serve and support your colleagues and your students.

Before developing a practical ethical perspective, it is important to consider more general ethical aspects that undergird teaching and most other helping professions.

General Ethical Aspects of Professional Behavior

In considering the many complex ethical issues that will face you regularly, be sure you are familiar with the more basic aspects of principled professional conduct. These aspects apply to most education settings and you will be expected, even as a novice teacher, to have an efficient working knowledge of these general ethical features. Such principles and guidelines are most often found in your school district's policy documents and in the ethical guidelines of professional organizations to which you belong. The more important general ethical aspects follow.

Responsibility

It is imperative that you act responsibly at all times in the execution of your professional duties. Remember that you are compelled to act ethically after due consideration of the ramifications of your ethical decisions. Possessing an acute sense of responsibility will assist you in making difficult ethical decisions and help you delineate your professional obligations from those of others. In the long run, remember that you bear ultimate responsibility for your work, your professional decisions, and how your professional behavior impacts your colleagues and your students and their families.

Competence

Another way of increasing your ethical standards of behavior is to ensure that you are the most competent professional possible given the level of your technical expertise and experience. Incompetent professionals and those who do not constantly strive to better themselves over time are at much greater risk for acquiescing to lower ethical standards than those who devote consistent time and energy to careful self-reflection and deeper understandings of principled behavior. It is in your best interests, therefore, to routinely maintain the highest expectations of yourself, your colleagues, and your students both in academic work and in ethical judgment. You can also increase your competence by availing yourself of every opportunity for professional interaction, by continuing education in your field and related areas, and by developing significant collaborative efforts with your colleagues.

It is also important, however, to remember that competence as a support for appropriate ethical judgment and behavior has its limitations. As long as you operate within the established parameters of what is permissible behavior in your field, you will likely increase your knowledge of ethical action. If you choose to develop some unorthodox or innovative professional style, do so only in terms of what is considered appropriate ethical and professional behavior. If, however, you choose to act in clear contradiction to established behavioral and ethical norms, you run a significant risk of serious damage to your professional integrity and trustworthiness.

Moral Standards

Individual moral standards as well as their influence on professional work vary from person to person. Generally, your personal moral standards will be of little concern in your teaching life unless they negatively interfere with your professional responsibilities, your conduct, and your professional decisions. However, as this book has repeatedly made clear, there are close links between who you are as a person and who you are as a teacher, so there is sure to be some reciprocal influence between your moral perceptions and professional behavior. Personal behavior, especially in public, has clear ramifications for what you do professionally. It is in your best interest that you consider your moral standards and any possible detrimental effect some of your views might have on your work.

Objective Professional Judgment

While complete objectivity in any professional endeavor is almost impossible, you will increase your ethical conduct by always doing your best to consider all information, collaboration, and decision making as objectively as possible. Engaging in objective professional conduct does not necessarily mean that you deny any personal emotions or perceptions and never consider them in your actions, but it does mean that you acknowledge your personal and professional biases, reflect carefully on their influence, and then put them aside to deal with current issues as impartially as possible. It is equally important that you actively and consciously constrain your personal or professional biases from dictating your decisions or actions unchecked by rational thought. Ineffective teachers often act out of their personal and professional prejudice—usually with disastrous consequences for all involved.

Condoning Unethical Behavior

In many discussions of ethical professional behavior, the focus is on your personal conduct. However, you can also increase your ethical integrity by doing your best to avoid condoning the unethical practices of those around you. In most instances, unethical actions by your colleagues will be rather subtle and debatable. You will need to reflect on the nature of their actions and then decide if any ethical decision or gesture on your part is warranted. In most questionable situations where you are not privy to all the details of a particular situation, it is probably in your best interest to refrain from overt opposition. However, where there are clear ethical violations among colleagues, it is your professional duty to refrain from condoning what transpires either by removing yourself from the situation or by making your disapproval known. Obviously, where there are clear ethical violations concerning students or their families, you are professionally bound to oppose such action in every appropriate manner possible.

Confidentiality and Privacy

Issues surrounding confidentiality and the right to privacy are at the heart of many ethical issues in teaching and other helping professions. Effective teachers routinely maintain the highest possible ethical standards in dealing with sensitive information and its dissemination because they understand the potentially negative consequences that may result from carelessness. Essentially, the notion of confidentiality assumes that not all information should be available to all persons, but only to those who need the information to make proper professional decisions for humane and effective intervention. Your ethical conduct demands that you maintain this standard in all of your interactions with your colleagues and your students and their families.

A basic assumption of confidentiality is the notion of sharing or revealing information only on a need-to-know basis. Confining the dissemination of information only to those persons who are directly involved with a particular decision or problem goes some way toward ensuring that sensitive information is not obtained by other parties who may, deliberately or inadvertently, use the information to negative effect. It is equally true, however, that the need-to-know basis is, at best, quite vague and relies on each professional's ability to decide who should be privy to confidential material.

Another safeguard related to confidentiality involves written permission for the dissemination of sensitive details. It is imperative that you obtain documented consent to release information about students, parents, or families to your colleagues or other agencies. When obtaining such written permission, you should explain the amount of information that will be released, to whom it will be released, the purpose for sharing such information, and the safeguards in place to ensure that confidentiality is not violated and is used only for professional purposes. It is also important to remind students (where appropriate) and their parents of the limits of confidentiality because no confidentiality safeguards are absolute.

Another way of maintaining confidentiality is by carefully considering what you submit to others in written reports and other sensitive documentation. Clearly, the advantage of disseminating written data is that you usually have more time to contemplate the ramifications of sharing the information than if you are sharing it verbally. Ensure that you edit written documentation carefully to include only the information that is absolutely relevant and for which you have consent to release. Carefully reflect on what the information might mean to others, and remember that written documentation is, in most instances, much more binding than any verbal report or discussion. Do your very best to avoid including tangential sensitive material or personal, subjective, or speculative judgments.

You may further protect confidentiality and the right to privacy of your students and their families by limiting your professional discussions and collaborative actions to only those people who are directly involved in the current collaborative situation. Limiting your discussions in this way not only helps ensure that confidential information remains among appropriate personnel, but is also a wise way to maintain focus on the topic under consideration. In addition, be sure that all professional conversations and discussions necessary in collaborative work occur in a private setting so that sensitive information is not inappropriately disseminated.

You should also take great care in the storage or disposal of confidential information, most often encountered in the form of reports and cumulative records. Always ensure that sensitive information remains in a secure location when it is not in use. When in possession of such information for your work, take great care not to leave documentation unattended or in places where unauthorized persons might find it. If, by chance, any confidential information is compromised, or if, for example, documentation is missing or lost, be sure to report these problems immediately.

Finally, it is important to remember that confidentiality in most situations is not absolute. While in your day-to-day professional work confidentiality will usually be respected and practiced, under the law there are generally three exceptions to absolute confidentiality. The first and most obvious is that confidentiality can be waived if the student or, more usually, the student's parents, authorize the release of confidential information. Second, in most helping professions, including teaching, confidentiality becomes a secondary issue where such information presents a clear and present danger to either your colleagues, the student, or their families. Third, under certain circumstances, courts of law can require professionals to divulge confidential information. These caveats to absolute confidentiality should also shape your ethical decisions regarding confidential matters.

Duty to Warn

As mentioned previously, there are some exceptions that initially appear to confound the basic tenets of confidentiality. However, at its core, ethical behavior essentially dictates that all options be weighed in any problematic situation and that the most beneficial potential outcome should dictate professional action. It follows, therefore, that another aspect of your ethical conduct is a duty to warn others if a student is a danger to himself or herself or if the student is a danger to others. Clearly, in such circumstances, the need to prevent further complications far outweighs the need to keep such information confidential. This kind of exception is clearly recognized under the law and is most often seen, for example, in professionals' obligations to report suspected child abuse or someone's suicidal ideation.

Nondiscriminatory Assessment and Intervention

The results of any educational assessment are likely to contain a great deal of valuable but sensitive information. Furthermore, no educational assessment is likely to be completely accurate, so what you do with the results are crucial for your ethical integrity. It is your responsibility to guard against any misuse of test results that will be to the detriment of your colleagues or your students and their families. First, ensure that all evaluation is carried out under optimum conditions and that the test protocol is scrupulously followed. This will guarantee the best possible result given the limitations of the test. Second, be absolutely sure that any test results are stored securely whenever they are not being examined, and that they are only examined by others on a need-to-know basis. Third, respect and encourage students and their families' right to be informed of the evaluation's purpose and to have the results explained to them carefully. Finally, it is important to indicate, where necessary, the limitations of the assessment or of the test that was used.

Welfare of the Student and the Family

An important way of demonstrating your ethical consideration is to conduct your professional life, wherever possible, in the best interests of those with whom you work. Do your utmost, for example, to secure the best possible services for your students and their families, clarify any potential conflicts of interest, and be sure to provide all necessary information to those who need it for appropriate action. In addition, be sensitive to any possible problems in collaborative relationships and habitually seek to build consensus for mutual gain. Furthermore, try to ensure the execution of only the most effective, least intrusive interventions, always basing your decisions on researched and documented best practices of your field. Be responsive to the perspectives of children and their families by monitoring all professional interactions around a given problem. Also, if it becomes clear to you that any interaction or intervention is clearly detrimental or negative, terminate such activities as soon as possible.

Professional Interaction

Another way of increasing your ethical stance in your work is to pay close attention to your professional interactions. It is vital to respect the professional privileges of your colleagues and to possess a working understanding of their obligations and authority. Pay close attention to initiating, establishing, and maintaining collaborative relationships not only with your colleagues, students, and students' families, but also with satellite agencies and professional organizations. In addition, spend time reinforcing others' good work and pay close attention to how you interact with colleagues in both public and private settings. Do your very best not to be unnecessarily confrontational with colleagues in public, and strive to project an image of professional consideration, tolerance, and refinement.

Due Process

Generally, due process can been defined as the legal right of parents and students to participate at every possible opportunity in the collaborative educational efforts and decision-making process for appropriate educational interventions. Due process is guaranteed under law, and your professional commitment to upholding all aspects of due process will increase the potential for close interprofessional collaboration and more effective educational and other interventions.

Aside from these underlying assumptions, all of which will help you maintain the highest possible ethical standards of interprofessional collaboration, you should develop a strong sense of how to make ethical decisions in difficult circumstances. While a vast literature is available relating to the more philosophical aspects of ethical decision making, you can develop a strong practical ethical sense by following a relatively straightforward practical approach to ethical dilemmas.

A Practical Approach to Ethical Considerations

Essentially, your ethical conduct should revolve around a single major consideration: What is the best course of action once all possible aspects of the problem have been considered? In order to arrive at such a decision, the following steps will help you situate a problem in its ethical perspective.

Reflecting on Personal Ethical Standards

Every person acts out of some set of ethical standards, which they have formulated and refined over time—standards that are characteristically both personal and professional. Reflecting on and understanding the motivation for these standards, as well as how they appear in action, is crucial to disciplined, ethical reasoning. In short, it will be difficult for you to be the best teacher you can be without first understanding who you are as an individual.

Reflecting on Possible Problematic Situations and Developing a Plan of Action

As part of your reflection, spend time thinking of potentially difficult ethical situations and how you would deal with them should they occur in practice. While this reflection will not always be entirely accurate, it will give you some inkling of the many alternatives you might face in ethical decision making and, perhaps more importantly, help you develop an ethical framework *ahead of time* that might be useful in a real life situation. The cases in this book will provide you with many opportunities for this kind of situational reflection.

Using Available Guidelines to Develop Ethical Perspectives

Aside from self-examination and active reflection of potentially difficult situations, there are several more concrete guidelines that will help you develop a broad professional code of ethics. For example, spend some time reviewing the laws that influence your professional behavior because they often provide answers to difficult yet common ethical and practical decisions. In addition, be sure to be familiar with the policies laid down by your state and local district regulations. If you are still unsure after consulting these sources, be sure to discuss the problem with a trusted, more experienced colleague or with an administrator.

Reviewing All Information Related to the Problem

Often ethical decisions or actions only become clear once you have carefully examined all the factual information related either directly or indirectly to the problem. Collecting and reflecting on such information is also a necessary preliminary step in any problem solving. Wherever possible, carefully consider information that is unbiased and undistorted by your or others' personal perceptions. Also, this step will help you establish whether you should seek out more information or whether you have enough information to proceed.

Deciding on the Primary Ethical Issue

Considering all the relevant and available information in conjunction with your personal and professional code of ethics will allow you to decide on the primary ethical aspects of the problem. Most ethical problems are quite complex and involve a series of interrelated and overlapping issues. After carefully considering the problem, one of these issues usually appears to be more important to address or solve than others, and this primary problem should, where possible, be addressed first.

Deciding on a Course of Action

After such extensive ethical consideration, decide on a course of action that takes into account not only the extent of the problem, but also the ethical impact your actions will have on the student, your colleagues, and the families involved. In addition, reflect on whether the outcome of your actions will be ethical for you and others involved in the problem.

Reflecting on the Problem, the Ethical Resolution, and Further Ethical Development

An important aspect of continued development of principled professional behavior is extensive reflection after the problem has been addressed and resolved. Failing to complete this step means that you will not learn as much as possible from any problematic situation, thereby possibly curbing your ethical growth and increasing the potential for repeating future ethical errors. Take time to think through what resulted in success or failure, the role you and others played in the final outcome, and, most importantly, how your ethical standards influenced the final outcome. This step-by-step practical approach will give you a more accurate perspective when you are faced with ethical decisions in your professional life.

These general ethical aspects of professional work in teaching are most useful when adopted and practiced consistently. They provide a sound basis for supporting your professional behavior in difficult ethical circumstances and will increase the potential of your demonstrated integrity in all aspects of interprofessional collaboration.

Summary

This chapter discussed the professional imperative of ethical conduct in collaborative dealings with colleagues and students and their families, and how this conduct generally applies to the context of teaching. Ethical decision making and conduct imply careful attention to a set of underlying general ethical aspects and rely on teachers' practical applications of an ethical decision-making process for principled interprofessional behavior.

Questions for Reflection

1. Consider who you are as a person and how who you are is likely to affect your professional behavior and decision making.

2. Reflect on what you consider to be your ethical standards of interprofessional collaboration. Consider whether these standards are adequate or appropriate for your work in teaching.

3. Consider the most unethical professional conduct you can imagine. Reflect on what your actions and attitudes would be if such conduct by a colleague, student, or parent occurred in your work setting.

4. Contemplate your professional ethical standards, examine the reasons why you hold yourself to these standards, and uncover where and how you learned that these standards were appropriate and acceptable.

5. Consider one part of your ethical attitude or behavior that you think needs improving. Think of ways that you can improve this professional behavior or attitude.

References

American Psychological Association. (1989). Ethical principals of psychologists. *American Psychologist, 45,* 390–395.

Crego, C. A. (1985). Ethics: The need for improved consultation training. *The Counseling Psychologist, 13,* 473–476.

Fannibanda, D. K. (1976). Ethical issues of mental health consultation. *Professional Psychology: Research and Practice, 7,* 547–552.

Gable, R. A., Arllen, N. L., & Cook, L. (1993). But—let's not overlook the ethics of collaboration. *Preventing School Failure, 37,* 32–36.

Goodlad, J. I., Soder, R., & Sirotnik, K. A. (Eds). (1990). *The moral dimensions of teaching.* San Francisco: Jossey Bass.

Herlihy, B., & Golden, L. (1990). *Ethical standards casebook.* Alexandria, VA: American Association for Counseling and Development.

Howe, K. R., & Miramontes, O. B. (1992). *The ethics of special education.* New York: Teachers College Press.

Newman, J. L. (1993). Ethical issues in consultation. *Journal of Counseling and Development, 72,* 148–156.

Pryzwansky, W. B. (1993). Ethical consultation practice. In J. E. Zins, T. R. Kratochwill, & S. N. Elliot, (Eds). *Handbook of consultation services for children* (pp. 329–348). San Francisco: Jossey Bass.

Raskind, M. H., & Higgins, E. L. (1995). Reflections on ethics, technology, and learning disabilities: Avoiding the consequences of ill-considered action. *Journal of Learning Disabilities, 28,* 425–438.

Reschly, D. J. (1988). Alternative delivery systems: Legal and ethical influences. In J. L. Graden, J. E. Zins, and M. J. Curtis. *Alternative delivery systems: Enhancing instructional options for all students* (pp. 535–552). Washington, DC: National Association of School Psychologists.

Strike, K. A., & Soltis, J. A. (1992). *The ethics of teaching* (2nd Ed.). New York: Teachers College Press.

6

Communication in Interprofessional Collaboration

Impediments to Effective Communication
Advice
False Reassurances
Misdirected or Inappropriate Questions
Wandering Interaction
Interruptions
Being Judgmental
Professional Orientation
Conflict
Mixed Messages
One-Way Communication
Minimizing Feelings and Insincerity
Fatigue
Hot Words and Phrases
Captive Listeners

Nonverbal Communication
Paralanguage
Facial Expressions
Gestures and Movements
Eye Contact
Physical Appearance
Body Sounds
Overall Demeanor
Physical Touch
Communication Tempo

Congruency

Written Communication
Purpose of Written Communication
Enhancing Written Communication
Confidentiality

Summary

Questions for Reflection

References

Introduction

Of the many aspects that impact interprofessional collaboration, perhaps the most important is communication between you, your colleagues, the parents and families of your students, and the students themselves. Many inexperienced teachers tend to take their communication skills for granted because communicating is such an integral part of their lives and some assume that any communication is effective communication. Communication, however, is a basic skill that must be exercised for constant improvement.

Your ability to communicate effectively is also a prime facet of your professional integrity. The extent and effectiveness of your professional communication will project to others the extent of your professional character, your willingness to collaborate, and the level of your communicative expertise. Perhaps most importantly, effective interprofessional communication means that more time can be spent doing your job with the fullest possible understanding of your educational tasks.

Communication occurs verbally, nonverbally, and through writing. In each area, it is important that you hone your communicative ability to impart information and nuance that is deliberate, clear, and useful. Remember, too, that all communication occurs in the wider context of your profession, including your collegial relationships, policy and work rule constraints, and your personal and professional code of ethics.

All aspects of verbal and nonverbal communication rest on a number of foundational elements that, together, form a communication cycle and include these elements: the sender, the receiver, the message, the communicative channel, feedback, the communicative setting, and noise.

Communication Cycle

Effective communication occurs in a reciprocal cycle that shapes the form and content of the information you impart and receive. Your working knowledge of this cycle will, to a great extent, determine the effectiveness of your professional communication. Not only is it important that you understand this cycle, but also that you remember it during any professional interaction.

Sender

All messages originate with the sender, the person who wishes to communicate the message. The sender makes a decision about what he or she wishes to communicate and then proceeds to send the message. If you are the sender, you are responsible for ensuring the best chance of the message being received and understood. First, carefully consider for whom the message is intended. Professional communication is more likely to succeed if the intended receiver is the person or persons for whom the message is most relevant. Second, as much as possible, make a conscious, considered decision about the kind of message you wish to send. A moment's reflection will help you carefully formulate what you are attempting to convey and lessens the chance of miscommunication or misunderstanding. Third, take some time to consider the context of the message; that is, carefully examine the environment your message will enter. Such consideration often shapes the way you communicate rather than the content of your message. Fourth, decide on the best possible way to convey your message. Given the context of the communication, what do you think would be most effective? Should it be verbal, nonverbal, or written? If the message is spoken, it is important that you monitor the nonverbal signals you are sending that either support or detract from what you are saying. If the message is nonverbal, it is important to establish the appropriateness and relevance of the nonverbal form the message will take. If the message is to be written, consider carefully what you will write and the possible impact it might have on the receiver. Fifth, phrase your message as clearly and directly as possible and do your best to keep your message appropriately brief. Shorter, clearer messages are less likely to be misinterpreted by the receiver than longer or vaguer messages. Sixth, concentrate on what you are saying or writing so that you will remember as much of the message as possible. This final step is important in terms of your collegial integrity because most professionals tend to respect people who remember accurately more than those who do not. It is also important to monitor what you are communicating in case you need to modify the mode or content of the message as it is happening. Irrespective of how or what you communicate, remember that once you have sent your message, it is immediately subject to a host of extraneous influences beyond your control.

Receiver

Messages move from the sender to the receiver, the person who is the intended target of the message. If you are the receiver of any professional communication, it is your responsibility to carefully consider what is being communicated and then to respond appropriately, either with a message of your own or to clarify the meaning of the original message. As the receiver of any message, it is important to remember that you are quite dependent on the sender for what you hear, see, or read. When you receive any verbal or nonverbal message, it is important to engage in active listening, a process whereby you purposely attend to the verbal and nonverbal messages coming your way.

Active listening is a skill that often remains uncultivated among ineffective communicators. While the sender of the message must ensure that each message has the optimum chance for understanding, even the best intentions of the sender can be thwarted by poor receiving skills. As the message receiver, you should actively consider the message, reflect on its content, relate it to your current knowledge relevant to the message content, and, if necessary, use feedback to the sender for clarification. All these efforts should occur before you carefully formulate and deliver a response to the message.

As with all other communication skills, active listening improves with practice. Not only does active listening increase your chance of fully understanding the message, but it also communicates to the sender your attention, concern, and willingness to hear what they have to say. Active listening, therefore, will likely build trust and collegiality while simultaneously enhancing your professional integrity. Active listening also increases communication by focusing on the sender and the message, rather than on your own thoughts and emotional state. Focusing on the sender and the message will also help you keep your own judgments of the communication or the sender in check, allowing you to receive and understand all the details before making a carefully considered response.

For explanatory purposes, the functions of the sender and receiver are usually separated. However, in your professional communication, messages are more often sent and received much more rapidly or even simultaneously. Communication, by definition, is mutually interdependent—senders rely on receivers acquiring understanding, while receivers provide senders with feedback indicating their level of understanding.

Message

The actual content of what the sender communicates is the message—the reason for initiating communication in the first place. Ineffective teachers sometimes fail to pay initial careful attention to the actual content of their messages and may spend considerable amounts of time attempting to clarify the content of their communication later. If you are the sender, there are several aspects to remember beforehand. First, evaluate why you need to send the message. Reflect briefly on the appropriateness of the message content, the importance of sending the message, and to whom the message is being sent. Second, consider the purpose of the message. You may, for example, assess whether the receiver or receivers truly need the information you wish to communicate and how their reception of the message will influence your and their future actions. Third, carefully consider the timing of your message. Often it is less the content or delivery of the message that interferes with communication than the time at which the message is sent. Some reflection about timing may increase your willingness to send the message while at other times such reflection might lead you to wait. Fourth, where possible, rehearse the message to yourself before sending it. Rehearsal allows you a brief moment to organize and edit your thoughts, thereby increasing the chances that your message achieves its purpose. Given these simple steps, your messages are much more likely to be accurately received and understood.

Channel

The mode through which the message moves from the sender to the receiver is often called the channel. In spoken communication, messages usually are conveyed by both the sound of speech and by nonverbal expressions and gestures. In written communication, the channel usually consists of hard copy documentation or technological channels, such as electronic mail. The route a message takes may affect the understanding with which it is received. Spoken messages are usually more direct and easier to formulate, but may be a disadvantage given the immediacy required to both formulate and receive the message. Written communication, on the other hand, while often more time consuming, does allow the sender and the receiver more time to formulate and consider the message's content and meaning.

Feedback

Communicative feedback is the reciprocal information sent to the sender by the receiver to indicate whether the message has been obtained and understood. It is unlikely, except in the simplest of messages, that any communication will be completely understood without any form of clarification. If you receive a message, it is your responsibility to respond to the sender in such a way that you indicate how much of the message has been understood, which parts of the message are less clear, and whether you need more information for complete understanding. Senders also rely on feedback to clarify what parts of their message were not as clear as they thought and to provide the opportunity for reshaping the message to increase understanding.

Setting

Sending and receiving messages occurs in a broader context that has the potential to increase or decrease the efficacy of the communication. Some contexts are naturally more conducive to communication than others. A message is more likely to be understood when the sender and receiver are concentrating on the message at hand and where there are few to no distractions that can deflect their attention from the communication. Settings influencing communication can either be internal (intrapersonal) or external (interpersonal).

Intrapersonal Setting

All communicators bring to their collaborative efforts influences that automatically prejudice their interactions. Perhaps the most crucial influence is your personal style of communicative ability and skill. Because we so seldom view communication skill as something that must be constantly honed and practiced, we tend to communicate based on a personal style established in settings other than our work, which are usually informal and less clear. In a professional setting, however, communication deficits that might be quite acceptable and appropriate for informal personal communication can be problematic. To improve your professional communication, it is important to reflect on your communication style. Carefully examine, for example, how you send and receive messages, what personal communicative behaviors enhance or detract from your communication, your personal communication strengths and weaknesses, how others generally react to your communication, and so on. Generally, then, communication styles tend to be highly personalized, and while a personal communicative style can be a distinct asset, it may also be a communicative lens that can lead to misunderstanding.

Another major influence on your professional communication arises from your intertwined personal and professional experiences, which are always present in any professional interaction. Who you are as a person, how you learned to communicate in your personal life, as well as your reactions to others' communications will influence how and what you choose to disclose. Such reactions are based on what you have learned about communication in the past. To improve your professional communication, examine your reactions to both the acts of communications you are involved in as well as the content of the messages. For example, monitor the communicative effects of reactions that have their bases in your personal attributes, such as anger, frustration, or enthusiasm. In addition, consider the influence of your professional levels of expertise and experience. What you have learned in prior collegial communication and the degree of communicative success will also play a part in how you shape and respond to any current communication.

Interpersonal Setting

Another area of influence on your communication involves factors that, while beyond your control and often unpredictable, can influence any communication no matter how well planned it might be. For example, an unexpected interruption, an unanticipated emotional response from the sender or receiver, the sudden appearance of new information during a communication that changes the whole flavor of what is being communicated, and so on, can drastically alter what you need to communicate or understand. Naturally, it is impossible to plan for all possible eventualities, but the unexpected can be reduced by careful attention to every facet of the communication cycle, your own reflection on how and what you communicate, and calm consideration of, and reaction to, the unexpected.

Noise

In most communication cycles, noise, also known as communicative static, refers to the many potential interferences that might distract both the sender and the receiver from effective communication. Generally, noise either appears as tangible, real-world distraction or as psychological noise. For example, attempting to communicate in a noisy room or while other attention-getting events are occurring increases the chance of misunderstanding for both sender and receiver. Also, if the physical surroundings are distracting—by being uncomfortable, for example—communication is likely to be adversely affected. Psychological noise may also cause ineffective communication and may be present in the sender, receiver, or both. For example, if the sender, receiver, or both are angry, upset, or exhilarated, these psychological states are likely to interfere with communicative accuracy.

It is equally true that, in many instances, it is impossible to avoid some form of noise in any communicative setting. To counter the effects of even the most subtle noise, monitor the communication setting closely and remove any obvious barriers to communication that might interfere with understanding the message.

Skills Enhancing Verbal Communication

Careful attention to the subcomponents of the communication cycle is only the beginning of effective interprofessional communication. There are also many skills that can undergird how well you make the communication cycle operate for you. It is unlikely that you will use all of these skills in every communicative interaction, but in most cases several are likely to occur simultaneously. Essentially, communication support skills fall into two broad categories: (1) a set of skills that directly enhance communication and (2) skill in recognizing impediments to effective communication. Each of the following skills, when exercised appropriately, will provide support for the elements of the communication cycle. They are especially important as tools in communicating with students and their families.

The set of skills supporting effective communication aims to ensure the sender and receiver that the message is understood or to establish whether further clarification is needed.

Communication Opportunities

Constructive communicators understand that one way of beginning effective communication is to allow other professionals clear, supported opportunities for communication. For example, during the initial stages of the interaction, and once it appears that some form of communication is under way, a simple signal for deeper communication often allows others to begin their communication about the topic at hand. Phrases such as "How can I help you?" or "What's on the agenda for today?" indicate that you are prepared to consider the topic at hand while simultaneously providing an invitation for further interaction.

Reflection

In most communication interactions, reflection, the reconsideration of the message for further clarification and understanding, allows both the sender and the receiver opportunities to reshape the content, meaning, and implications of the message. Reflection can take many forms. For example, the sender or the receiver may restate their understanding, embellish the original message for more accurate understanding, or allow a few moments of silence for considered intrapersonal reflection for further comment.

Stating the Implied

Reflection often relies on some kind of overt sharing of message meanings that remain unstated but are nevertheless important. The meaning and purpose of any interprofessional communication can often be intensified by the sender and receiver explicitly discussing what implicit meanings and implications the message might have. Not attending to these underlying implications can sometimes result in confusion and misunderstanding that will need to be addressed later.

Summarizing

Another useful technique for improving communication involves summarizing what has been communicated or your understanding of the message content. Often messages are intricate or lengthy, and a brief summary of the main ideas can help establish continuity for improved understanding.

Paraphrasing

Paraphrasing by the sender or the receiver involves a basic restatement, in their own words, of what they understand the communication to be. This technique is important because it is an effective way of reinforcing understanding and providing an opportunity for each party to correct any misunderstanding.

Clarification

In most communication, and in spite of the best efforts of senders and receivers, experienced teachers understand that the possibility of some misunderstanding still exists from overlooked or hidden factors that have influenced the message content. In almost all cases, therefore, some level of clarification is necessary, usually via direct feedback. Senders often clarify their original message by restating the message in a slightly different way, or by adding or deleting some detail. Receivers often clarify what they are understanding by asking questions, restating what they have heard as a reality check, and by generally sending information to the sender indicating that they are checking message accuracy.

Silence

Many inexperienced teachers are uncomfortable with silences during spoken communication and may feel the need to fill the void with small talk or material quite irrelevant to the communication at hand. Silence, however, is an important and necessary component of effective communication that allows both the sender and the receiver time to assimilate the communicated content, to reflect on its meaning and implications, and to formulate appropriate responses. Also, appropriate silence during communication may reduce the potential, for example, for interruption and cross communication, both of which substantially increase the possibility of misunderstanding.

Pragmatics

Pragmatics refers to our sense of the appropriate social use of language in different circumstances. Not only is the content, delivery, and clarification of interprofessional messages crucial, but also the appropriateness of the language used to convey the message content. One way of learning to communicate effectively in your profession is to use language appropriate for the communicative occasion. Not only should you be able to use appropriately professional language, but also you should develop great flexibility in moving from more to less formal professional language depending on your communicative circumstances. For example, it is likely that you will be able to communicate effectively with your colleagues using many technical terms commonly associated with your profession, but such technical communication with your students or their parents might be confusing and distracting. Effective teachers shift with ease from more to less formal professional communication without losing the message content.

Time

Experienced, competent teachers tend to be very busy people whose time is precious. They also understand that time is a prime factor in formulating, sending, and understanding professional messages, so they habitually estimate the amount of time it will take to convey a message and for the receiver's response. Effective teachers also develop an acute sense of when time is being wasted in any communication and are skillful at refocusing the communicative interaction. Remember to balance your time resources between allowing enough time for careful communicative interaction and a sense of when time is being wasted.

Timing

In order to improve your interprofessional communicative skill, it is important to develop a sense of timing, that is, the ability to judge *when* to communicate. While an acute sense of timing is probably largely learned through trial and error, effective teachers know that *when* they communicate is often as important as *what* they communicate. Some useful pointers can help you develop such a sense of timing: First, be aware of and assimilate as much information as possible about the context in which you are about to communicate. For example, if the persons with whom you wish to communicate are paying attention, focused, and supportive, these indicators will increase the likelihood that communication is appropriate. If, however, all the contextual indicators are working against you, such as if those with whom you wish to communicate are inattentive, distracted, or in some psychological or emotional state that detracts from the potential effectiveness of your communication, you might be better served by postponing communication until later. Second, develop an extensive working knowledge of the people with whom you work, including a sense of their personalities and general demeanor. This knowledge will help you judge more accurately whether they will be more or less likely to consider your message. Third, monitor your own psychological and emotional state to gauge whether your current state will be more or less likely to enhance the accuracy and delivery of your communication.

These skills will likely be needed in various combinations in any communicative interaction and relate, for the most part, to verbal communication. Verbal communication, however, is also mediated by nonverbal communication, which conveys an equally important message that will either confirm or refute the verbal content. Effective communicators pay as much attention to their nonverbal as to their verbal communication for optimum understanding.

While all of the factors discussed so far tend to enhance interprofessional communication, understanding, and meaning, most effective teachers also remain acutely aware of the following factors, which can be detrimental to any communication effort.

Impediments to Effective Communication

All effective communicators are well aware that there is a set of factors that may detract from effective communication. It is important that you remain vigilant for the appearance of these impediments and deal with them effectively so as to assure the accurate transmission and reception of communicated messages.

Advice

Every teacher, from time to time, is tempted to offer unsolicited advice. Giving advice is usually well intended but can result in ineffective communication for several reasons. First, the person receiving the advice might not wish to be advised, or they might misinterpret the purpose of the offered advice. Second, offering advice can sometimes result in the recipient becoming confused or feeling obligated to comply with the suggestions. In either case, future impediments to communication and professional collaboration are possible. Perhaps the gravest danger in offering advice, however, is that the receiver might act on your suggestions that then produced disappointing or contrary results. In this case, future professional communication is likely to be damaged.

A somewhat more delicate problem arises when you are asked for your professional advice. Indeed, in some cases, making suggestions and adding different professional insights can benefit your colleagues greatly. In this case, it is *how* you offer the advice that might impede effective communication. Should you judge that your advice is being actively solicited, consider your messages carefully and convey them as accurately as you possibly can. It may be a good idea to emphasize that the information you provide is, at best, a potential alternative, but that it is the responsibility of the person asking for advice to make the final decision.

False Reassurances

Effective teachers understand that there is little use in interprofessional communication for providing false reassurances. Ineffective teachers often use false reassurances as a means of avoiding difficult professional issues or to disguise their incompetence. An important aspect of professional integrity is that professional judgments and comments remain as truthful as possible. Only by avoiding false reassurances is it possible to arrive at effective professional interventions that will be in the best interests of your colleagues, parents, and students.

Closely related to false reassurances is the practice of some ineffective teachers to communicate in clichés. Clichés are stereotypical generic phrases or opinions that are, by nature, poor communication tools. Clichés tend to ferment confusion and misunderstanding as they are not accurately descriptive or specific. Communicating in clichés may diminish your professional integrity among other teachers who might assume that you are incapable of original, accurately descriptive communication. Both practices—providing false reassurances and communicating in clichés—often create the perception of a general disregard for the opinions, feelings, and knowledge of other teachers, factors in and of themselves that are likely to lessen the effectiveness and accuracy of professional communication.

Misdirected or Inappropriate Questions

While feedback in the form of relevant, focused statements is an essential tool for effective interprofessional communication, misdirected or inappropriate feedback can create a great deal of confusion and irritation. For questions to be answered appropriately and accurately, they must be directed at someone who can provide the answers. Directing questions to persons who do not have this knowledge will mean wasting valuable energy and time finding a more appropriate source. Also, persistently directing questions to inappropriate people may result in a loss of professional integrity. Many ineffective teachers ask questions at inappropriate times, or simply ask questions indicating that they have not thought through what they wish to know. There are even a few teachers who ask questions that are entirely inappropriate in content or completely irrelevant to the communication under way. Obviously, such inappropriateness is a great hindrance to effective professional communication.

Wandering Interaction

When any two people communicate, there is always the potential for being sidetracked into discussing peripheral issues that detract from the original intended purpose of the communication, waste time, and frustrate more focused colleagues. Remaining focused can be enhanced by combining all the elements of the communication cycle with highly active listening skills. Should the discussion wander in spite of your best efforts to remain focused, it may be necessary to gently prompt a return to focus by a brief statement reminding others to keep on track.

Interruptions

Effective communication is most likely to occur in a setting free of interruptions and distractions. While it is not always possible to engage in professional communication in such ideal circumstances, experienced teachers do their best to reduce interruptions to a minimum.

Interruptions generally take two forms. In the first instance, interruptions might be external to the communication, that is, interruptions might intrude into the communication from the context in which the communication is occurring. For example, when meeting with parents, you may be interrupted by a student or another teacher. Such external interruptions almost always disrupt communication, even if they only occur for a very short time. In the second instance, interruptions might be internal to the communication. For example, interrupting someone who is communicating with you rarely allows you increased understanding of the message being conveyed to you. Such interruptions indicate an unwillingness to engage in active listening and also denote a certain lack of respect for the other person's point of view. Interruptions usually precipitate restatements, unnecessary clarifications, and generally disrupt the flow of communication from one professional to another.

Being Judgmental

As with unsolicited advice-giving, judgmental teachers assume that they have the unalterable and only correct opinion on any given topic and are usually quick to volunteer their perceptions. Being judgmental, however, is very different from making an informed, appropriate professional judgment based on your knowledge, experience, and level of professional expertise. Being judgmental interferes with effective communication because such behavior does not consider any other aspects, meaning, or alternative explanations for the topic being discussed. Judgmental teachers can further inhibit professional communication because they are usually so concerned that their own opinions are heard and asserted that they often fail to consider other important information, which might assist in their making more informed professional decisions.

Being judgmental may also have another significant, yet often unintended consequence: It may precipitate hurried decision making or actions that in the long run can prove to be more detrimental than supportive. Hurried professional decisions may also mean that more energy may need to be spent on more communication later to address the problems caused by the quick and probably ineffective or irrelevant earlier decisions.

The most effective way to avoid being judgmental is to suspend decisions about any professional situation until adequate information has been accrued. Resist the urge to pass judgment before all possible information has been gathered.

Professional Orientation

All teachers are socialized into their occupations through their preparatory training and their work with their colleagues in their field. Each profession has its own history, professional and technical language, and perceptions about how to solve professional problems. In addition, all teachers are trained to make independent, effective decisions for intervention from their professional perspectives. For example, the problems in school experienced by a hyperactive child might be treated by a pediatrician through medication, while a behaviorist might recommend a well-defined program based on the principles of applied behavior analysis.

Ineffective communication may occur when teachers from distinctly different disciplines work together on a common problem. Such difficulties are most easily resolved by proficient communication skill on the part of both senders and receivers. In addition, these difficulties can be avoided by your elementary understanding of the professional orientations and job responsibilities of your colleagues.

Conflict

Conflict is an inevitable part of any job and often of any particular collaborative task, and resolving conflict is a key to productive working relationships. Professional conflicts must be resolved not only to better serve students, but also to preserve and strengthen productive working relationships with colleagues. Resolving conflict generally provides greater insight into the professional problem at hand and also enhances understanding of others' perspectives. Unresolved conflict can become a constant distraction from your professional obligations and often leads to further communication problems and an increased risk not only of damaging your professional relationships, but also of shifting your professional energies away from the students you are supposed to serve.

Mixed Messages

Ideally, communicators would all convey messages that are unambiguous, direct, and easy to understand. Given the complexity of multiple communication channels, potential distractors in the communication setting, and the possibility that the sender might not have formulated his or her message very clearly before communicating, misunderstandings from mixed messages often arise. Ideally, the sender's verbal and nonverbal communication should be congruent, as this allows optimum opportunity for understanding from the receiver. If verbal and nonverbal communication are incongruent, the receiver is likely to be distracted by this disparity, thereby exacerbating an already unclear situation.

To avoid sending mixed messages, it is important to be skilled in all the components of communication mentioned in this chapter. Being acutely aware of your verbal and nonverbal actions, along with careful reflection on what you wish to communicate prior to beginning the interaction, will assure you and the receiver the best chance of understanding with the least amount of redirection, clarification, or confusion.

One-Way Communication

Communication, by definition, is a reciprocal process. Unidirectional attempts at communication, when only the sender engages in communicating a message, and where no response is required or allowed, is, at best, ineffective, and, at worst, counterproductive. Unidirectional communication also places the entire power of the communication with the sender. Because it is the reciprocal nature of communication that makes it effective, unidirectional communication is often viewed as dictatorial, as highly opinionated, and as a clear threat to interprofessional collaboration.

Minimizing Feelings and Insincerity

Most communications either implicitly or explicitly involve some form of emotional content that can interfere with the intent of the communication. For example, if a message is conveyed with a great deal of feeling and obvious emotional intensity, communication can be disrupted if the receiver minimizes the sender's depth of feeling or discounts emotional context altogether. Insincerity can be avoided by being aware that most messages carry an emotional component. Listen carefully to the message you receive, and evaluate the nature of the emotional underlay. For example, is the sender angry, enthusiastic, concerned? How does the emotional content match the factual content of the message?

In addition, communication that is either intentionally or unintentionally insincere reduces professional integrity and the likelihood of further meaningful professional communication. Often such insincerity is not overt or deliberate, but more likely the result of inattention, distraction, or disinterest.

Fatigue

Communication takes effort. Effective teachers understand that physical or psychological fatigue can seriously impair interprofessional communication. It is important that you monitor your physiological, psychological, and emotional status and evaluate your level of fatigue. If you are tired, you should make a careful decision either to modify your communication accordingly and be aware of the possible influence your fatigued state might have on professional communication or defer the communication until you are more rested.

Hot Words and Phrases

Hot words and phrases are emotionally laden expressions that have a particularly deep emotional significance for communicative participants, inappropriately raising positive or negative emotions, which in turn can be significant barriers to understanding. Experienced communicators spend time reflecting on what words or issues are especially significant for them and are vigilant in their interprofessional communication for the appearance of such phrases or words. In addition, experienced communicators know that in many instances, the person uttering the hot word or phrase is often unaware of the emotional content their communication evokes and also that occasionally conflicts can arise when such words or phrases are used deliberately.

Captive Listeners

While teachers assume that almost all communication is voluntary or responsive, a common exception involves communicating with a captive audience. While such communication may not be entirely unidirectional, it should be handled differently than communication in most other settings because the receivers are not as free to respond as they might otherwise be. Should you be communicating with captive listeners, such as in a classroom or in leading a seminar, it is your responsibility to communicate as effectively as possible—even more so than you usually would. Be alert for signs of miscommunication with your audience, encourage feedback, and allow time for assimilation and clarification of your message.

Nonverbal Communication

Nonverbal interaction imparts a great deal of other information than our verbiage. Unlike verbal communication, our nonverbal actions are continuous and usually observable, revolving around both our actions and the communication setting. There are many aspects to nonverbal communication, most of which are characterized as "body language." Only the most common features are discussed here as enhancers or inhibitors of nonverbal communication. It is in your best interest to monitor them all carefully in yourself and others for improved interprofessional communication.

Paralanguage

Paralanguage, while it occurs in the context of spoken language, is usually considered a nonverbal clue to communication. Paralanguage refers to the sounds of communication that accompany verbal communication such as voice pitch, quality, and volume as well as the rate of verbal delivery—in sum, how things are said as opposed to what is said.

Facial Expressions

Facial expressions can convey a host of emotions that impart clear information to others. A lifetime of social interaction teaches us to carefully observe the facial expressions of those with whom we interact to gather information about the intent of the communicator and whether the facial expressions are congruent with the verbal message being received or given.

Gestures and Movements

Physical movement can also convey a series of intended or unintended nonverbal messages. For example, continually shifting position, relaxing or tensing the body, and tightly folded arms all provide information as to our psychological and emotional states.

Eye Contact

Eye contact is possibly the most significant component of nonverbal communication because of the communicative status we assign to whether people return our gaze or not. Eye contact is so important that it is a major communicative variant across cultures. In some cultures, eye contact is expected, and if avoided, communicates disrespect or disinterest. In other cultures, the opposite is true.

Physical Appearance

Our manner of dress, grooming, and level of cleanliness, especially if carried to any extreme, provides information about how we view ourselves and how we wish to be viewed by others. Experienced communicators are aware that we sometimes judge people unfairly by their appearance. For example, we might have certain biases toward persons who appear either highly attractive or unattractive.

Body Sounds

While less often addressed, body sounds are also a powerful communicator of our feelings and psychological state. For example, sounds such as sighing or humming all convey clear meanings according to the contexts in which they are used.

Overall Demeanor

A communicator's overall manner and bearing, which includes all or most of the nonverbal aspects mentioned here, convey an equally strong nonverbal message to colleagues and students. For example, being poorly dressed and groomed, stooped over, and avoiding eye contact sends a very different overall message than if you are dressed and groomed appropriately, walk tall, and consistently cultivate eye contact with your peers.

Physical Touch

Physical touch, as we learn from our personal lives, is one of the most compelling forms of positive or negative nonverbal communication. In professional settings, physical touch is equally powerful but can also assume an entirely different, most often negative, meaning between teachers or between teachers and students. Experienced teachers are acutely aware of the power of touch and consider its use very carefully, if at all.

Communication Tempo

Communicative interactions can proceed at differential rates. For example, some communicative interactions might be lively and packed with information, while others might be more leisurely and meandering. Variations in communication tempo can often be responsible for causing misunderstanding. For example, if the communicative tempo is too quick, important details can easily be lost, or if the tempo is inordinately slow, the participants might become distracted or bored.

Congruency

Effective communicators understand and are constantly aware of the significance of the match between verbal and nonverbal communication, often called congruency. A high degree of congruency between what is said and the nonverbal aspects of communication indicate that the communicator is genuine, focused, and oriented. Such a match increases the probability of messages and responses being understood. On the other hand, when any communicator is verbally expressing one sentiment while nonverbal clues indicate other, less congruent meanings, the potential for misunderstanding, mistrust, and distraction is increased. When such a contradiction is clear, it is probably more important to attend to the nonverbal message as this is more difficult to control voluntarily and is more likely to be expressing the true communicative intent.

Written Communication

Most effective teachers are acutely aware of the skills necessary to communicate verbally and nonverbally. Fewer teachers, however, work as hard on their written communication, a major communication channel for the exchange of information. Written communication and information should be handled in such a way that it is easily accessible to authorized persons, should contain relevant and necessary information from credible sources without untoward embellishment, and should be documented in such a way that it enhances communication rather than inhibits it.

Purpose of Written Communication

Professional written communication serves a number of purposes. First, written communication provides a permanent record of professional decisions and processes and a host of other important information. Such permanent records are important for many reasons, including, in many cases, their value as legal documents admissible as evidence in courts of law. Second, written communication allows the transport of information from one professional to another over time. Written documents are repositories of professional thinking, problem solving, and collective decision making, which often focus directly on the person receiving the intended intervention or services. Third, written documents provide a trail of professional action that can be accessed at any time for historical and current information related to interventions with students.

Enhancing Written Communication

Just as effective teachers strive for error-free performance in all other areas of their work, such effort is necessary in written communication. Poorly written and error-filled communication not only increases the potential for mis-communication or misunderstanding, but also reflects negatively on the writer's integrity, work standards, and attention to detail.

Among the more important prerequisites for effective written communication are correct and appropriate grammar, accuracy, and communicative clarity. In order to ensure that written communication is error free, effective teachers proofread, revise, and edit their work carefully, understanding that their written communication will be a tangible record open to repeated scrutiny by other teachers, parents, and often students themselves. Not only is it imperative that your writing be error free, but also that your style of communication reflect an orderly presentation that is sufficiently detailed without being overly wordy, appropriately focused without being too narrow or broad, and written to the audience for whom it is intended.

Where possible, effective written communicators prefer word-processed material to handwritten documents. Word-processed work is not only more legible, but also often easier to correct, edit, and rewrite, and, with a little practice, much faster than handwriting. In addition, such work may be more accessible than other forms of communication by being available, for example, as part of a computer database. Be careful, however, to avoid informal fonts, formats, or unnecessary graphics, which might detract from the content of the communication.

Another way of increasing the effectiveness of written communication is to use, where appropriate, a standard format which you, your colleagues, and your students find understandable. Such formats provide a level of uniformity that makes written communication easier and quicker without losing any of the necessary clarity. Equally, being unnecessarily tied to a standardized format can impede communication through watering down content or by not being sensitive enough to the needs of the communicators.

Effective communicators understand that a key to quality written communication is the writer's ability to use professional language effectively, yet simply and clearly. Accomplishing such writing takes a great deal of practice but can be achieved. One way of ensuring the effectiveness of your professional written communication is to use the professional vocabulary of your field, which communicates technical detail in a common language that is understood by your colleagues, and, possibly, by parents and students you serve. However, it is also important to avoid unnecessary jargon, including acronyms and abbreviations, that may not be familiar to the reader.

Another effective written communication skill involves using language that is neutral, nonjudgmental, and written in the active voice. Do your best to be more specific rather than general, more concrete than abstract, and more definite and decisive than vague. It is also important to make every word you write add to the impact of your message. Do not overstate your message and do your best to state your message positively without being unrealistic or untruthful. It is important at some point before your final communication product becomes available to other readers that you decide what content to include or omit in the interests of clarity and of the intended audience, because you will almost always have more information than needs to be communicated. Such reflection allows you to formulate the style, detail, and breadth of what you wish to communicate.

Your written communication can also be improved by omitting from your writing hearsay, judgments that have no basis in fact, and any content that is unverifiable. It is therefore more effective to rely on behavioral descriptions than on unsubstantiated general statements. If general statements are unavoidable, it is best to explain them. Remember to avoid, where possible, abstractness and ambiguity.

Confidentiality

A major issue related to written interprofessional communication concerns the confidentiality of written material. Experienced teachers are acutely aware that documentation, being a permanent product and record, is more durable, and therefore, more open to breaches of confidentiality than spoken communication. A number of relatively simple, yet often ignored measures will ensure confidentiality of your interprofessional written communication. For example, avoid leaving documentation in any place where it might be viewed, inadvertently or deliberately, by people who should not have access to that information. In addition, documents not currently being used should be stored in a safe place, preferably in a locked, secure place to which access is controlled and limited. Should your work require that copies be made for several colleagues, limit the number of copies and ensure that the copies reach only their intended destination. All originals and copies should be marked as sensitive material.

From time to time it may be necessary to mail confidential information. Mailed confidential information should be sent under seal and by registered mail. If it becomes necessary to destroy confidential information for any reason, it should only be disposed of after all names and identifying information have been blacked out. This material should then be shredded or destroyed by other means which assure that the information is unreadable. Finally, computer disks and sensitive information in computer databases that are no longer needed should be erased.

Summary

Interprofessional communicative skill is pivotal for effective collaboration with your colleagues, parents and families, and the students you serve. Verbal, nonverbal, and written communication skills are all important tools that will help ensure your collaborative effectiveness. Effective communicators understand and monitor their participation in the communication cycle while simultaneously developing strong supportive skills and an awareness of issues that can impede communicative activity.

Questions for Reflection

1. Carefully examine your communicative attitudes and skills. List what you feel are your communicative strengths and weaknesses. Think of ways to increase your strengths and to compensate for or eliminate your communication weaknesses.

2. Practice monitoring various aspects of the communication cycle in any communication, professional or personal. Develop a habit of consciously thinking about communication while you are doing it.

3. Monitor and reflect on the emotional content of your communication. Think of ways to appropriately lessen the impact of emotion in the manner and content of your communication.

4. Pay close attention to nonverbal behavior in yourself and others during any communication. As the communicative interaction develops, evaluate the level of congruency between verbal and nonverbal messages. Consider reasons why verbal and nonverbal messages are more or less congruent and what this implies for any further communication.

5. Examine written communication, both formal and informal, and evaluate its content for clarity, obvious bias, accuracy, attention to detail, and understandability. Reflect on ways to improve the written communication.

References

Blyler, N. R., & Thralls, C. (Eds). (1993). *Professional communication: The social perspective.* Newbury Park, CA: Sage.

Brill, N. (1978). *Working with people: The helping process* (2nd Ed.). Philadelphia: J. B. Lippincott.

Dettmer, P., Thurston, L. P., & Dyck, N. (1996). *Consultation, collaboration, and teamwork: For students with special needs* (2nd Ed.). Boston: Allyn & Bacon.

Friend, M., & Cook, L. (1996). *Interactions: Collaboration skills for school professionals* (2nd Ed.). New York: Longman.

Hybels, S., & Weaver, R. L. (1986). *Communicating effectively.* New York: Random House.

Klopf, D. D., & Cambra, R. E. (1983). *Speaking skills for prospective teachers.* Englewood, CO: Morton Publishing.

Sugai, G. M., & Tindal, G. A. (1993). *Effective school consultation: An interactive approach.* Belmont, CA: Wadsworth.

7

Conflict Management and Resolution

Introduction

Professional conflicts arise out of competing, incompatible professional needs for acceptance and action. There is little point in imagining that such conflicts do not exist or that they will be resolved without careful consideration. How you cope will depend on your view of conflict. When acknowledged and properly addressed, conflict can help teachers define issues more clearly, increase professional involvement, and strengthen professional relationships. Resolving conflict collaboratively is also likely to increase everyone's sense of ownership of an agreed-upon solution, increase their ability to see others' points of view, build trusting professional working relationships, and better prepare everyone involved for other conflict situations. If problematic situations remain unsolved, however, conflict may well escalate to the point where alternative solutions become restricted or virtually impossible to implement. Furthermore, unresolved conflict can make collaborative work unpleasant and, perhaps more importantly, will often detract from the real work at hand: achieving professional goals to provide the best service delivery possible to your students.

Sources of conflict are often initially ill-defined. Conflict often begins with a simple hunch that things are "not right." Some people attempt to act on these hunches. Whether such action produces outcomes that exacerbate the problem or result in workable solutions is usually quite unpredictable. The most effective way for resolving any real or suspected conflict is to define the conflict in terms of a problem that can be solved either individually or within the collaborative group. If serious legitimate conflicts are left unattended, professional collaboration is jeopardized. On the other hand, if you react to a perceived problem that may not really exist or that may be far less serious than you perceive, you may engage in unnecessary courses of action, which further deflect your focus from effective service delivery.

Conflict occurs for many reasons, some of which may be obvious; other causes are, at best, obscure. For example, conflict may arise when too little information is provided, if information is inaccurate or incorrect, or when too much information makes decision making confusing. Professionals prepared from different theoretical perspectives might also clash over methods of intervention, treatment, or evaluation. Whatever the nature of the conflict, however, some areas of conflict seem easier to resolve than others. Conflicts arising out of inaccurate information, for example, are generally much easier to resolve than struggles over values or cultural differences.

While the origins of interprofessional conflict are quite varied and unpredictable, several major causal areas are important to remember when any dissonance arises in your collaborative work, including conflict among and within you or your colleagues and your students and their families.

Causes of Conflict

Most conflictual situations appear to have something in common: they arise among professionals who are all, at least in their perceptions, attempting to do the best job that they can. Conflict can originate either between people with different agendas, between people with the same agendas, or within individuals.

Conflict between Teachers with Different Agendas

It is common for teachers to have different perceptions of what is important for effective intervention. Conflict, therefore, often arises when a decision must be made about which goal is to be adopted by the collaborative group. Inevitably, this means that some goals will be adopted at the expense of others.

Conflict between Teachers with Similar Agendas

Often teachers may actually have a similar goal but find that they disagree about how to reach that goal. Conflict can arise in disagreements about the methods, techniques, or feasibility of an intervention. In addition, conflict among teachers with similar goals may arise when they cannot all equally access their goals. For example, all teachers may agree that a certain student should be placed in a mainstream class, but this is not possible given the school schedule.

Conflict within Teachers

Sometimes teachers experience internal conflicts among their own competing professional goals and agendas. While such dissension does not always affect others, intrapersonal conflict does have the potential to influence communication with others. For example, you may see great value in two effective interventions and be unable to decide which you will support when discussing these alternatives with your colleagues. Your indecision might mean a delay in providing input to your colleagues and the final outcome.

In addition, nonprofessional conflicts within you or your associates may affect working interactions and decisions. For example, if you are depressed, angry, or elated, your personal psychological and emotional state will tend to influence your professional interactions and decisions. Experienced teachers learn to take these perceptions into account to contain them as much as possible while engaging in their professional activities. Conflict may also be generated by the style in which it is managed.

Conflict Management Styles between Teachers

Individual teachers handle conflict in different ways. Some styles of managing conflict are more productive than others and it is important to have a working knowledge of which management styles impede or support your collaborative work. The most important management styles are generally acknowledged to be those of competing, avoiding, accommodating, compromising, and collaborating.

Competing

Competitive teachers generally operate under the premise that they must overcome any and all opposition to what they believe to be the most appropriate or effective actions. Almost always, they tend to see their solutions as the most important and will work very hard to ensure that they "win." Many teachers who use this style tend to rely, for example, on power plays such as uncompromising demands, refusing to listen to others' viewpoints, or win/lose ultimatums. They sometimes refuse to engage in team efforts if their ideas are not consistently implemented. This style of conflict management is not always negative. If you feel *very* strongly about some important issue, you may want to use this style to further your agenda. However, if you use this style often, it will tend to alienate you from your colleagues.

Avoiding

Some teachers try to avoid conflict at any cost. They may remain silent in spite of having some very good ideas, or they may defer to other team members at their own expense. Avoidance as a routine way of handing conflict is usually counterproductive as it weakens your ability to assert your professional opinions, many of which may be valuable to your colleagues and your clients. However, this style may be appropriate where conflict is so bitter that a "time-out" is necessary, or if you feel that you cannot provide a feasible, immediate solution. As with a competitive style, however, constant use of this style may damage your professional relationships.

A major disadvantage of competitive and avoidant styles of conflict management is that they rarely allow for conflict resolution. Both styles tend to draw attention to the conflict itself rather than to what can be done to move beyond it to more productive professional action.

Accommodating

Teachers who manage conflict by accommodation tend to put aside what they think is important. They do not propose their own professional points of view, but tend to ensure that others' points of view are espoused. Such an approach might be appropriate if the issue under consideration is unimportant or if the situation appears to be unalterable. However, repeatedly accommodating others' professional views at the expense of your own might make you resentful or angry, which in turn will reduce your professional effectiveness. Accommodation is preferable to competitiveness and avoidance, however, in that it is more interactive and less likely to be resented or ignored.

Compromising

Practitioners who compromise give up some of their ideas with the expectation that others will do the same. Thus, when teachers compromise, agreed-upon solutions tend to result in a partial ownership by everyone. Compromising is a more direct conflict management style than competition, avoidance, or accommodation. It is most appropriate when time for conflict resolution is limited or when two parties appear deadlocked. Using this style takes more communication and negotiating skill than competition, avoidance, or accommodation.

Collaborating

Collaboration goes a step further than compromising in that it encourages high levels of assertiveness and cooperation to generate new solutions and decisions arising from the conflict. A collaborative style provides a high degree of ownership for everyone involved. It works less well, however, when only some teachers are committed to the style. It also relies heavily on voluntary professional participation.

Very few teachers use one style of conflict management for resolution all the time. Different professional settings, the behavior of colleagues, or the nature of the collaborative problem, for example, may all influence a choice of style. However, as an *habitual* form of professional interaction, some styles are preferable to others. In addition, all styles of conflict management have concomitant consequences because they affect all or most other members of the collaborative group. Remember that whichever style you choose, you will model that style to your colleagues and clients.

Consequences of Conflict

If conflict is handled appropriately, some positive consequences might result. Appropriately effective conflict resolution through communicative debate can often increase the sense of professional belonging and community that plays such an important role in professional motivation and effective collaboration.

Conflict resolution also tends to generate alternative solutions to the presenting problem and increases opportunities for cooperation and mutual support while simultaneously encouraging shared ownership of future problems, solutions, and successes.

However, how conflict is handled can also result in some negative repercussions. Just as heated discussion and debate can fruitfully lead to new insights and professional cohesion, it has the potential to precipitate a great deal of animosity and resentment. For example, if you or your colleagues feel that you have not been recognized, or that you do not have a stake in collaborative decision making, your motivation to engage in future professional interactions may be lessened or, in extreme instances, you might consider complete withdrawal from, or opposition to, the collaborative process. Unresolved hostility, then, may lead to the destruction of the collaborative effort. Chronic conflict may also mean that you or your colleagues become less willing to pursue effective future problem solving and conflict resolution.

The Responsive Context of Conflict for Problem Solving

The context in which conflict occurs almost always has a direct bearing on the course of the conflict and on the manner in which it is resolved. However, this does not necessarily mean that participants in conflict situations are entirely unable to influence the course of events. It is important to look for clues and information that will shed light on the various facets of the conflict. The more complete the information, the more likely it will be that you are able to understand the true nature of the conflict and be able to decide on an appropriate course of action. Dealing effectively with conflict involves evaluating the seriousness of the conflict, gathering information to resolve the conflict, actively resolving the conflict, and understanding your position in the conflict situation.

Evaluating the Seriousness of Conflict

Some teachers feel that all conflict situations should be completely resolved. Reacting to conflict, however, is often involuntary and may or may not be appropriate. An important professional skill is to learn how to assess the level of conflict and its possible consequences to decide whether action is warranted or whether inaction is a more appropriate professional behavior. All conflict management for resolution, therefore, should begin with these two questions: Is there truly, in your perception as well as in the perception of others, a conflict situation? Is this conflict worth pursuing or resolving? Such a decision involves a host of factors that will vary from situation to situation. If, indeed, some kind of conflict exists, the following are some guidelines you may wish to consider.

Response Intensity

Not all conflict situations require the same response intensity. In some situations you will be able to live with the consequences or implications of an unresolved problematic situation while in other instances you will need to take immediate action. Consider the consequences of your actions and weigh all the issues you can possibly think of. Try to think not only of the immediate ramifications of your decision, but also of what it will mean interprofessionally in the future, and what ramifications, if any, are likely for your students and their families.

Prioritizing Conflicts

It is important to prioritize the seriousness of conflicts. Because time and energy for conflict resolution are finite, you should gauge the relative importance of professional conflicts and devote your attention and skill only to the most serious conflicts. You should prioritize any conflicts in light of what might happen with future conflicts or with what has happened with past conflicts.

Conflict Frequency

Consider how often you engage in conflict management and problem resolution. Some ineffective teachers insist on frequent, elaborate conflict management strategies for each and every disagreement, no matter how minor. Because not all conflict situations generate similar intense emotions in your colleagues and because not all conflict situations are equally important, engaging in continual indiscriminate conflict resolution can result in diluting the efficacy of solving future major problems. Preferably, conserve your energy and skill for issues that really matter and where a failure to resolve the conflict may result in serious consequences.

Investing in Conflict

Consider your personal and professional investment in the conflict situation. It is essential that you consider the personal and professional costs involved in engaging in conflict resolution. Some areas of conflict, although worthy of your attention, may demand an inordinate amount of your personal and professional capital. Unnecessarily devoting excessive professional energy to some conflicts may mean less attention to your professional commitments or to other more important conflict situations.

Gathering Information for Conflict Resolution

Managing conflict is a complex task requiring careful consideration of as many situational variables as possible. Comprehensive knowledge of all the facets of any conflict will help you to generate appropriate solutions and to remain engaged, and therefore effective, in these situations. This, in turn, will make it more likely that you will engage others cooperatively for problem solving, thereby establishing a common ground for conflict resolution and effective intervention.

Types of Information

You are unlikely to be able to collect all the possible information necessary for a complete picture of any professional conflict. However, the more information you can obtain, the more likely it will be that you are able to examine the extent of the problem and consider appropriate optional solutions. Pay careful attention to as many facets of the situation as you can. For example, obtain all the factual information possible (reports, evaluations, documents, and so forth), examine your own perceptions of the problem, and learn as much information as possible about others' perception of the problem (including what emotions they bring to the situation). Try to distinguish, as far as possible, the real core problem from the many emotions and biases surrounding the core problem.

Factual Information.   Conflicts sometimes arise out of misinterpretations of factual information. It is therefore important to collect as much of the factual information pertaining to any conflict as possible. For example, ensure that you have collected all the documents, reports, and hard evidence that might be relevant. Often these kinds of conflicts are the easiest to resolve because facts can readily be checked for accuracy or interpretation.

Perceptual Information.   Your perceptions and those of others are usually highly subjective and slanted toward what will give some kind of advantage. These perceptions are often not shared by others, but provide a fertile area for misunderstanding and conflict. You should consider two basic sets of perceptual information: your own perceptions and the perceptions of others.

It is important that you monitor yourself continuously regarding your *own* emotional state as you gather information for conflict resolution; that is, wherever possible, avoid inserting your own strong emotions into an already complex situation. Try not to appear argumentative or disagreeable, as this will usually exacerbate the situation and impede progress toward resolution. Also, do your best to put aside any preconceived notions about the person or the issue with which you are dealing. Exercising such skill takes considerable practice, but is essential if the true source of the conflict is to be uncovered and addressed.

Most conflicts will involve a greater or lesser emotional component among your colleagues, which may detract from getting to the core of the conflict. It is always important, therefore, to set the conflict in the context of the professional and personal emotions it arouses among your colleagues. For example, are the parties involved angry? Resentful? Hurt? Are they cooperative and enthusiastic? Are some teachers feeling left out? Are some of your colleagues competing for attention? Try to establish exactly the source of the conflict and the factors that are causing the problem.

Interactive Aspects of Conflict Resolution

Simply collecting information about and around the conflict is usually not enough to generate possible solutions. Once you have gathered as much information as possible, it becomes necessary to interact with your fellow teachers on a number of personal and professional levels for effective resolution.

An essential element of conflict management and resolution involves teachers' ability to remain engaged with each other long enough to consider alternative actions for resolution. Ideally, when conflicts arise, each professional presents his or her point of view and indicates which parts of that perspective he or she is prepared to negotiate in the interests of resolving the conflict satisfactorily. While such a "win-win" solution is what all teachers should strive for, it is unwise to assume and expect that every professional conflict will result in a happy compromise. In many instances, conflict can entrench individual perceptions and some participants, no matter what is at stake, may be reluctant to compromise their views in any way. Furthermore, always bear in mind that because of individual professional perceptions, how "win-win" is defined by one professional may not be the same for another professional involved in the same conflict.

Unfortunately, some conflicts will result in one of two other possible outcomes, namely, a "win-lose" or a "lose-lose" situation. "Win-lose" solutions occur when compromise breaks down, allowing some participants to establish their agendas at the expense of those who fail to convince the team to adopt at least some of their perspectives. "Lose-lose" situations often occur when it appears that the conflict is unsolvable, generally because individuals are unable to agree on any common ground.

Being New in Conflict Situations

Spending extended periods of time in work situations allows teachers to learn the personal and professional characteristics of their colleagues. Such knowledge is likely to include an awareness of the behavioral limitations and strengths of other practitioners in conflict situations. The less time you have spent in any work situation, the greater the disadvantage if any conflict arises. First, many skills necessary for conflict management and resolution are improved over time. Inexperienced teachers are less likely to possess these sophisticated coping skills because of the brevity of their professional experience. Second, inexperienced teachers are less likely to possess an accumulation of knowledge about the history of interprofessional dynamics at play in conflict situations. Successful conflict management requires as much knowledge as possible, accumulated over time, of the professional and personal characteristics of all participants. Third, novice teachers are more likely to react out of pure emotion than careful consideration of the issues involved in any conflict situation. Such ill-considered reactions might delay effective conflict resolution or may exacerbate an already delicate circumstance. Fourth, novice teachers may not be as readily aware of available resources that might be used to manage the conflict or solve the problem.

Finally, one of the most important aspects of avoiding conflict or for addressing conflictual issues successfully involves the health of your professional relationships. Healthy professional relationships reduce the likelihood of unresolvable conflict and will allow you and your colleagues to focus more on service to students and their families rather than being distracted by side issues that are often generated by less healthy professional relationships. New teachers entering a work setting for the first time encounter several disadvantages, which they must take into consideration if they are to succeed in building professional relationships that will last and develop over time. For example, novice teachers do not have two essential forms of contextual experience: working in the field over time and inexperience in their current work setting.

It is difficult to make up for inexperience when entering your first job. You may have gleaned some experience from your preparatory coursework and field experiences, but day-to-day work is a very different proposition. For example, your interactions with students, families, and colleagues will be more varied and sustained than field experiences. In addition, you will be coping with the pressures of learning what your job and its context require. Thus, the two necessary ingredients, experience in working with other teachers and experience of the job setting, will be largely absent.

Also, different work settings are dictated by different sets of interprofessional, institutional, and community influences. Any new professionals, experienced or otherwise, will need to adjust to the context-specific variables produced by their jobs. Effective adjustment will tend to be more difficult for novice practitioners who have not had the opportunity to practice these adjusting skills in other settings. Novices also face other unique adjustments. They are usually enthusiastic and brimming with a great deal of theoretical knowledge acquired from their preparation programs—qualities that can be both advantageous or disadvantageous, depending on how carefully they gauge the context in which they work and assuming that they wish to make a good impression. Enthusiasm and knowledge will be an advantage if they are matched to the professional subtleties and pressures of the workplace. Eagerness and excitement coupled with a willingness to learn and serve are generally highly regarded professional qualities. Some novice teachers, however, unintentionally create conflict by appearing arrogant, unteachable, and by acting as if they have nothing to learn.

Experienced teachers entering a new job situation often have slightly different aspects to consider in managing and resolving conflict in their work environments. These teachers will undoubtedly have experience in working with other teachers in the field. However, to a greater or lesser degree, they are likely to have less information about the other contextual factor, namely, how to use their experience in a specific new environment. Thus, these teachers must strive in their new work environment to forge professional links with as much diligence as novices, both in terms of overcoming dissonant professional orientations and of learning institutional expectations.

Conflict might also appear when teachers bring to a new job a professional orientation that does not match their previous professional position. Conflict may arise when educational philosophies, treatment approaches, or service delivery strategies are incompatible. Successful teachers possess a repertoire of skills that allow them to adjust to new work situations with a minimum of conflict in this area.

Finally, the philosophy and expectations of the new institution may be somewhat incompatible with a new teacher's previous work setting. Effective teachers actively learn as much as they can about their new institution in the shortest possible time. This knowledge often helps in reconciling personal or professional goals with those of the overall establishment.

Establishing Ground Rules for Professional Interaction

Attempting to manage and resolve conflict is difficult unless there is at least an implicit collegial agreement about ground rules for professional interaction. For example, any colleague has the right to air concerns and to be listened to carefully, no one person should dominate collaborative interactions, and conflict resolution should deal with the current, immediate conflict rather than other past issues. The following ground rules may also be helpful. First, it is important to model appropriate interactive behavior that will help solve the conflict. Expecting such behavior from others is difficult if you are not engaging in acceptable professional and personal interactive behavior yourself. Second, in some conflict situations, you or your colleagues may often be angry or upset to the point at which communication for resolution is impaired. If this occurs, it may be necessary to talk about the manner in which the discussion should proceed or to limit what will be discussed. Once the discussion rules have been either implicitly or explicitly decided on, it is important that everyone involved adhere to them as far as possible. Once again, this will model professional behavior for other people involved and will communicate good faith and a willingness to solve the conflict. Third, effective conflict resolution also depends on participants remaining alert to the general drift of the discussion and not becoming embroiled in distracting side issues.

Styles of Conflict Management

Conflict management and problem-solving skill do not imply that you cannot express your own point of view or that you cannot disagree with others. Rather, it is often the *manner* in which you convey your position that leads either to resolution or future conflict. Thus, developing a style, or habit, of managing conflict is important. For example, with a little reflection and tact, you are more likely to accomplish your goals than if you choose to be argumentative. In order to assert your ideas or opinions, try to discuss your point of view clearly and succinctly. Remember to speak from your point of view rather than against the positions held by someone else. Try not to argue or become defensive when your views are challenged or discounted. Be vigilant and try to extract meaning from what is said to you that will shed light on the problem. Above all, stay calm and separate what you say or hear from your personal emotions as much as possible.

There are two other pivotal issues to consider when attempting to manage conflict or problem solve. First, many teachers, when the conflict becomes intense, overdo notions of empathy to the point where they some-times agree with things they are opposed to, or make claims or promises that they are unable to support. Denying your discomfort in what others say or making exaggerated promises could provide some respite from difficult situations in the short term, but may damage your overall professional integrity.

Second, you may be involved in some professional interactions where practitioners take ownership of other people's problems in an attempt to either end the conflict or to ingratiate themselves to their colleagues. Taking owner-ship of others' problems may have several debilitating effects. For example, it may mean that those who truly do bear responsibility for the problem will abdicate their obligations to the person who takes ownership. People who take such ownership will then be saddled with work or tasks that are not rightfully theirs to complete. Such conditions usually lead to resentment and anger. Furthermore, commandeering others' problems does not afford the person responsible the opportunity of exercising their professional talents to solve the problem and to learn valuable work lessons in the process. In some instances, teachers take ownership of others' problems as a means of increasing profes-sional stature when, in fact, it accomplishes the opposite in the long run. Generally, repeated ownership of others' problems will lead to a lowered sense of professional self-esteem and a lack of credibility, and will communicate that you are not able to determine the boundaries between yourself and your colleagues.

Difficult Situations and Working with Difficult People

Experienced teachers do their best to build and maintain healthy professional relationships as an effective way of avoiding conflict. Where conflicts do arise, they demonstrate a wide array of skills that make it more likely that any future conflict will be handled appropriately. They are also skilled at judging when to pursue resolution and when to pause until a more favorable time for conflict resolution is possible. In practicing your conflict management skills, several considerations can help clarify and address most conflicts you encounter in your work:

1. When engaging in conflict resolution with your colleagues, students, or their families, it is usually counterproductive to minimize the problems they raise. Whether the problem is truly trivial or not, simply dismissing it will communicate a certain professional insensitivity. Instead, carefully consider-ing the extent of the conflict will create the best atmosphere for resolution.

2. If conflict appears intense or immovable, it is often useful to assume a "one down" position, because many people who engage in conflict often expect to be challenged and opposed. They may be hostile and feel the need to assert their authority over others. If you assume a less threatening position by communicating interest, calmness, and empathy, you will be more likely to diffuse an already tense and counterproductive situation.

3. In other situations, resolution may be more likely at a later date. Deferring resolution is appropriate when the conflicting parties appear deadlocked or when emotions are running high. Some conflicts can be eliminated after a "cooling off" period. This tactic, however, is ineffective if the deferred conflict remains unresolved in the future, allowing the conflict to be a recurrent barrier to effective professional conduct. Furthermore, a "cooling off" period may not be appropriate in any situation in which an immediate decision or solution is necessary.

4. It is equally true that not all conflicts can be solved easily. One way to solve more intractable problems is to use a mediator—a neutral third person who will serve as a buffer between the conflicting parties. Be sure, however, that the mediator is respected and credible to all of the parties involved. Finally, in some other instances, conflicts might be truly unsolvable. Judging that a conflict situation is irreconcilable is valid only after repeated interprofessional engagements that attempt to resolve the issues and after appealing, where possible, to a neutral third party for help.

Unresolved conflicts generally take two forms: Conflicts that are unlikely to be resolved due to intractable contextual conflicts—such as institutional policies and mandates, historically difficult attitudes or perceptions—and unsolvable conflicts with colleagues.

Experienced teachers seek to manage the conflicts arising out of situations beyond their control by novel solutions or effective teamwork and by working for change at higher levels of the organization. Such efforts are usually long term and require a commitment to change that may well span a whole professional career. However, in the day-to-day sense of professional work, conflicts requiring long-term solutions tend to be tolerated and accommodated in the best way possible. To effect some form of change over the long term, consider some or all of the following tasks:

Gathering Information
Working for long-term change requires that you amass as much information about the problem situation as possible. Seek information from as many sources as possible and resolve to continue collection of data *over an extended period of time.*

Building Alliances

Institutional reform requires that teachers form groups with a common aim or goal. Such groups can more easily activate the policy change process necessary to accomplish major institutional changes.

Joining Professional Organizations

Many professional organizations aim to be on the cutting edge of policy implementation and reform. By becoming an organizational member, you will access a group of like-minded people who will also be attempting professional reform.

Interpersonal Conflicts

Simply put, you will infrequently, but quite possibly, encounter in your career teachers with whom conflict appears continually unavoidable and unsolvable in spite of your best efforts at professional resolution and cooperation. In most professions, there are a few people who, for a variety of personal and professional reasons, seem to spend most of their time embroiled in one conflict after another and who seem to resist any attempts to modify their combative professional interactions. How you decide to work with these difficult professionals will dictate, to a large extent, the level and duration of conflict that is likely to occur. Given the constraints of your job and your level of experience, you will probably have to work with difficult people from time to time. Should this occur, some or all of the following strategies may be helpful.

Focus on the Immediate Task. Many interprofessional conflicts can be avoided or minimized by concentrating on the task at hand rather than on the people attempting to complete the task. You may be deflected from your professional obligations if you allow extraneous factors to interfere in your professional decision making and creativity.

Communicate Clearly. Concentrate on providing direct, clear, and thoughtful communication in dealing with difficult colleagues. As miscommunication diminishes, so will the potential for conflict.

Be Proactive. Be alert for any signs of conflict or the potential for conflict. Should these arise, do your best to rectify the situation as quickly as possible to avoid escalation of the conflict to more serious and debilitating levels.

Build Consensus. Collective ownership of problem-solving strategies and solutions to professional problems reduces the chance of conflict by encouraging participation in communal settings. Fellow teachers are far less likely to be disagreeable when they perceive that they have a stake in the outcome and that their input has been carefully considered.

Confront as a Last Resort. You may find that even your best efforts do not result in resolution of conflict with another professional, and that some kind of head-on confrontation becomes necessary. If this is the case, you may choose to do so either in a professionally public forum or privately.

Terminate. In a very few instances, and in spite of all your best efforts, it may be necessary to terminate your professional relationship with someone who refuses to cooperate or who actively works against anything you attempt to accomplish. Such instances are quite rare. Termination of a professional relationship, especially with anyone who works in your immediate setting, must be considered very carefully and might have grave consequences for your professional future. It should be seriously considered only after extensive, persistent attempts to rectify the conflict and then only in consultation with other colleagues with whom you have an enduring close professional relationship.

Reflection for Future Conflict Resolution

The conflict resolution skills that successful teachers acquire over time are honed by repeated trial-and-error learning that continues throughout their professional lives. Trial and error, however, are only useful if combined with careful analysis of professional behavior in those situations. An important professional behavior, therefore, relates to practicing reflective skills in dealing with conflict *as it occurs and after the conflict is resolved.*

Reflection during Conflict

One of the most difficult skills to acquire is active professional reflection *while the conflict is occurring.* Many conflicts remain unresolved because the participants avoid reflection through active listening and self-monitoring as they are attempting to process the information generated by the conflict. Instead, some teachers react out of their emotional attachment to the issues at hand, become reactive, or ineffectively use proaction by trying to anticipate what will happen next so that they may gain the advantage. All of these reactions distract them from important clues for resolution, which may appear during the conflict. Reflection during a conflict revolves around three key concepts: self-monitoring, monitoring others, and context monitoring.

Self-Monitoring

As conflict occurs, it is essential that you monitor your thoughts, emotions, and communications. For example, as you monitor your thinking, are you focusing on the current issue? Or, are you beginning to think of ways to gain the advantage? Are you bored with the situation? Do you find yourself distracted and daydreaming? What opinions do you have about what is happening in the conflict situation? Are these opinions based in fact and, as far as possible, are your opinions untainted by speculation or premature conclusions? It is also important to monitor your emotional state. For example, are you angry, disappointed, or exuberant? Are you aware of your emotional attachment to the issues surrounding current conflict? Are you reacting to "hot words" that might override your ability to listen carefully or to center on the real conflictual issues? What was your emotional state immediately prior to the conflict situation?

It is also very important that you monitor how you are communicating. Be sure to incorporate your active listening skills. Carefully monitor the cadence of your speech and try not to interrupt. Are you asking clarifying questions? Do you appear interested? Are you conveying a general sense of involvement? Is your nonverbal behavior matched to the content and delivery of your speech? These and other similar questions will be helpful in your involvement in any professional conflict.

Monitoring Others

Not only must you carefully monitor your own motivations and way of seeing the world, but if conflict is to be successfully resolved, you must pay careful attention to others' perceptions and behaviors as well. Reflect, if you can, on other teachers' communicated thoughts, their style of communication, and their emotional state. For example, are their thoughts logical and well considered? Are they willing to consider other views and opinions and to reflect upon these opinions appropriately? Are their concerns appropriate? Does the conflict seem to be on a personal rather than a professional level? What strengths and weaknesses can you identify in what they are saying? Are they expressing their views clearly?

It may also be helpful for you to establish the emotional content of the conflict. For example, what is the primary emotion exhibited by the speaker—anger, frustration, despondency? Is the speaker reacting appropriately to anything that is being said by anyone else? Does it seem like it would be best to focus on certain less volatile parts of the issue, which would evoke a less emotional reaction? What was the speaker's emotional state prior to the conflict? It will also be helpful to monitor how the speaker is communicating. For example, is the speaker using effective communication skills? Is the speaker presenting his or her point of view articulately? What is the state of the speaker's nonverbal communication? Does the content of what the speaker is saying match the speaker's nonverbal signals?

Context Monitoring

Conflict does not occur in a vacuum. The context in which conflict occurs is often important if you are to get a clear understanding of the underlying issues and work toward resolution. What happens in a conflict situation can be influenced by a host of factors over which you generally will have no control. However, knowledge of these factors can often be helpful in any potential solutions for greater professional cooperation. The following factors might have an effect on a current conflict.

Prior History of Conflict. Many conflicts have a prior history that is likely to have a bearing on the current friction. You will be more effective in conflict situations, therefore, if you have some knowledge of how conflicts have been handled in the past and possibly some insight into the patterns of conflict management and resolution. For example, some teachers might have histori-cally irreconcilable personal and professional differences that are resurrected in each new conflict and that, while appearing not to have any direct bearing on the current issues, will nevertheless tend to contaminate the conflict. A prior conflictual history may also revolve around seemingly intractable policy and institutional issues. Conflict among teachers may also arise from a history of outside influences such as the nature of the relationship with students or their families, other professional institutions or services, or larger societal issues such as colleagues' or families' personal values.

Communication Skills. How teachers communicate with each other during times of conflict will directly influence solutions to the problem. Clearly, the best chance for conflict resolution lies with each professional exhibiting a highly competent set of communication skills, which allow the conflict to be understood from several points of view.

Personal and Professional Settings and States. In many instances the degree of friction, and possibly the outcomes of any conflict situation, may be influenced by what happens shortly before the conflict arises. Again, these factors are varied and not always easy to pinpoint, but being aware that such factors exist, and where possible establishing what they are, will affect how the conflict is managed or resolved. For example, were the participants upset or angry prior to the beginning of the conflict?

Conflict is also much more likely to be resolved if the participants are reasonable, logical, open, and willing to work toward a common solution. However, this ideal situation is not always possible. Professionals usually come to conflict situations in various states of personal and professional willingness to engage in problem solving. Some might be cooperative and willing to work for a solution while others might be distracted. Others might enter the situation resentful and irritated, some might have experienced some personal problems just prior to the current conflict, while others might be overly enthusiastic or unreasonably optimistic, and so on.

Institutional Demands and Policies. Almost all professional conflicts are set within the context of what is considered appropriate and effective by the professional institution in which you work. Thus, in conflict situations, these factors may shape any response to conflict. Often institutional constraints are a source of ongoing conflict among teachers who feel that they have a better solution to a particular problem than the solutions implemented in their work context. Conflict, therefore, sometimes occurs when professional visions clash with institutional decree. There are also many practical behaviors in which you may engage that can have a positive bearing on any conflict situation.

Practical Hints

The following behaviors can support you when you become involved in a conflictual situation. Practice these behaviors as a way of increasing your resolution skills and of shaping conflict for positive rather than negative ends.

Staying Calm
Often conflict evokes emotions ranging from fright to anger. It is important that you remain as calm as possible to carefully interpret the nature of the conflict and to prepare appropriate responses.

Making Notes
The psychological noise generated by interprofessional conflict may distract you from remembering everything that is communicated. Making brief notes will help you remember what was said and provide added information that might be useful for solving the conflict.

Not Taking Remarks Personally

Taking any part of the conflict personally will reduce your ability to obtain a clear picture of the core conflictual issues. In most conflict situations, however, there is also a chance that, as emotions become heightened, some comments may be meant to be taken personally. You will gain little understanding for resolution by responding to these comments. If you feel that certain personal remarks must be addressed, it is probably best to address them at a later time when you are calmer and removed from the current situation.

Considering All Options

Remember that in any conflict situation, there is usually more than one option for action or inaction. You should decide, for example, whether you should respond, remain silent, how involved you need or want to be in the current situation, or whether it may be appropriate for you to call a time-out.

Responding Carefully

Conflict situations tend to evoke ill-considered responses from the participants because of their heightened emotional involvement. If you choose to respond or communicate in a conflict situation, do so only after carefully considering what you want to say and how you wish to say it. It is imperative that you think before you speak. Also, the manner of delivery is often even more important than the content of your communication.

Gauging Progress

The purpose of working through conflict is to move toward resolution or at least a workable compromise. It is important, therefore, that you are able to judge whether the current conflict appears to be moving toward some kind of resolution. If it appears that resolution is feasible, you would probably want to remain engaged. On the other hand, if you judge the situation to be intractable with little or no hope of resolution, you may want to disengage and work for solution at a later time.

Postconflict Reflection

A crucial professional skill for conflict resolution involves learning how to reflect on a problem that has just been solved or left unresolved. Reflecting on conflict situations is hard work, but well worth the effort in the long run. Novice teachers, especially, tend to be relieved when a professional crisis is over and hope that such an event will not occur again. Experienced teachers, however, know that it is more than likely that a similar conflict, or at least a conflict with some similar elements, will occur in the future. It is imperative, therefore, that you learn from conflict situations *after the fact.* Make professional reflection for conflict resolution an integral part of your professional behavior and commit to increasing your skill as you mature professionally.

Reflection on a conflict and how it was handled is useful for a number of reasons. First, it is probable that hindsight will allow you a more realistic assessment of the situation than your evaluation at the time of the conflict. You will be less likely to be emotionally involved and the perspectives of others may be clearer. Second, you will have time to examine and reflect on each facet of the conflict at your own pace, which might provide additional insights and perspectives not obvious at the time of the conflict. Third, such reflection will allow you to examine your professional behavior given your personal state during the conflict—this will help you assess your professional strengths and weaknesses for future reference.

Summary

Coping with conflict for effective resolution is a complicated and often imprecise professional endeavor. However, there are a host of factors which, should you be able to acknowledge and understand them, will give you a fair chance at arriving at a solution. Actively seeking to resolve conflict will allow you and your colleagues to refocus on your primary objectives of service delivery options that are best for your students and their families.

Questions for Reflection

1. Consider your personal responses to conflict. Reflect on how these responses will support or impede your performance in interprofessional conflicts.

2. When you find yourself in any conflictual situation, practice all the hints discussed in this chapter to maintain your psychological and emotional stability.

3. Practice postconflictual reflection by considering previous interprofessional conflicts you have had, how you resolved them (or failed to resolve them), and what, in retrospect, you could have done more effectively.

4. Decide which conflict management style is closest to the way you usually react in a conflict situation. Consider whether any other style would be more appropriate and how you could incorporate the new style into your professional behavioral repertoire.

5. Reflect on professional behaviors in others that would lead you to consider termination of a professional relationship and think carefully about how you could work for a more successful resolution of such a circumstance.

References

Burnett, R. E. (1993). Conflict in collaborative decision-making. In N. R. Blyler & C. Thralls, *Professional communication: The social perspective* (pp. 144–162). Newbury Park, CA: Sage.

Dettmer, P., Thurston, L. P., & Dyck, N. (1993). *Consultation, collaboration, and teamwork for students with special needs.* Boston: Allyn & Bacon.

Filley, A. C. (1975). *Interpersonal conflict resolution.* Glenview, IL: Scott Foresman.

Fine, M. J., Grantham, V. L., & Wright, J. G. (1979). Personal variables that facilitate or impede consultation. *Psychology in the Schools, 16,* 533–539.

Friend, M., & Cook, L. (1992). *Interactions: Collaboration skills for school teachers.* New York: Longman.

Heck, S. F., & Williams, C. R. (1984). *The complex roles of the teacher: An ecological perspective.* New York: Teachers College Press.

Morsink, C. V., Thomas, C. C., & Correa, V. I. (1991). *Interactive teaming: Consultation and collaboration in special education.* New York: Macmillan.

Ross, D. (1989). First steps in developing a reflective approach. *Journal of Teacher Education, 40*(2), 22–30.

Schon, D. A. (1983). *The reflective practitioner: How professionals think in action.* New York: Basic Books.

Schon, D. A. (1987). *Educating the reflective practitioner: How professionals think in action.* New York: Basic Books.

Schon, D. A. (Ed.). (1991). *The reflective turn: Cases in and on educational practice.* New York: Teachers College Press.

Sugai, G. M., & Tindal, G. A. (1993). *Effective school consultation: An interactive approach.* Belmont, CA: Wadsworth.

Wickstrom, K. F., & Witt, J. C. (1993). Resistance within school-based consultation. In J. E. Zins, T. R. Kratochwill, & S. N. Elliot, (Eds). *Handbook of consultation services for children* (pp. 159–178). San Francisco: Jossey Bass.

8

Problem Identification and Problem Solving

Introduction

Professional problems are a very real and often necessary part of any work endeavor. Effective teachers know that problems arise from multiple and often interrelated sources, which can, to a greater or lesser degree, interfere with the timely delivery of services or unfocus interprofessional relationships. Problems encountered in professional life are likely to range over a wide continuum of seriousness from momentary, easily solved predicaments that are not very demanding to very intense, protracted, and often complicated situations that might require attention over a long period of time. For example, a simple misunderstanding between colleagues, parents, or students can usually be resolved quite easily. On the other hand, some problems might require extensive input from others, a coordinated, well-planned intervention, and significant commitment for successful solution.

There are almost always a few problems that are either insoluble or that can only be solved with a disproportionate concentration of resources, time, and energy. One characteristic of professional maturity, therefore, is the ability to distinguish among various kinds of problems and to act accordingly.

Many novice teachers are vaguely aware that problems in professional practice are a given fact of their work, yet the frequency of these problems, their intensity, and perhaps their interrelatedness, are often underestimated. Attempting to deal with professional problems while simultaneously attending to the complex adjustment of beginning teaching can often be quite challenging. As a new teacher, it is your responsibility to understand the nature and characteristics of potential professional problems and to deal with them to the best of your ability, level of experience, and willingness to learn.

In order to resolve problems effectively, you should develop a clear, practical evaluative approach to problem solving. Only by understanding that problem solving is undergirded by several important principles and by evaluating all aspects of any professional problem will you increase the likelihood of finding a solution.

Undergirding Principles of the Problem-Solving Process

Engaging in the problem-solving process requires a great deal of commitment, hard work, and focus. Most of the principles discussed next will govern your effectiveness in solving problems in your teaching.

Respect

A major underlying feature facilitating problem solving is interprofessional respect for the perceptions and viewpoints of others. Developing such a sense of respect does not mean that you should ignore or agree with any point of view that you strongly oppose, but it does mean that you should cultivate the ability to listen to what others have to say at each step of the problem-solving process. Cultivating interprofessional respect to others will increase the chances of reciprocal respect and collegiality from your colleagues.

Information

Generally, the more information brought to bear in considering a problem and possible solutions, the better. Relevant information increases the chance of a close match between the problems and the offered solution and also allows a wider consideration of possible intervention alternatives. It is rare that you will be inundated with so much information that decisions for interventions are impeded by the amount of information available.

Problem Orientation

Remember that your collaborative peers may view the problem and possible solutions from a variety of professional and personal perspectives. The advantage of this diversity is that greater numbers of possible solutions are likely to be offered for discussion. On the other hand, varying perspectives can also result in misunderstanding and increase the possibility for interprofessional conflict.

Communication Skills

It is imperative that in collaborative efforts to solve professional problems all the parties involved exhibit exemplary communication skills. Carefully structuring messages, listening attentively to what is being communicated, and providing feedback are all crucial.

Positive Atmosphere

The collaborative problem-solving process is sure to be more effective if you and your colleagues engage in problem solving in a supportive and positive manner. While critiquing ideas during discussions is a highly legitimate endeavor, refrain from making such interaction a personal battle. Instead, agree with your colleagues where possible, be proactive and thoughtful when necessary, and give credit to others when it is well deserved. Also, practice being assertive rather than aggressive and encourage consensus and collegiality wherever possible.

Conflict Management

Inevitably, the problem-solving process sometimes generates confusion and disagreements. When these conflicts arise, be sure to use your communication and conflict resolution skills to the best of your ability. Being skillful in these situations will increase the chances that any friction will, in the end, be productive rather than divisive and will also model for your colleagues that conflict is not necessarily destructive. Potential areas of conflict can also be avoided or their impact lessened if you are empathetic, honest, and provide meaningful, goal-directed feedback to the ideas presented in the process.

An Evaluative Approach to Problem Solving

Any professional problem should be addressed, wherever possible, in the interests of more effective collaboration and for the betterment of professional relations. Failure to do this might result in several difficulties. First, collaboration can be seriously impeded at many levels if problems are not solved in a timely and satisfactory manner. For example, problems between team members or between teachers and parents and families, or misunderstandings with students, can all detract from the original purpose of the collaborative effort. In addition, inattention to problem solving often results in what was originally a manageable problem becoming much more entrenched and difficult to solve over time. On the other hand, attending to problems impulsively rather than with a good sense of timing can sometimes create more difficulties than the original problem. Spontaneously attempting to solve a problem without first establishing who owns the problem, for example, or who is responsible for its solution, can create a host of other distractions and misunderstandings that would not have occurred had you established such ownership before acting.

Second, exceptional teachers develop an acute sense of problem ownership that allows them to clearly distinguish between problems they are responsible for solving, those over which they have no control, or those problems for which others have responsibility. Developing an awareness of problem ownership is one of the most effective ways of maintaining your professional and personal integrity in your work. If, after serious reflection, it is clear that the problem is yours to solve, or that you are one of several professionals necessary to solve the problem, then further solution-oriented action is obviously warranted. This aspect of problem solving is usually understood in some rudimentary form by most professionals. However, novice teachers tend to have more difficulty in distinguishing problems for which they are responsible and those for which they are not. Consequently, many novice teachers take responsibility for problems that are not of their making or feel obligated to assume responsibility for others' problems as a means of building their integrity. While a hallmark of effective professional behavior is responsibility for one's actions, taking responsibility for and attempting to solve others' problems often leads to a diminution of professional integrity. For example, your professional standing can be adversely affected if you are seen as attempting to rescue less competent teachers or interfering in problematic situations that are obviously unrelated to your professional obligations, experience, or level of expertise.

Third, it is important to distinguish between problems that are soluble and those that are not. Obviously, it is your individual and collaborative responsibility to solve any problems with which you are directly connected or for which you will be held accountable. However, you will find that in most professional work there are a series of problems that appear to be insoluble or at least will consume inordinate amounts of time and energy. Effective teachers understand that their time, energy, and expertise are finite and so they develop an evaluative sense to distinguish which problems they are likely to solve and which are beyond their ability to unravel.

Essentially, most professionals work in one of two general behavioral modes in dealing with some difficult work situation. If teachers engage in problem solving prior to the occurrence of a problem as a way of avoiding the problem or to lessen the impact of the problem when it occurs, they are said to be acting in a *proactive* way. Acting proactively in anticipation of a potential problem has a number of advantages. Clearly, proactive measures allow a wider consideration of possible alternatives unfettered by the constraints of a problem that has already happened. Furthermore, studying potential solutions to possible problems allows tentative solutions to be applied hypothetically and evaluated without the pressure of immediate action. Also, proactive actions permit decisions for intervention to be weighed over time, thereby providing valuable opportunities for reflection and revision prior to implementation.

However, proaction also has several drawbacks. For example, the luxury of proaction is often impractical because the vast majority of teachers' time and energy is spent addressing problems that have already occurred. In this sense, proaction might be considered a distraction from the reality of dealing with day-to-day problems requiring more urgent attention. Furthermore, proaction, when it is possible, is always speculative and may therefore define solutions and construct interventions that are irrelevant to any real-world problem. Proaction, therefore, might be seen by some as irrelevant or a waste of precious collaborative time. In addition, many professional problems are unique, complex, and unpredictable, thereby making it difficult to anticipate the nature, influence, or course of future problems.

Proaction, while generally seen as advantageous, usually occurs less often than reactive professional behavior. Given this practicality, almost all teachers spend much more time in their work in a *reactive* problem-solving mode. In this mode, teachers react to professional problems that have already occurred and that demand their attention. Again, the advantages and disadvantages of reactive problem solving mirror those discussed with proaction. One advantage of working reactively is that your problem solving will address difficulties that have already occurred, thereby allowing for solutions that are entirely focused. Another advantage of reaction is that it is often seen as time efficient because teachers are usually more comfortable in spending their professional time on real problems than speculative ones. Furthermore, because the nature of the problem is already known, irrelevant speculation of some hypothetical, unknown difficulty—which might not ever occur in the real world—is usually avoided.

Working reactively, however, also has several distinct disadvantages. For example, once a problem has occurred, alternatives for resolution are limited by the nature and extent of the problem, while other solutions are omitted by default. Also, in reacting to a problem that has occurred, there is little or no time to consider the ramifications or relevance of proposed solutions or interventions. Furthermore, opportunities for valuable reflection on any given problem are more limited as these are constrained by the need to solve that problem.

Steps for Collaborative Problem Solving

In order to solve problems effectively, it is necessary to move through a series of steps that begin with defining the problem and end with a careful evaluation of whether the proffered solution accomplished its goal. While it may be possible to solve problems, at least partially, by ignoring these steps, practicing problem solving through a logical, reflective process is much more likely to increase the potential for a satisfactory solution while simultaneously enhancing your professional integrity. The following steps provide a sequence for solving most of the professional problems you are likely to encounter.

Step 1: Is There a Problem to Solve?

A common novice error in problem solving is the assumption that a problem exists before verifying whether this is actually the case. Such impulsive assumptions can be detrimental to your professional performance in a number of ways. For example, impulsivity in professional behavior often leads to wasted time, energy, and effort. In addition, your professional integrity suffers if you attempt to solve problems that either do not exist or which are irrelevant to your work. Furthermore, such irrationally swift action communicates that you may lack the ability for careful reflection and that you are impulsive and inappropriately reactionary.

On the other hand, some professional problems demand rather quick action, so extensive reflection might not always be necessary or appropriate. These problems, however, have solutions that tend to be self-evident and often commonsensical.

There are several critical factors to consider in establishing whether or not a problem exists:

> *Is there really a problem?* Begin by resisting the notion that because you or others perceive that there is a problem that a problem automatically exists. All teachers perceive their professional world through their own personal views and biases, and quite often, if you take a moment to reflect on the validity of the alleged problem, other explanations might be more likely. For example, what is first raised as a professional problem might be a professional or personal bias that has little base in fact or which is irrelevant to your work.
>
> Another way to decide whether a problem is legitimate is to ascertain how many of your colleagues agree that the problem exists. While it is always possible that highly relevant problems can be restricted to one or a few teachers, it is generally true that the more people who agree there is a problem, the more likely it will be that a genuine problem exists. In this regard, however, it is also important to remember that a group of individuals might raise a particular problem as a means of furthering their own hidden professional and personal agendas, or for reasons that have little to do with actually resolving the issue.
>
> If, after careful consideration of all the information at your disposal, you conclude that it is likely that a problem exists, you should then establish who owns the problem and the ramifications of the problem for your collaborative work.

Whose problem is it? A common difficulty, especially among novice teachers, is confusion about who actually owns and is responsible for any professional problem. If you attempt to solve a problem that is, for all intents and purposes, owned by someone else, you run the risk of setting a precedent that will adversely affect your future professional integrity. For instance, if you insist on attempting to solve issues that are not your responsibility, you might then be expected to solve others' problems in the future or you might be seen as interfering in the professional obligations of others. In addition, attending to others' problems will divert energy and effort that should be focused on problems that you are directly responsible for solving as a collaborative professional.

Remember that it is often tempting to try to solve all problems evident in your work setting, especially if you are highly motivated and if you can see solutions to the problem that appear to have escaped others' attention. You might also be tempted to solve others' problems because of the positive reinforcement this sometimes provides (albeit in the short term), or you might feel such action necessary in the best interest of the collaborative group or the students.

On the other hand, deciding whether to solve others' problems when those problems affect either the collaborative team or the student requires a more refined judgement. In most instances, you or your colleagues will need to weigh the possible ramifications of allowing the problem to continue or whether it is necessary to intervene. Should you decide to solve the problem in the best interests of your collaborative colleagues, remember that this runs all the risks already mentioned above regarding taking ownership of problems that are not your immediate responsibility.

Once problem ownership has been established, it will usually become clear whether further action is warranted. If so, the next decision involves evaluating whether action is possible given the nature and extent of the problem.

Even if there is a problem, is it soluble? It is important that even when you are certain that a professional problem exists, that you then carefully examine the nature and extent of the problem to determine whether solution is possible. Many teachers become frustrated by spending significant amounts of time, energy, and effort attempting to solve problems that are either insoluble or which are not worth their time and effort. You will be more likely to avoid such misdirected activity by evaluating several key areas that will indicate the feasibility for solving the problem. First, ask yourself what will happen if the problem remains unresolved. Obviously, in some instances such an evaluation will indicate immediately that action is necessary. Perhaps more importantly, however, asking this question will demonstrate that in other instances no further action is appropriate. Second, assess whether the problem is worth any or all of the effort you might have to expend to solve it. Effective teachers take time to reflect on their finite resources and to match these to only the most important problems in their setting. Third, assuming that the problem is worth solving and that you are willing to do so, decide whether there are enough other resources in your work setting to solve the problem. Finally, solving the problem will most often need to be accomplished in cooperation with others, so it becomes necessary to evaluate whether other key players contributing to the solution are willing to commit *their* energy and effort with you to solve the problem.

Step 2: Identifying the Problem

By the end of Step 1 the existence and relevance of a professional problem will have been established. However, much work remains in order to solve the problem effectively. Now the problem must be specifically identified and delineated. Identifying the problem is probably the most important step in the entire problem-solving process as all that follows proceeds directly from how the problem is conceptualized and defined. If the work at this stage is carefully done, you are likely to uncover the exact nature of the problem as well as any related interventions. On the other hand, if you or your colleagues fail to complete this step carefully, you run the very real risk of matching less appropriate interventions to a poorly defined problem, which will delay effective resolution of the problem and force you to return to this step later.

When defining a problem, it often helps to remember that problems should be clarified through collaborative discussion, negotiation, and consensus. Before moving on to possible solutions, all participating parties should agree that there is, indeed, a problem, engage in an evaluation of the factors contributing to the problem, and examine how the problem appears from various professional points of view. Such consideration will bring the problem into focus, generate areas of agreement, and identify areas of disagreement about the problem that will need to be resolved before moving to the next step in the problem-solving process.

Experienced problem solvers understand that during these critical discussions, several practical skills are paramount. First, inevitably, initial discussion of the nature of the problem will generate areas of disagreement and even conflict. This is a necessary part of defining the problem and should be seen as an essential precursor to problem identification and definition. Second, it is important to describe the problem as accurately as possible. The more accurately you describe the problem or its contributing elements, the greater the potential for effective communication and a concomitant reduction in the potential for misunderstanding. Third, do your best to discuss the problem in language that is both concrete and specific. This will increase the likelihood that you will be immediately understood and that you will also, therefore, waste less time restating previously unclear comments or observations. Fourth, bring as much relevant information as possible to bear on defining the problem. The more information you have about the nature of the problem, the more likely it will be that you will be able to define what the problem really is. Fifth, it is usually helpful to define the problem in terms of measurable rather than vague or subjective outcomes. Concentrating on measurable features of problem identification and definition allow for more accurate assessment of whether the problem has been solved. Sixth, allow adequate time for the identification process to run its course. Because many professional problems are complex, it is unrealistic to schedule little time for these discussions.

Finally, it is important to understand that defining the problem cannot go on indefinitely. While it is extremely important to define the problem as accurately as possible, persistent engagement at this step after the problem has been defined or where further discussion yields diminishing returns should be avoided. Generally, it is possible to move to the next step of the problem-solving process when consensus is reached on the nature, extent, and contributing factors of the problem under discussion.

Step 3: Generating Potential Solutions

There is little point in considering possible interventions and solutions without first having an accurate definition of the problem. Once this has been accomplished, however, it is important that you and your colleagues then consider a wide variety of alternatives that might have some bearing on the problem. Initially, it is important to consider relatively nonspecific, wide-ranging solutions even if at first they appear less than ideal. Initially considering many possible alternatives is appropriate because it provides a broad set of options that will likely generate other ideas and also build an expansive menu of choices that can be considered more specifically later. Also, it is to everyone's advantage to have as diverse a problem-solving group as possible. By including persons from dissimilar professional and personal backgrounds, you increase the potential for a rich assortment of possible courses of action.

At this juncture, several barriers might impede the flow of potentially useful suggestions. For example, brainstorming ideas to solve problems often raises contradictory viewpoints, thereby raising the possibility of strong dis-agreement or conflict. Be sure, therefore, to keep the focus on simply listing ideas and suggestions rather than making judgments, at least at this point, about their worth.

Another common issue encountered in this step is related to the amount of time that is spent generating the ideas and suggestions. Effective teachers understand that while enough time should be allocated for the task, too much time spent on brainstorming can also be counterproductive. Clearly, too little brainstorming time is a much more common problem than too much time. Thus, interactions should be kept tightly focused and goal oriented. Not allocating enough time to this step increases the chances of omitting poten-tially effective solutions. On the other hand, wasting too much time here might also mean having less time to spend on the next important steps in the process.

Step 4: Evaluating Potential Solutions

By this step, you should have as much information as possible about the problem and the potential solutions. Now it is feasible to begin narrowing down your options through a more careful analysis of each suggestion, idea, or proposed intervention. First, it is necessary to study carefully the entire set of assembled suggestions without making any judgments as to their worth for the final solution. Once everyone has familiarized themselves with the entire list, each individual item can be evaluated. Here, too, it is important to remember that time is influential—the longer the list of suggestions, the less time you will have for discussing each one. For each item, discuss the advan-tages and disadvantages in as much detail as possible. Carefully evaluate the resources needed for each item and whether these are readily available. After considering these two issues, you will see clearly that several ideas or sugges-tions generated in the previous step will be either irrelevant or inappropriate. These can then be omitted from further consideration.

At this point, you and your colleagues will have a reduced list of possible solutions that are much more closely matched to the problem. However, two more considerations are crucial in delineating the final pool of options from which a solution might be chosen: feasibility and intrusiveness. In terms of feasibility, further evaluation of each option should be discussed as to whether it is possible to implement the given suggestion or idea. Many ideas and suggestions, while possibly creative or relevant, might be impossible to execute for a wide variety of reasons, including ethical considerations, the perceptions or wishes of parents, or legal or policy constraints. Intrusiveness should also be an overriding consideration in that while some solutions might hold great potential for solving the immediate problem, they might be so intrusive as to create more problems than what they are able to solve. Solutions that have more disadvantages than advantages, those that require excess or unavailable resources, and those that are impossible to implement or that are overly intrusive should then be deleted from the list.

Step 5: Selecting the Solution

By now in the problem-solving process, your collaborative efforts will have produced several well-defined, focused, and viable alternatives for implementation. In conjunction with your colleagues, a final decision must be made as to which alternative is best. Given that much of the collaborative evaluation of these alternatives has already taken place, selecting one option above several other equally viable options should not be difficult and may be based on which intervention might be most convenient, the professional preference of the collaborating parties, and the general goodness of fit with the preferences of the parents, family, and student. All that remains after this step is the actual implementation of the intervention and an evaluation of its efficacy.

Step 6: Implementing the Solution

If all the preceding steps have been carefully negotiated, implementing the appropriate intervention is the next logical step. The collaborative team should decide on the parties responsible for implementation and any final adjustments before the intervention should be made. It is also important at this point for you and your colleagues to determine the length of time the intervention will be in place and what criteria will determine partial or complete success.

   If you are responsible for implementing the solution, be sure that you are completely familiar with the technical, professional, and collaborative aspects of your task before implementing the solution. In addition, ensure that you have all the resources you need and determine an alternative plan of action to address any problems that may arise during implementation. Experienced teachers also understand that as a matter of professional courtesy and in the interests of remaining focused, it is a good idea to report progress or lack thereof to your colleagues on a regular basis. Reporting the status of the intervention allows those involved in the original problem-solving process to be informed as to the solution's progress, to assist you if any problems arise, and to offer encouragement and support. If you fail to keep your colleagues informed, you increase the likelihood of professional isolation and the possibility of damage to your professional credibility. Once the intervention has been implemented, the final step of evaluating its efficacy remains.

Step 7: Evaluating the Outcomes

There is little point in expending a great deal of professional and personal energy to identify and define a problem, evaluate a variety of options, and then implement what appears to the most appropriate solution without, at some point, evaluating the efficacy of what has been implemented. Experienced teachers will tell you that, in many instances, this final, important step is often overlooked or poorly done. Evaluating the outcomes of the proposed solution will establish whether the collaborative problem-solving effort was successful in the long run. By the time the solution is implemented, all involved parties should have discussed and decided upon how to measure the final outcome.

Assessment of the outcomes will reveal one of three general results. First, the implemented solution might be a complete success. If this is the case, due credit should be given to all those who contributed to the process and careful note should be made of why the solution was successful. Second, the solution may have been partially successful. If this is the case, careful analysis of which aspects were successful as well as a careful review of which aspects were unsuccessful—and why—should be undertaken. Following such scrutiny, collaborative problem solving to address the unsuccessful aspects and the initial solution should be rectified through the steps just described. A third possibility exists: that the entire implemented solution produced no successful outcomes whatsoever. Complete failure to solve the problem may occur for any number of reasons. However, experienced teachers know that the most likely reason is that the problem-solving process, outlined in Steps 1 through 6, was not effectively completed. Obviously, such a complete failure signifies a need to return to Step 1 and repeat the process much more carefully and thoroughly.

Summary

Problems in professional work are common, varied, and require energy consummate with the extent and seriousness of the problem. All attempts at problem solving should follow a series of steps beginning with an assessment of whether there is, in fact, a problem and then carefully proceed through the problem-solving process to a final step of evaluating how effectively the problem was solved.

Questions for Reflection

1. Reflect on your personal views on what constitutes a professional problem and whether your perceptions of professional problems match those of your peers.

2. Consider how you have solved problems in your personal life, and identify whether you use similar approaches in attempting to solve professional problems.

3. Select what you consider to be a major professional problem that might arise in your first year of teaching. Use the steps of the problem-solving process to practice how you would solve that problem.

4. Consider each step of the problem-solving process and what professional pitfalls might arise as you use the steps to solve a professional problem.

5. Think of ways you could model and teach the steps of the problem-solving process to colleagues who fail to use them or to whom the steps are unknown.

References

Brubaker, D. L. (1970). *The teacher as decision-maker.* Dubuque, IA: William C. Brown.

Kabler, M. L., & Genshaft, J. L. (1983). Structuring decision making in multi-disciplinary teams. *School Psychology Review, 14,* 150–159.

Margolis, H., & Brannigan, G. G. (1987). Problem solving with parents. *Academic Therapy, 22,* 423–425.

Zins, J. E. (1993). Enhancing consultee problem-solving skills in consultative interactions. *Journal of Counseling and Development, 71,* 185–190.

9

Working with Parents and Families

Introduction

The role of parents and the family has become much more prominent in education over the last thirty years. Teachers have increasingly incorporated families in educational decision making, intervention, follow-through, and evaluation based on the realization that other people important in the student's life often possess unique support characteristics and information intricately tied to the success of any educational endeavor. The new prominence accorded parents and families can be traced to a complex set of factors, including significant demographic or sociological and legal changes.

The demographic portrait of the family has changed markedly in recent years. Many sociological indicators consistently reflect that in our society we have more single parent families, more absentee fathers, higher incidences of spouse and child abuse, more divorce, and a host of other factors potentially detrimental to the welfare of children. In addition, schools report sharp increases in family-related problems, student aggression against peers and staff, a general decline in literacy rates, and, in many school districts, increased dropout rates. These extraordinary demographic and sociological changes have triggered legal mandates at the local, state, and federal levels that attempt to address family problems by increased support for helping agencies, more punitive criminal law, and codification of the responsibilities of the helping professions and the rights of children, parents, and other guardians.

Recently, teachers' views of parental involvement in school issues have also changed. In the past, many professionals tended to view parents as the major cause of their children's problems, often resulting in educational interventions being limited to the isolation of the classroom. Many parents were dissociated from what happened to their children in school, and consequently, collaboration between parents and school professionals was, at best, irregular. Many teachers believed that they knew what was best for students and, at least implicitly, did not see parents as an important source of help and support. Historically, many professionals believed that parents should defer to teachers in education-related matters. Over time, however, parents who felt alienated from the educational process and especially from collaborative efforts in educating their children began to advocate actively for increased participation in educational matters. Concurrent with significant parental advocacy at all levels, it became increasingly clear to researchers and teachers that attempting to solve students' problems in isolation at school was ineffective. Instead, the need arose to address the complex needs of children within a larger context of both the school and the family. These changes, along with demographic, sociological, and legal changes previously mentioned, slowly allowed parents a more assertive role as full participants in the collaborative process.

Seeing that these historic changes will impact your collaborative work, it is important that you operate from a professional mind-set based on some general practical assumptions in working with parents and families.

Assumptions in Working with Parents and Families

Working with parents and families can be both a rewarding and a frustrating experience. In all your dealings with parents, remember that they are likely to be collaboratively inexperienced. Whereas teachers have learned their professional functions through rigorous training and a deliberate socialization into their field of expertise, parents have little to no formal training in handling problems with their children or working with teachers. Some parents and families deal with these problems more effectively than others.

Several key undergirding issues can enhance or damage your working relationship with parents and families. First, it is appropriate that you work under the assumption that parents generally wish to cooperate with you and your colleagues in the best interests of their child. Beginning with such an assumption invites parents and families to collaborate, communicates that you are willing to consider their point of view, and conveys the expectation that they are valued collaborators in solving their child's problem. Cessation of the collaborative relationship with parents and families should only be a last resort when all other efforts by you and many other persons have completely failed to produce any workable response—a circumstance that will not happen more than a few times in any teacher's career.

Second, begin your work with the family with the assumption that the parents and other family members know a great deal about the student that you might not know. Parents and caregivers usually possess a great deal of important information that can expedite effective treatment interventions. This knowledge has a profound effect on the selection, implementation, and evaluation of any specific strategy for change in student behavior. For example, the professional team might devise what, to them, appears to be a very efficient and focused intervention only to discover that, given the circumstances or wishes of the family, the intervention is inappropriate. Without the information and input from the family, implementation of the intervention might have caused more problems than it resolved.

Third, it is crucial to understand the distinction between what you know about each student and what the parents know about their child. These perspectives are likely to be different but overlapping sets of information. Be careful, therefore, not to assume that you know more about the child than the parents or other family members do. While this may be partially true in that you know how the child behaves at school, the child's behavior in nonschool settings might be markedly different.

Fourth, students only spend minimal amounts of time under direct supervision of any professional and a much greater proportion of their time in other situations where family members are in much closer contact. Professionals rely heavily on the support of families and caregivers to carry through with interventions outside school and when direct professional supervision is impossible.

Fifth, the nature of each educational intervention is often modified or changed according to the unique needs and configurations of each individual family. For example, one family might need intensive intervention because of some serious problems with the student and family members, while another family might simply need minor interventions to prevent more serious problems. It may also be that the unique make-up of each family could result in different interventions or levels of intervention depending on the number of people in the family, each person's roles and status in the family system, and the extent to which family members reciprocally influence each other and events in their day-to-day lives.

Sixth, you have a professional obligation to include families wherever possible in the entire decision-making process that leads to effective intervention with their child. Family members, especially parents, have a legal and ethical right to be fully aware of the potential implications of any intervention and their responsibilities before, during, and after any intervention.

Seventh, guard against stereotyping parents for any reason whatsoever. Remember that there is a great deal that you do not know about parents' and families' lives, homes, and attitudes. If you sincerely wish to be helpful and supportive, view each family as a separate entity with its own unique set of strengths, weaknesses, and life history. Maintaining this position will keep you focused on each student's welfare and reduce the likelihood of wasted energy on aspects of the family that are perhaps unchangeable or irrelevant.

Eighth, while it is essential that you accord families and parents appropriate respect, it is equally important not to be overwhelmed or intimidated by parents who might be aggressive, overly passive, or in some way socially inappropriate. Just as parents and families can be very supportive of your efforts and the efforts of other professionals, you should not be distracted into side issues such as continual disagreements, power struggles, and other maneuvers that derail you from implementing effective interventions with the student. Remember that irrespective of such asides, your ultimate function as a professional educator is to provide quality service and assistance to each of your students. Do your best, therefore, to avoid getting angry, frustrated, or defensive. Focus instead on what elements of the situation are positive and helpful for the student, and, after careful consideration of their value, give lower priority to issues that are negative and less relevant.

Ninth, in all of your interactions with parents, be forthright about your limitations as a professional. Experienced teachers understand that many parents, facing difficulties with their child, often see teachers as having all the answers to the problem. Of course, you are obligated to fulfill your professional duty according to your experience, technical skill, and collaborative expertise, but parents must sometimes be reminded that there are practical, legal, and ethical parameters within which you must operate. Reminding them of this aspect of your work will help avoid misunderstandings and more clearly communicate your role in assisting them and their child.

Finally, also be aware that in any collaborative venture with parents and families, there is a continuum of involvement that overlays any action you, the parents, or your colleagues may take. The continuum of parental involvement can stretch from absolute noninvolvement on the one hand to excessive overinvolvement on the other. Parents operating at either extreme may become a very real obstacle to effective intervention. While there are very few parents who are entirely absent from some form of educational involvement, you will encounter such individuals from time to time. It is much more common, however, to encounter parents who, while initially uninvolved or overinvolved, can be encouraged to participate more appropriately.

Most parents that you will work with are likely to be more than willing to engage in any form of collaboration for the benefit of their children. Wherever parents may fall on the continuum of involvement, it is important to remember that there are many reasons, often unknown to school personnel, for any level of involvement or disengagement. Not all of these reasons are negative, but it is important to establish, as best you can, the reason for their level of involvement in the collaborative effort.

Given these general assumptions about your work with parents, it is important to have a general understanding of their perspectives based not only on their involvement with the school, but also on their varied functions as caregivers to their children.

Family Aspects Influencing Collaboration

Several factors influence the nature and extent of parental roles in working collaboratively with teachers, including survival functions and the role of families throughout the developmental lifespan and the levels of cohesion and adaptability to changes within the family.

Survival Functions

Parents and families are engaged, for much of their time, in a host of survival functions which, depending on how well these functions are executed, have a great influence on the level of parents' participation in any collaborative endeavor to solve problems with their child in school. For example, survival functions include efforts to fulfill economic needs. Energy expended to meet economic necessities can have a clear effect on the level of involvement of parents and families in collaborative efforts. Thus, if the economic needs of the family require a single parent to spend a great deal of time at work, there will be little time available for working with school personnel.

Another survival function relates to meeting the day-to-day needs of the family and includes routine chores and daily living obligations. For example, if a family must spend inordinate amounts of time attending to the complex needs of a seriously handicapped child, there may be less time for involvement with teachers and the school. In addition, parents and families also have socialization and recreational needs that require time and focus. Greater or lesser attention to these needs will affect the amount of time devoted to other areas of need with their children. Many other survival functions include how families cope with a broad range of common family problems and vocational or educational needs of each family member.

Life Span Involvement

Parents, families, and siblings characteristically have a deep and lasting involvement with any individual child that is almost impossible, and certainly impractical, for teachers to simulate. This aspect reinforces the notion that parents and families should be deeply involved in any interventions and also underscores that others in the family system possess considerable knowledge important for all professionals involved in solving the problem.

Essentially, family involvement with a child stretches over a lifetime and moves through quite clearly definable phases. During infancy and preschool, for example, family and parental efforts are usually concentrated on meeting the child's physical and health demands and establishing the rudiments of a parental relationship. When the child enters school, parents maintain the physical and parental foci while simultaneously concentrating on the educational needs of the child, including parental and family involvement with teachers. By the time the child reaches adolescence, parents and families again make a major readjustment as the adolescent begins to define his or her self-identity. It is during adolescence that parental influence begins to wane and the parameters of the parent/family–child relationship are redefined more in terms of adult interaction. When the adolescent leaves school, the final transition to adulthood begins with concomitant stressful changes in the dynamics of the family system.

Cohesion

Cohesion generally refers to the level of emotional distance between family members and is gauged on a continuum from high enmeshment to complete disengagement. The nature or extent of cohesion often varies according to the unique circumstances of each individual family. Assessing the level of cohesion is important for problem identification and effective intervention with students. On the one hand, parents and families who are overly enmeshed with the problems of their child might hold inaccurate perceptions of the problem and might also impede progress toward effective intervention. On the other hand, parents and families who are completely disengaged from the student's problem may be unlikely to make collaborative efforts to solve the problem. Generally, teachers prefer a level of cohesion that allows parents and the family to be meaningfully involved without being so involved that the potential for conflict or serious misunderstanding is increased.

Adaptability

Adaptability refers to the family's ability to adjust to the many changing and often difficult issues of family life. Some families appear to possess more skill at adapting to change than others and to possess a greater repertoire of appropriate behaviors for problem solving. The more adaptable the parents and family, the more likely that you and your colleagues will be able to define any problems and intervene effectively.

Cohesion and adaptability are usually given lower precedence in working with families yet they are crucial to your understanding of how much a family might help or what issues they see as important when collaborating with helping professionals. These two factors are equally important to you as a teacher because they are practical issues that can be improved on as you work with the family and teach them more about the functions necessary for effective family living and support of educational interventions.

Family interactions can also be understood within a systems-oriented approach—that is, the broader context of how family members interact as part of a social system.

Systems Approaches to Collaboration and Intervention

A systems perspective involves viewing any collaborative work we do with students, their families, and other professionals as an interrelated set, or system, of personal interactions with numerous connections. In order to be an effective collaborator, it is important to consider two interrelated areas that will impact your work—that is, a system-oriented view of (a) the family and (b) interprofessional collaboration.

System-Oriented Views of the Family

A major influence in collaboration with families has been a general acceptance of the family as a microcosmic social system that is highly interconnected and mutually influential. Such a view of the family assumes that changes in any one system member usually results in some greater or lesser change in all the other system members. A systems approach has important implications for intervention and interprofessional collaboration in two very important ways.

First, a systems view dictates that whatever problem the student is exhibiting affects others in the system, including family members, the student's peers, and relationships to professionals rendering assistance. Proposed interventions and possible solutions, therefore, have to consider the student and his or her problems in a highly detailed context. Such a view necessitates the incorporation of many people for effective problem solving and has many advantages over other modes of professional behavior. For example, involving many interested and influential parties allows for a comprehensive "big picture," which is much more likely to be accurate than if fewer individuals are involved. In addition, the more family and helping professionals are involved, the more likely it will be that a full array of intervention options are considered. Also, involving as many people in the family system as possible will generally provide the best chance of continuity between interventions activated at school being reinforced and supported at home.

Second, family systems, by definition, are influenced by several areas of human interaction that are more or less important to the social functioning of the family. These areas are commonly delineated as the marital, parental, sibling, and extrafamilial roles.

Marital Roles

A major influence on relationships within the family system is the personal relationship between the parents. Because the family operates as a system, the health of the relationship between the parents will directly affect the relationships among all other members of the family. The greater the health of this relationship, the more likely collaboration will exist with educational and other helping professionals for effective intervention. Clearly, should such a relationship be dysfunctional or damaged, or should one or both parents be absent, a concomitant negative effect on any collaborative efforts is likely.

Parental Roles

How parents or caregivers perform in their role as parents is also critical to relational dynamics within the family. The ability to cope with the stress of parenting, approaches to limit setting, the giving and receiving of affection, discipline, and so on, will all influence collaborative outcomes.

Role of Siblings

The role of siblings in relation to the rest of the family is generally less well understood than the function of parents. However, siblings of the student having problems in school can often play an important part in the dynamics of the family, and understanding this is important in tailoring effective interventions. Many factors such as siblings' ages, their ability to cope with the problem sibling, their maturity level, their ability to cope with the family stress caused by the problem student, and their willingness to be involved will influence the level of siblings' participation in problem identification and intervention.

Extrafamilial Roles

Other persons in the wider context of the family might also play an important, influential role and may also be instrumental in supporting the efforts of helping professionals. Relatives, friends, and family acquaintances form the widest circle of influence that you should consider as you attempt to solve any problems your students might have.

Such a systems view, however, belies several significant drawbacks. For example, in most intervention settings, it is not possible to involve all persons who are part of the professional and family system, creating the potential that important insights or help crucial to any intervention might be lost. It may also be that too many people might become involved, creating the potential for confusion, conflict, or faulty communication. Furthermore, you and your colleagues may not have the time to manage unusually large numbers of participants or the vast amounts of information that such involvement might generate.

Systems Views of Interprofessional Collaboration

A second aspect of a systems view is directly related to interprofessional collaboration. As you begin to work with your colleagues, it will quickly become apparent that social and relational aspects of your work cannot be ignored, and, indeed, must be appropriately maintained and strengthened if working with students is going to be optimally effective. In terms of a systems view of your collaboration, you will find that your collaborative behavior is likely to have a greater or lesser effect on all of your colleagues. You have a responsibility, therefore, to consider reasonably what your actions will mean to your colleagues, the likelihood of how they will react, and what such actions and reactions will mean for the larger system of working with students and their families. In addition, you should bear in mind that what might appear to be, in your judgment, an action of little consequence, might, to your colleagues, be much more significant.

In summary, a systems view of your work will help much more than hinder your professional efficacy. Careful attention to the effects of your actions and to the actions of others on your colleagues and your students and their families will set the stage for effective interaction and intervention while simultaneously ensuring that the focus of all involved remains appropriate, well defined, well implemented, and carefully evaluated for maximum effect. While monitoring a high level of awareness of the interactions of any family system, it is equally important to note and to work to lessen any barriers to effective collaboration with parents and families.

Barriers to Parental and Family Collaboration

When parents and teachers engage in interprofessional collaboration, they often identify a range of collaborative impediments that affect the quality of the educational decisions that need to be made. In order to be an effective collaborator, you must be aware of these barriers so that they may be overcome or at least neutralized.

There are numerous reasons why engaging in collaboration is sometimes problematic. Both parents and teachers agree, for example, that logistical problems such as inability to attend meetings, communication problems, and lack of time may interfere with the collaborative process. Parents may also feel that they are not equal partners in the process and may therefore be unwilling to participate in collaborative activities. Parents also sometimes cite feelings of inferiority when interacting with teachers and other helping professionals. Parents may, furthermore, see themselves as being at a collaborative disadvantage because they are unfamiliar with school policies and the legal implications of any educational decisions or interventions that might affect their children.

Teachers, on the other hand, often view a lack of parental and familial collaboration as stemming from a lack of motivation. Teachers also sometimes believe that parents' uninvolvement comes from their lack of appreciation for teachers' judgment. Teachers also report that parents sometimes do not appreciate the professional constraints within which they are obligated to operate.

Generally, therefore, many aspects of collaboration with parents and family members can potentially be disastrous. As an effective teacher, particularly in the early stages of working with any individual family, it will be your responsibility to be aware of and, where possible, to avoid such barriers. Once a firm and trusting collaborative relationship has been established, you will be largely responsible for diminishing these barriers by making parents and family members aware of them and for soliciting their help in removing such impediments.

Professional Responsibilities in Working with Parents and Families

Most professionals assume certain responsibilities when working with parents and families. Parents also have important obligations that will support intervention for effective educational change. The responsibilities below are not exhaustive but describe many of the primary duties of any competent teacher involved in interprofessional collaboration.

Providing Information

One of the basic and more traditional responsibilities of any effective teacher is to provide information to students, their families, and your colleagues. A crucial element of providing information, of course, is knowing what information to provide and when to provide it. Some inexperienced teachers might provide too much information, much of it irrelevant or repetitive, while others might not provide enough. Deciding how much information to provide can be facilitated in a number of ways. First, carefully attend to information you are clearly obligated to provide based on your professional preparation. Second, be familiar with your school's policies regarding the dissemination of information to students, their families, and your colleagues. This will help you remain within the legal and ethical guidelines of your work. Third, enlist advice and suggestions from trusted, experienced colleagues about how, when, and with whom information should be shared. Recommendations from your colleagues may be an effective shortcut to appropriate information sharing. In addition, seeking out such advice will provide an opportunity to build interprofessional relationships and to learn from others. Fourth, wherever possible, consider the ethical implications of what sharing this information will mean. Generally, as discussed elsewhere, a rule of thumb regarding information sharing is to do so only on an as-needed basis, thereby somewhat restricting the information's unnecessary availability.

Interpreting Information

It is insufficient simply to provide appropriate amounts of information to students, parents, families, or your colleagues. In most instances, some level of explanation is required given that many collaborative problems originate in the misunderstanding or misinterpretation of information. In addition, given that information is characteristically variable, ranging from the simplest material requiring little or no explanation to highly complex technical infor-mation that requires extensive interpretation, it is important that you consider the extent to which explanation might be needed.

Interpreting information to students and families is crucial to inform them of issues surrounding educational problems and interventions. You will be responsible for explaining a wide range of information that they may not understand or that they may seriously question. Effective teachers develop great skill in interpreting information at the level of the families' and student's understanding.

When interpreting information to parents, there are several ways you can ensure that you do so accurately and in an understandable way. First, prepare what you wish to share ahead of time, making sure that the information you will deliver is appropriate and relevant, as well as conforming to all the policy and ethical guidelines of your profession. Second, ensure that you understand what the information means and the purpose for which you are sharing it. It will also be to your benefit to reflect on the problematic aspects of the information in anticipation of any questions the family might ask. Carefully preparing in this way will reduce the potential for confusion while simultane-ously giving you a better understanding of the information and of how to convey it. Third, be sure, where necessary, to make notes as prompts or reminders for reference during the conference. Fourth, while it is not often necessary to learn all the information by rote prior to delivering it, you should be so familiar with it that you present a coherent explanation devoid of convoluted asides or illogical explication. Fifth, it is usually a good idea to remind yourself that students and families are unlikely to possess most of the technical background that assists you in understanding information. Do not assume that families possess even rudimentary technical knowledge that will help them make sense of what you are trying to explain. If you anticipate that questions might arise for which you have no answer, do your best to establish where such answers might be found before you meet with the family. Sixth, present information in small amounts and allow adequate time for those hearing the information to assimilate what you are saying. Encourage students, parents, and other family members to ask questions. From time to time, summarize and paraphrase what you have just reported. Seventh, make notes during the meeting as a reminder to clarify points that might need further explanation or follow-up. Finally, it is always a good idea to plan some time at the end to address any lingering concerns or to answer other questions.

Interpreting information to your colleagues entails similar professional behavior but with one other very important element—your colleagues have the advantage of professional orientation and training. It is best, however, not to assume that all of your colleagues will find the information you are sharing understandable or relevant. While such information might be important from your perspective, your colleague's training and their professional perceptions might be quite different. It is your responsibility not only to anticipate such instances, but also to have some knowledge of your colleagues' professional orientations. Engaging in such professional behavior will increase your colleagues' understanding of the significance of the information you present. It will also help ensure that they are more willing to consider such information, and, therefore, be able to bring *their* professional expertise to bear on the information for effective problem solving.

Reporting Evaluation Results

A specific responsibility in sharing and interpreting information involves reporting evaluation and assessment results to students, families, and your colleagues. Many experienced teachers see this aspect of information sharing as one of the most important parts of their job. Reporting evaluation results is especially important as many decisions for intervention that affect everyone involved are directly shaped by such results.

There are several underlying assumptions about sharing and interpreting test results that you must keep in mind. First, your colleagues and your students and their families expect that any evaluation has been carried out accurately and according to the principles of psychological and educational assessment. Test results and what they mean, therefore, can only be as accurate as your testing competence. It is your responsibility to ensure that any test you give is within the scope of your expertise, that you have attended to the numerous pitfalls of test administration, and that you have conducted the test to the best of your professional ability. Second, those around you will assume that you understand what the results mean and that you will be able to explain them in a detailed but understandable way. Finally, they will expect that, based on the results you have obtained, you will be able to make relevant recommendations to improve the student's performance.

As with any other informational issues, the basic distinction between students and their families on the one hand and professionals on the other must be kept in mind: Students and parents will need the results explained and interpreted in an understandable, preferably nontechnical way, while colleagues in other fields will need some orientation as to how you are viewing the results. Where possible, you should shape your interpretation to the professional backgrounds of your colleagues.

Bearing this distinction in mind and adjusting the level of your explanation according to your audience, remember some other guidelines. First, you might explain the need for the evaluation and why completing such an evaluation will benefit the student. Second, explain the purpose of the evaluation as a way of establishing current levels of performance rather than as a "pass/fail" test with negative connotations. Third, explain how the evaluation relates to what the student does in class. Fourth, present the test results carefully, slowly, and as far as possible, in nontechnical jargon. Fifth, at all stages of the presentation, allow time for clarifying questions. Sixth, try not to present too many evaluation results in one session as this increases the possibility of misunderstanding or conflict. It is also true, however, that you may have to include more results than are comfortably understandable due to time constraints or the limited availability of the participants. If you present a considerable amount of information, do your best to provide manageable portions in turn and then spend some time explaining the connections between the various results and how they, in combination, provide a broad evaluative picture of the problem at hand. Finally, during your reporting session, be sensitive to others' reactions to your presentation and assure them of your availability to revisit the results at a later time should they wish to do so.

Gathering and Understanding Family Information

Another area of information gathering involves what you can glean from families themselves. Information from and about the family is also important when shared with your colleagues who will be involved with you in collaborative decision making. It is important, for instance, to obtain information about the specific needs and strengths of the family, which will vary according to their individual circumstances. You should also gather as much information as possible about the family as an interrelated social system, as such knowledge might be important for how any particular problem is defined or approached. Effective teachers know that how each family member behaves individually *and* as part of the family system holds many clues as to what types of interventions might be appropriate. Consider, too, how the family system reacts to the problems at hand and how they appear to be coping (or not coping) with their current circumstances.

Understanding Family Diversity

This chapter has already noted the changing configuration of the family over the last generation. You will be a far more effective professional if you devote some time and energy to understanding the many diverse kinds of families, family systems, belief systems, ethnic and cultural backgrounds, and so on, of the students you serve. Astute understanding of these highly variable factors will enable you to perform your work more effectively for a number of reasons. First, gathering information on family diversity will help you understand the family "from the inside out," that is, to gain the family's perspective of their relationship with you and your colleagues. This view might provide a radically different slant to how you approach collaboration with the family and in working with the student. Second, knowledge of the uniqueness of the family you are dealing with will help you match effective interventions to their unique characteristics. Third, a careful assessment of the unique characteristics of each family will assist you in confronting any biases or mistaken impressions you might have that could potentially impede effective collaboration or intervention implementation. Fourth, gathering information about the family will increase the chances of engaging them in meaningful, efficient action to solve the current problem and increase their potential support of the professionals involved. Fifth, gathering information from the family will increase your interactions with them and thereby facilitate a collaborative relationship that will benefit all parties in the future.

Communicating Effectively

Highly developed communication skills for collaboration are imperative. Experienced, effective teachers will tell you that some of their colleagues, though significantly skilled in many technical aspects of their work, are not skilled communicators, thereby losing integrity and a concomitant perception, by others, that they are ineffective. There is little use in being a highly competent teacher without being able to communicate with families or colleagues.

Meetings and Conferences

If you need to meet with others to disseminate information, be sure that you plan the meeting carefully ahead of time. First, it is important to notify parents, families, and your colleagues of when the meeting will be held. Usually, the more time between notification and the meeting, the better, as timely notification allows advance planning. Second, it is imperative that you prepare thoroughly for the meeting. Your careful preparation will allow you to spend meeting time concentrating on sharing and interpreting information for others rather than attempting to learn the information in the meeting. In addition, being prepared for the meeting will raise others' perceptions of your professional integrity, which will likely translate into their increased confidence in your abilities. Third, as a very important part of your preparation, decide on what you want to achieve in the meeting and how you will achieve it. Here it is important to reflect on any possible snags that might arise and plan how to deal with them. Fourth, be sure that the setting for the meeting is available, as comfortable as possible, and that it will be conducive to achieving the goals you have set for the meeting.

Several aspects of the meeting itself can increase the chances of effective communication with families and parents of your students. First, where possible, it is important to have had some other contact with the families and other involved colleagues prior to the first meeting so that you will have already established some degree of relational familiarity. Second, strive ahead of time to build whatever rapport circumstance allows. This is especially important prior to the meeting and at the beginning of the meeting as a way of orienting the attendees and to reduce the often formal and somewhat distant attitude that most people initially display in a contrived setting. Third, once everyone appears relatively comfortable, and assuming that you have attended to common social functions such as introductions, begin the meeting by discussing the purpose of the meeting, what your goals for the meeting are, and how everyone attending the meeting is related to those goals. Present your information and intermittently allow for discussion and clarification. Fourth, be vigilant about the passing of time and bring the meeting to a close with a summary of what has transpired and by providing or soliciting information for any follow-up to the meeting.

After the meeting, it will be to your benefit to spend some time reflecting on how successful the meeting was so as to devise ways to improve future meetings. During the postmeeting period, you may also need to share the outcome of the meeting with other colleagues, prepare any written summaries or reports, and engage in any follow-up activities you think will improve communication and access to information for families, students, and colleagues.

Other Opportunities for Communication

Effective teachers know that many other less formal opportunities for communicating can be very useful in working with families and other professionals. For example, you might consider an "open door" policy whereby colleagues, parents, and families have informal access to you. Such a policy has distinct advantages as it communicates that you are approachable and willing to collaborate without formal notification. However, such a policy can also be detrimental in that unexpected visits can interfere with your other duties and in that you may not always be as prepared as you would like to be.

Another way of enhancing communication is to take the initiative before the beginning of school, or early in the school year, to establish working relationships with parents, families, and colleagues *before there is a need to do so because of a specific problem.* Proactively establishing communicative rapport is a clear advantage because when specific problems arise, many aspects of the collaborative relationship for problem solving are already in place, allowing you to devote more of your time and energy to the problem and possible solutions rather than being distracted by having to establish these social connections first. Proactively establishing rapport, however, is also time consuming and may, in some instances, be unnecessary.

One way of establishing rapport ahead of time is to engage in home visits of your students. Visiting students' homes, if possible, is an excellent way of communicating you care and for gleaning a great deal of information that might not otherwise be available to you. Such visits will almost always enhance your credibility and allow you a closer working relationship with students, parents, and families. On the other hand, home visits are time consuming and labor intensive. In addition, such visits might not always be possible, and there is always the possibility that some families may misconstrue your perfectly good intentions as being overly inquisitive or threatening.

Finally, use any school function as a golden opportunity to communicate with parents and families. PTA meetings, cultural or sporting events, and so on, all provide valuable moments for learning about your students, their parents, and their families. Effective teachers know that such information is often useful when problems arise and in shaping interventions for maximum effect.

Instruction to Families

Another function you will need to fulfill is to provide instruction to families and parents in matters related to their child's well-being in school. Generally, this can most easily be accomplished by being supportive of appropriate parental and family behavior as it relates to the student's problem and by tactfully advising some parental actions and perceptions over others. In addition, at each step in solving the problem, you will need to spend time explaining to parents every aspect of the collaborative process. This is an extremely important responsibility, as time spent teaching parents collaborative skills will encourage them to participate, insure that they are well informed, and strengthen the collaborative relationship.

In all aspects of your work with parents and families, strive to build mutual respect and inculcate a clear sense of collegiality and trust rather than any kind of adversarial relationship. Remember that one of the most effective means of assisting and supporting students is to have the parents, and preferably other family members, where appropriate, involved in every phase of solving the problem. Effective professionals spend a great deal of time and energy on this aspect of their collaborative effort. It is equally true that working with parents will be greatly facilitated if they choose to accept certain responsibilities throughout the collaborative process.

Parental Responsibilities

In most instances, parents understand that their active support for teachers' efforts with their children is valuable. Many parents will be supportive of any collaborative educational effort and will work actively to support their children in school. While you may also encounter truly uncooperative parents from time to time, it is much more likely that parents are willing to do their part but do not know how to proceed. In these instances, it will be your responsibility to model appropriate and effective collaborative behavior. Parents also bear some responsibility in the collaborative effort, including efforts to increase their parenting skills, cooperation and support for what teachers are doing in school with their child, information sharing, active participation in educational decision making, and advocating for their child to educational and other service personnel.

Parenting Skills

Like most human interactions, effective and appropriate parenting skills must be learned. Parenting encompasses an extraordinarily complex set of sustained social tasks that, to a greater or lesser degree, span parents' lives. Many parents have adequate social support systems such as extended families and especially their own parents who assist them in learning how to parent children. However, not all parents are so fortunate, and you are likely to encounter parents whose parenting skills are ineffective or inadequate. In these cases, educational professionals should provide whatever help is necessary to increase effective parenting skills. It is also the parents' responsibility to be aware of their skill weaknesses and to do their best to improve these areas. By improving skill weaknesses, parents can make significant contributions to their child's welfare, especially in school. Increased parenting skill is more likely to result in more collaboration with teachers and schools, closer attention to their children's needs and problems, and their own increased sense of efficacy.

Cooperation and Support for Educational Efforts

Parents bear a reasonable responsibility to cooperate with teachers and the school's educational efforts. It is unlikely that educational endeavors will be limited to school hours given that most teachers strive for the generalization of academic and social skills to noneducational settings. Any interventions executed in school, therefore, will have a greater chance of success if they are also implemented or supported by parents at home. Parents are most effective when, after collaborating with teachers and other support personnel, they agree to support educational interventions at home. For example, parents can assist teachers by supervising the student's homework and other out-of-school educational activities, by providing educationally enriching experiences, and by modeling appropriate educational pursuits themselves. Parents can also be supportive by modeling and demanding high levels of socially appropriate behavior and by providing appropriate sanctions for their children's socially inappropriate actions.

Information Sharing

Families are also responsible for providing as much relevant information as possible to teachers in order to solve educational problems effectively. However, experienced teachers will tell you that while such information is often crucial, eliciting information from parents can sometimes be difficult and frustrating. For example, parents may be unaware that their knowledge is very important to any collaborative effort. Other parents may not wish to share family information that they consider sensitive. Often, the more severe the student's problem, the more likely it is that parents might withhold information. Given that relevant information is a key to effective intervention, your professional behavior in eliciting information must be impeccable, balancing the need to know on the one hand with a professional, trusting relationship with parents on the other.

Active Participation

Parents' active participation in their child's education is quite variable—from being overly and inappropriately involved to not being involved at all. Ideally, parents should participate in their child's education—based on the specific needs of each individual child, their level of parenting skill, and teachers' recommendations—by providing needed family information that might be important for educational decision making and intervention.

Advocacy

Advocacy can best be described as the promotion of a certain point of view with the aim of having that position adopted to meet certain specific ends. In educational terms, advocacy relates most often to parents' ability to express their wishes and promote their point of view concerning what they see as best for their child in school. Many parents are able to articulate such advocacy. Other parents, however, find it difficult to advocate for their own or their child's positions. In such instances, it is your responsibility to advocate on the parents' behalf and also to model and teach collaborative skill so that parents might become their own advocates in future collaborative ventures.

Summary

Collaborating with parents and families is a complex and pivotal task if students are to be well served in schools. In order for collaboration to proceed effectively, teachers should be aware of the many barriers in working with parents as well as their professional obligations in supporting parents and encouraging parents' participation in education decision making and intervention. Parents also bear a clear responsibility in the collaboration process and in their willingness to support the teachers' and the school's endeavors.

Questions for Reflection

1. What is your impression of parents' attitudes and actions around educational collaborative activity on their children's behalf with teachers and the school in your community? Is this impression accurate?

2. Consider systems aspects of parents and families that you know, including your own. What aspects of these parents and families appear to be supportive of educational collaboration? Which aspects appear detrimental to such collaboration?

3. Examine as many ways as possible to establish a working relationship with parents and families. Weigh the effectiveness of each approach against any disadvantages the approach appears to generate.

4. Reflect on a systems approach to interprofessional collaboration with parents and families. What problems do you foresee in such endeavors?

5. Explore the advantages and disadvantages of parents' and families' active participation and collaboration with teachers and other school professionals. Delineate what you judge to be the ideal level of parental involvement in collaborative educational activities with teachers and the school.

References

Alper, S. K., Schloss, P. J., & Schloss, C. N. (1994). *Families of students with disabilities: Consultation and advocacy.* Boston: Allyn & Bacon.

Aronson, J. Z. (1996). How schools can recruit hard-to-reach parents. *Educational Leadership, 53*(7), 58–60.

Berger, E. H. (1981). *Parents as partners in education: The school and home working together.* St. Louis, MO: C. V. Mosby.

Davern, L. (1996). Listening to parents of children with disabilities. *Educational Leadership, 53*(7), 61–63.

Elkind, D. (1995). School and family in the postmodern world. *Phi Delta Kappan, 77,* 8–14.

Falik, L. H. (1995). Family patterns of reaction to a child with learning disability: A mediational perspective. *Journal of Learning Disabilities, 28,* 335–341.

Green, S. K., & Shinn, M. R. (1995). Parent attitudes about special education and reintegration: What is the role of student outcomes? *Exceptional Children, 61,* 269–281.

Harry, B., Allen, N., & McLaughlin, M. (1995). Communication vs. compliance: African-American parents' involvement in special education. *Exceptional Children, 61,* 364–377.

Herzog, M. J. R., & Pittman, R. B. (1995). Home, family, and community: Ingredients in the rural education equations. *Phi Delta Kappan, 77,* 113–118.

Jackson, D. N., & Hayes, D. H. (1993). Multicultural issues in consultation. *Journal of Counseling and Development, 72,* 144–147.

Kroth, R. G. (1985). *Communicating with parents of exceptional children: Improving parent-teacher relationships* (2nd Ed.). Denver: Love Publishing.

Masino, L. L., & Hodapp, R. M. (1996). Parental educational expectations for adolescents with disabilities. *Exceptional Children, 62,* 515–524.

McIntyre, T., & Silva, P. (1992). Culturally diverse childrearing practices: Abusive or just different? *Beyond Behavior, 4,*(1), 8–12.

Moore, D., & Littlejohn, W. (1992). Trends toward increased family-school collaboration. *Contemporary Education, 64,* 40–45.

Reyes, O., & Jason, L. A. (1993). Collaborating in the community. In J. E. Zins, T. R. Kratochwill, & S. N. Elliot, (Eds). *Handbook of consultation services for children* (pp. 305–328). San Francisco: Jossey Bass.

Rutherford, B., & Billig, S. H. (1995). Eight lessons of parent, family, and community involvement in the middle grades. *Phi Delta Kappan, 77,* 64–68.

Sontag, J. C., & Schacht, R. (1994). An ethnic comparison of parent participation and information needs in early intervention. *Exceptional Children, 60,* 422–433.

Stone, C. R. (1995). School/community collaboration: Comparing three initiatives. *Phi Delta Kappan, 76,* 794–800.

Trivette, C. M., Dunst, C. J., Boyd, K., & Hamby, D. W. (1996). Family-oriented program models, helpgiving practices, and parental control appraisals. *Exceptional Children, 62,* 237–248.

Turnbull, A. P., & Turnbull, H. R. (1990). *Families, professionals, and exceptionalities: A special partnership* (2nd Ed.). New York: Merrill.

Cases for Reflection and Practice

Trouble at the Top

Alone in the Dark

Deja Vu All over Again

To Do or Not to Do

Nature versus Nurture

The Broken Bond

The Rising Storm

Carmela's Predicament

A Question of Color

James's Uncertain Future

Help for Jay

Requiem for Amy

Frozen at the Precipice

Jessica's Wrath

Caught in the Middle

Trouble at the Top

Chief Protagonists
JAY LARSEN, former principal
JUNE BROCK, principal

When Jay Larsen retired as principal of Bellevue Academy, we all wondered what his replacement would be like. Jay had been principal for as long as anyone in town could remember. In the late 1960s, First Presbyterian Church decided to build the first private school in the area. At that time, Watson City was showing signs of healthy economic growth, and there seemed to be a demand among new residents for some alternative to the local public schools.

Jay Larsen was there from the beginning. In time, Jay became part of local folklore—his energy, innovation, and enthusiasm were common knowledge and universally admired. When Jay announced that he would retire at the end of the school year, it dominated the local news coverage for several days. A parade was organized in his honor, and he received every civic award the city could find. The mayor even invented a new leadership award that in future years would bear his name.

Of course, Jay was a hard act to follow. We knew, too, that his successor would face a different Bellevue. Watson City had continued to grow over the years and while the community was still blessed with very little crime, there were clear signs that strong leadership would be necessary. Recently, there had been a marked escalation of petty misdeeds and vandalism, which were attributed to several Bellevue students.

The search for Jay's successor began immediately after his announcement. The search committee, headed by the Reverend Fulbright, consisted of several senior church leaders, a member of the city commission, several members of the school board, and a prominent local attorney who was also the chair of the PTA. It was clear from the start that the committee wanted new blood, energy, and a strong hand at the helm. After what seemed like an eternity of speculation and a steady procession of candidates, the regional church council, at the recommendation of the search committee, announced the appointment of June Brock as the next principal of Bellevue.

The search committee's selection quickly divided the school staff and the city. Obviously, the board had opted for youth and vigor over experience. Some teachers felt that June was a poor choice because of her lack of experience. Others, myself included, felt that perhaps her relative lack of experience was not necessarily negative, but instead that her qualifications and high energy would allow Bellevue to build on its already sterling reputation. As wonderful as Jay had been, we all knew that Bellevue could still improve in many ways.

June was new not only to our school, but also to the responsibilities of being a school principal. June came to Bellevue immediately after completing her specialist degree in school administration at the local state university. As far as we could tell, prior to her full-time specialist degree, she had had four years of teaching experience as a ninth-grade earth science teacher in a neighboring state. It soon became clear that it wasn't June's academic qualifications that swayed the search committee, but rather that she had researched discipline policies and strategies extensively while doing her graduate work. June's interest in school discipline was one of the primary reasons for her landing the job.

A young woman of twenty-seven, June appeared quite stern from the start. She spoke in precise, clipped sentences that gave us the impression that she was measuring every word. She made it clear at our first faculty meeting that her mandate from the school board and the search committee was to "whip Bellevue into shape." To say that we were a little baffled is an understatement. Almost everyone on the faculty had served the school for years. We knew that parents and the community were very pleased with how we did our work. Twice a year, the community organized teacher appreciation days to which both public and private school faculty were invited. Personally, I believed that one of the major perks of my job was that we handled problems among faculty, parents, and students quickly and effectively. There were no warring factions, little political maneuvering, and generally very little conflict. We knew better than June that a few minor problems had cropped up in Jay's last few years but they appeared to be isolated incidents and only involved a few of the school's 600 students. We agreed that we needed to be vigilant, but June's harshness seemed out of place.

The changes that were supposed to "whip us into shape" were swift, if not clear. June whipped us, that was sure, but it wasn't into any better shape. By the end of the first semester, what had been a happy, cooperative, and spirited staff was frayed to the breaking point.

The first hint of what was to come appeared in the third week of school. Jay had scheduled the annual open house the year before and, as usual, it was to run from 9 in the morning until the close of school at 3:30. We were all proud of how hard we worked for this annual event. It was the initial opportunity of the year to show off our wonderful school. For years, in beautifully decorated classrooms over soda and homemade cookies, the open house allowed us to renew acquaintances with parents and families from the year before, welcome new parents to our building, and work hard at recruiting for the next year. We spent long hours prior to the open house making sure that Bellevue was as close to a showpiece as we could get it. We generally succeeded, although we knew that for quite a while afterward we would be exhausted from the effort. Unfortunately, we assumed that this year would be no different. How wrong we were.

A week before the open house several of us came to the faculty lounge for lunch to find letters from June in our mailboxes informing us that the date of the open house had been changed and that the hours had been extended from 9:00 in the morning until 9:00 at night, with lunch and dinner being provided in the school kitchen. We were stunned. Obviously, June had never tried to work with parents and young children entering and exiting the school all day! At our faculty meeting the next day, we voiced our reservations over the unexpected rescheduling. June listened stoically. Teacher after teacher raised very valid points: Why hadn't the faculty been consulted about the change? Why a big change so close to the event? Did June realize that we had all planned our teaching around the original date? Did June realize how difficult a twelve-hour shift would be? Did she understand the extra load on the kitchen staff? Had she ever spent twelve hours at a stretch dealing with families and children?

Eventually the teachers' questions ended. The room was hushed as we waited for June's response. She was flushed. I noticed a slight tremor in her hands as she raised herself ramrod straight and said: "I believe the change in time and day were necessary because working parents should not have to make special arrangements to visit their children's classrooms during regular school hours." She took a deep breath and continued: "There will be times when I will make decisions for the benefit of the school with which you as teachers will not agree." Then, turning on her heel, she left the room.

This first change precipitated several others in short order. Soon, without any consultation with the teachers, June implemented substantive changes in weekly faculty bulletins, parent newsletters, monthly calendars, school stationery, the dates and times of workshops and in-services, supervision and recess duties, bus scheduling, and policies in school registration. She even changed how faculty meetings were run. These many changes, of course, had quite predictable results. There was quite a bit of confusion among students, parents, faculty, and staff. Most of the disorganization could have been avoided had June taken time to observe how well the previous procedures were functioning before instituting any changes of her own. That didn't seem to be her style, however.

Eventually, matters came to a head in a faculty meeting where we heatedly questioned the changes. Many of the new rules were unclear and we openly challenged June as to whether all these changes were necessary in such a short time. Her response was terse: "I want to let everyone see my own personal style and let them know that a new principal is in charge." These and other similar comments did little to win her our respect. It didn't help that from her first day on the job her office door remained closed with an appointment sign-up sheet for us to complete if we wished to speak to her.

Other instances were even more frustrating. True to her training, June instituted (without any input from the teachers, of course) a new discipline policy. Before we could send problem students to June, we now had to complete extensive documentation on the nature and scope of the inappropriate behavior, complete with dates and times of previous occurrences and detailed evidence of at least three attempted interventions. June had devised complicated forms for this documentation, and we soon came to use this process only as a last resort. The paperwork simply wasn't worth the time and effort.

We were also reluctant to refer students to June for another reason. On those rare occasions when a teacher did submit a request for help, June insisted that the Reverend Fulbright be present. In almost every instance, this resulted in immediate dismissal of the student from the school. Many teachers were incredulous—while these students needed to see June, their inappropriate behavior hardly warranted expulsion. Several teachers attempted to intervene to avoid a student's expulsion, but June was immovable and the school board supported her to the hilt. In June's first year, expulsions from Bellevue rose dramatically. The local news media were quick to document these events for the whole community to see.

The junior high teachers felt the impact of this "discipline" more than other grade levels and found it increasingly difficult to remain optimistic. Things became so harsh that they requested a meeting with June and members of the school board to find some compromise. Instead, the school board established a committee to research the problem and to make recommendations for future incidents. That was the last the junior high teachers ever heard of the issue.

June also influenced extracurricular policy. A major change was to require that only students who were on the A and B Honor Roll be allowed to participate in after-school activities. June's stated purpose was to place a higher emphasis on academics. We tried to calmly voice our opinion when the matter was raised in faculty meetings. We were careful to tell June that we understood the purpose of the policy but felt it would most likely undermine the self-esteem of those students who were only able to excel in sports. The restrictions were also quite unrealistic. We felt that, at most, only those who were failing academically should have been precluded. Eventually, the school board sided with us and approved the policy with the changes we had recommended. It was only a small victory.

June soon moved on to other areas of our previously tranquil school life. Another policy she developed and implemented caused perhaps the most frustration of all, and it was the policy that had the least to do with education—the adoption of a dress code. June decreed that students were not to wear shorts to school unless the temperature exceeded 70 degrees by noon. Predictably, many students became preoccupied with getting frequent temperature readings!

The "temperature policy" created unbelievable chaos. After several days of complaints from teachers, June agreed, as a matter of compromise, to announce the temperature periodically throughout the school day. As soon as the temperature reached the "shorts" threshold, the students could then leave class with their teacher's permission to change! Some of my colleagues at other schools had a hard time visualizing what now occurred most days at Bellevue: 600 students in mass exodus to change as soon as the threshold temperature was announced. The compromise was worse than the original solution. The whole idea took away valuable teaching and learning time and the students were continually distracted by trying to determine the temperature reading.

As the "temperature policy" continued, we revolted again. June relented again, with worse results. Her new solution was that the students were only allowed to change into shorts at noon, during their lunch time—as long as the temperature threshold of 70 degrees had been reached! The cafeteria turned into a zoo. Most children did not have enough time to eat and stand in line for their turn to change in the bathrooms. Of course, throughout all these twists and turns, if any child was brazen enough to come to school in shorts when it was not "the right temperature," they had to call their parents for a change of clothes. By this time, most teachers were ready to forego tact and professionalism but managed to arrange a meeting with the school board to discuss the wisdom of this policy. We recommended that the entire dress code as well as the "temperature policy" be dropped. That was several months ago—we have heard nothing further.

As I look back on these distracting events, which have kept Bellevue Academy from functioning as effectively as it once did, it is obvious that the problems were not simply due to June's lack of experience. She wanted power, and plenty of it. She thought she could get what she wanted by refusing to discuss the reasons for her decisions and by refusing to admit when she had made a mistake. She was spurred on by her position in the hierarchical structure of a private school.

In spite of all the rancor, we kept trying to discuss our differences calmly and openly with June and chose our battles carefully. Some of us met individually with June in hopes of appearing less threatening. Her response was always the same: "I'll think about it." She didn't see the problem. Many of the faculty acknowledged that developing the skills to run a school effectively takes time and experience, but our help was continually spurned.

At the end of June's first year, we gave up and appealed directly to the Reverend Fulbright and the church council to mediate our differences. They refused because they felt that, given time, June would improve her leadership skills.

We have given June the benefit of the doubt, but at this point, at the end of her second year, there has been no improvement. Several of us are seeking legal recourse to ensure that a replacement be found as soon as possible.

Alone in the Dark

Chief Protagonists
THELMA CRABTREE, student
MRS. CRABTREE, Thelma's mother
STEVE LOPEZ, assistant principal
ALAN STEAN, teacher

I was sitting in my classroom waiting to see if any of my students' parents would appear for the October parent teacher conferences. This was my first year at Junction High and I wasn't sure what to expect from either the parents or the faculty. My classroom phone rang. It was Steve Lopez, the assistant principal.

"Is a Thelma Crabtree one of your students?"

"Yes, I have her for social studies and geography."

"I just got a call that someone saw her biting her mother out by the road. Does that make any sense to you?" He asked.

"I have never met Mrs. Crabtree," I answered. "Thelma is always cooperative but very quiet in my class. Biting her mother seems very out of character."

"I don't know either Thelma or her mother. Would you mind taking care of it?" Steve asked.

I stepped outside to a rather strange sight. Two women, both looking dishevelled and agitated, were standing by the road at the corner of the school lot. I recognized one as Thelma, my quiet, conscientious fifteen-year-old student, and I assumed the other was her mother. As I approached, Thelma was

185

holding tightly to the corner of Mrs. Crabtree's sweater, appearing for all the world like a little girl desperately clutching her mother's apron strings to save herself from a threatening world.

"Hello, Thelma," I said as calmly I could, approaching the silent pair. I looked at her mother and said, "I'm Alan Stean, one of Thelma's teachers. Would you like to come to my class?"

"I wanted to, but Thelma wouldn't let me," Mrs. Crabtree explained in a bewildered voice. "It took me thirty minutes to get from the car to the corner of the school, one step at a time. When we got here, Thelma refused to move and started biting me."

I turned to the quiet, frightened girl and asked, "Did you bite your mother?"

Thelma explained, "Carrie (one of the school psychologists) told us both that Mother wasn't to come in the school and talk to the teachers. I can't let her in there."

Mrs. Crabtree turned to Thelma and pleaded, "I just want to ask the teachers if there is anything that I need to do for you. I need to know how much material to buy for your home economics project. It's alright."

Without speaking, Thelma bent down and started biting her mother on the upper arm through her sweater. As Mrs. Crabtree tried to turn away, she cried out, "Ow! Ow! Ow! Thelma, stop! Why are you doing this? OK! OK! We won't go into school."

Thelma stopped biting her mother and started sobbing, "You know you can't go in there."

It became clear to me that Thelma was holding her mother's sweater for support and also to keep her from getting any closer to the school. I was shocked. I had never seen Thelma do anything remotely aggressive. This seemed more a desperate attempt to satisfy the conflicting instructions she had received from the important adults in her life than aggression toward her mother. I watched Mrs. Crabtree try to reorient herself and regain her composure. I started to realize that this was a bigger problem that what it appeared.

As Thelma continued to sob, I told her, "Your mother has a right to know how well you are doing in school. Have you told her that you are getting As and Bs in my classes?"

Thelma's trembling became more noticeable as she answered, "No. You aren't supposed to be talking to her either."

Mrs. Crabtree, trying to be positive, said, "I know that you are good in school. If you won't tell me what is happening in school, the only way I can find out is to come here and talk to the teachers."

Thelma bit her mother again. I moved toward them but I was afraid to intervene for fear that I might make the situation worse. I told Thelma to stop but I don't think either of them heard me as they engaged in a curious dance around each other.

Finally, the dance stopped.

"You can't go on biting your mother. We need to talk and find a way to work this out."

Thelma did not reply.

Mrs. Crabtree thought aloud: "High school can be scary. I guess there are a lot of things that are different here than at the middle school. I don't want to upset Thelma but I need to know if she is doing OK."

"Thelma's teachers say that she is very quiet in class," I told Mrs. Crabtree. "As of last week when I talked to them, she was getting good grades in all of her classes. Do you know what Thelma means when she says you aren't supposed to go in the school?"

Mrs. Crabtree asked her daughter, "If you are doing so well in school, what harm would it do if I went in for a minute to ask your home economics teacher how much material I need to buy?"

Thelma's only answer was to bite and pinch her mother again. Thelma stopped long enough to say, "I have to pee."

Mrs. Crabtree rubbed her arm and explained.

"Whenever Thelma gets upset, I worry that she will pee in the car before we get home. It's a half an hour drive back home, and we left home two hours ago."

"Thelma, Do you need to go into the school to use the rest room?" I asked.

"She'll go into the school if I leave her," Thelma answered, pointing to Mrs. Crabtree while looking down at the ground. "Even though she knows she shouldn't."

"Well," I said, playing for time, "we can stay out here and talk until you get back."

Thelma turned and wouldn't face me again. She was becoming more distressed and confused by our inability or unwillingness to follow the simple instructions she had received from Carrie. "No! You aren't supposed to talk to him either. Let's go home!" She pleaded.

"I guess we should go," Mrs. Crabtree said.

I knew further efforts were unlikely to be successful. I asked Thelma, "Can you wait to use the bathroom until you get home?"

Thelma nodded yes.

"Are we still friends?" I asked.

Thelma stared at the ground and shook her head.

"Maybe by the time we get back to class tomorrow we will be able to talk about this," I said hopefully.

Thelma shook her head and started pulling her mother's sweater toward the car.

"I guess we should go. You won't pee will you? You promised," Mrs. Crabtree pleaded.

Thelma shook her head from side to side.

As they turned to leave I said, "It was nice meeting you, Mrs. Crabtree. I hope we can talk and be friends again tomorrow, Thelma. Being your friend is important to me."

The pair shuffled away.

Returning to the building, I was worried that I had unintentionally violated Thelma's trust. She was a quiet girl who only talked when spoken to and then always in a monotone. She never interacted with other students in my class. At lunch time each day I could count on seeing her standing alone in the hall five minutes after being dismissed from my class. I had worked hard to develop a friendly, supportive relationship with Thelma.

Steve Lopez stopped me in the hall. "Well, was your student really biting her mother?"

I briefly related what had happened.

"It doesn't make sense," said Steve, "I don't think there's any constraint keeping Mrs. Crabtree out of the school—she has custody of Thelma, so she should have the right to talk with us."

"Carrie's not here right now," said Steve, "but check with Doris Dexter. I think she has had some dealings with Thelma in the past."

Doris was in her office.

"I remember Thelma. She's the big dumpy girl with old dirty clothes that just hang on her. I've seen her shuffling down the hall. The first time I met her was when she came back to school after a year on a psychiatric ward. It seems that she drove a spike through her foot and then wouldn't let anyone touch her foot to treat it."

"Until this morning, Thelma has always been really quiet and cooperative," I said. "This morning I felt that she must have been feeling the same way she did when she drove the spike through her foot. I'd hate to think of her doing anything drastic like that again."

"The first time I met with Thelma's father," Doris continued, "was the only time I have ever been afraid for my personal safety in dealing with parents. Mr. Crabtree acted so irrationally that I was sure I was going to be beaten up at any moment. In fact, I remember removing my watch and glasses—at least they would be safe even if something happened! But back to today. I can't imagine what Carrie might have meant or said to Thelma to give her the impression that we weren't allowed to talk to her mother."

I talked with Carrie a few weeks later, and the picture of the day in the parking lot became a little clearer.

"I asked Thelma's mother to wait in the car on Thursdays when she picks Thelma up after school and brings her to counseling. They need to work on separation. In a few years, Thelma will be out on her own and they need to start working on that. Mrs. Crabtree insists on meeting Thelma at the school door or even at the classroom door. She claims that Thelma won't be able to find the car on her own. Mrs. Crabtree always arrives at our meeting scratched and bruised, so we haven't been very successful yet. The rule wasn't intended to restrict the mother's access to the high school staff."

When Thelma returned to class, she refused to talk to me or do any work. She sat quietly at her desk waiting for the class to end. When I tried to discuss the incident by the road she would only say, in reference to what Carrie had told her, that I had lied, that I had broken "the rules" and her trust. Nothing seemed to help.

I felt as if I was in a room with the lights off—as if in my dealings with Thelma I would unwittingly destroy something. At the same time, I desperately needed to get to a door and let some light in.

In spite of my best efforts, I never did.

Deja Vu All over Again

Chief Protagonists
JIM GRADY, assistant professor
REBECCA STONE, professor
STAN GALLO, department chairperson

Jim Grady took the job at Alpha State University to start his new career as a university professor. The job seemed like a good fit. After several weeks in his new position, he felt that he had adjusted very well. Several faculty members had commented on his ability to work hard and that the students were impressed with the way he handled his classes.

Sitting in his office several months later as the snow fell heavily outside, Jim smiled when he remembered how nervous he had been in the search committee interview. He had no idea what they were going to ask. Like all first-time job applicants, Jim thought the interview would be much worse than it actually was. He even found himself enjoying the debate with the panel as they grilled him on various aspects of teaching and academic research.

The night before the search committee interview, Jim had dinner with influential members of the search committee, including Rebecca Stone. He had gotten wind that she differed with him on several important issues in special education. The dinner had gone well, but Jim made a mental note of their apparent disagreement. He wondered if perhaps she had read an article he had written the year before, which laid out his position very clearly on many of their intellectual disputes. Halfway through the interview the following day,

Jim was ready for the delicate but direct question Rebecca posed: "Jim, tell us your views of including all students with disabilities in regular classrooms."

Jim pondered for a moment, reflecting that his impression of the dinner disagreement was accurate. He knew his answer would be directly opposed to her views on the subject, so he reminded himself to respond carefully. "I know that this is a controversial area, Rebecca. I think that it's true that we keep too many kids in special education for too long. We need to find ways of changing that, and the move to inclusion seems to be quite promising. On the other hand, I'm concerned that we often seem to talk in this debate about 'all children' being included. I think that for a small portion of the special education population, the regular classroom is probably an inappropriate, and perhaps even a discriminatory setting. I think 'all' is a label that will do some kids a disservice."

Rebecca glanced knowingly at several of the other committee members: "So you don't think the general education class is the place for all students? Who should decide who will make it into the general education class and who should not? Who, in fact, has the right to make that decision?" Rebecca sat back expectantly, waiting for an answer.

Jim could not recall what he had answered, but he left the interview feeling that whatever he had said, it wasn't what Rebecca wanted to hear.

Two weeks later, Jim happily accepted the job at Alpha State. By the time he had settled into his new apartment and had gotten his office straightened out, he had met and talked with all the faculty. There were seven full professors in special education while Jim and Gerry Patterson, who had been at Alpha State a year longer, were assistant professors. He knew he would like working with them all.

The week before classes began, Rebecca and her husband invited Jim over for dinner. Dinner was congenial enough, but the conversation soon turned to ideas of difference and the extent to which people with disabilities should be included in the mainstream. The debate became quite lively. Rebecca pressed hard. As the conversation progressed, Jim started to feel that every word he said had some great significance that was escaping him and that if he put a foot wrong, some kind of conversational trap would spring shut. He chose his words with increasing care. Rebecca kept on using the example of a child with spina bifida as the hypothetical for their conversation about inclusion. Jim argued that no matter what the level of inclusion, it was ludicrous to assert that most or all children with spina bifida, given their generally profound impairments, were the same as other children who did not have such physical and intellectual problems, and that denying this difference would have negative consequences for the impaired child. Soon it was time to leave. Jim was relieved. Perhaps he had dodged the bullet after all. As Jim exchanged the usual pleasantries of saying goodbye, the trap sprang shut: "Well, Jim," Rebecca observed, "we see things very differently."

"Sure," said Jim sincerely, "but it's great that we can agree to disagree."

Rebecca smiled knowingly. "You'd feel like us if you had a grandchild, as we do, with spina bifida . . . "

Driving home, Jim felt used. He chided himself for not anticipating the outcome of the conversation but he was also angry that he had been set up. He started to feel a little uneasy. First it was the interview dinner, then the question in the formal interview, and now another polite, but pointed clash.

Jim hadn't had too much time to ponder this distraction. His first quarter went by in a whirlwind of activity. While he tried to learn as fast as he could, he knew that his first year would require many adjustments and would include a fair share of mistakes. He realized, too, that he was the new kid on the block and that the full professors, all of whom had been at Alpha State at least a dozen years, were likely to have firmly established professional and personal relationships. He watched, listened, and tried to keep his mouth shut.

As Jim had suspected, Rebecca was a force to be reckoned with. Jim made friends in remote parts of the university who didn't know Rebecca, but they had all heard of her. She clearly had many powerful connections within the university, around the rest of the state university system, and in the state department of education. She had just received an award as state professor of the year. In the department, Rebecca was a strong influence in faculty and committee meetings. She had opinions on everything and was generally very well informed. Several times he heard students complaining about her abruptness. Some students said openly that they found her aggressive. It seemed that Rebecca almost always got her way either for things she wanted or for people she favored. Jim was soon to learn this firsthand.

Early in his second quarter, Stan Gallo, the departmental chair, met with Jim. They held similar views on many special education issues and decided to write a federal grant together. Over several weeks, they worked diligently to hammer out the plan for the grant. One Wednesday afternoon, with the project well advanced, Stan stopped by.

"I'd like to propose a change." Stan began, "Rebecca got wind of what we were doing and she wants to be part of the grant submission."

Jim didn't react, but his recent history with Rebecca made him wary. It didn't help that he knew Stan was close friends with Rebecca and her husband.

"What did she have in mind?"

Stan settled into a chair and began. "Well . . . "

Jim listened carefully. He knew that Rebecca was a successful grant writer and it was clear that she was well positioned in the university. She was also a competent scholar. He was sure that her participation could add some clout to their grant. As he listened to Stan's explanation, though, Jim realized that what Rebecca was proposing fundamentally changed the conceptual framework of the proposal. They would have to start from scratch. By the time Stan finished, Jim could tell that Rebecca's insistence was more about her not wanting to be left out of some research activity than in being a contributor to what they were proposing. It turned out that Rebecca had some data already collected and wanted to add it to what Jim and Stan were proposing. The problem was that her data were from a different project—it didn't fit at all.

Jim decided that this was not a battle he wanted to fight. He agreed to Rebecca's contribution. The grant, substantially changed and less coherent, Jim thought, was submitted two weeks later. Jim wasn't at all surprised when a notice arrived saying that the grant had been rejected.

If that had been the end of it, Jim reflected, he wouldn't have been in his current predicament. His mind slipped back to what had happened shortly after the ill-fated grant-writing exercise.

The only condition attached to Jim's acceptance of the job at Alpha State had been that he teach all the courses in special education research methods. The undergraduate course was the problem. It was required of all special education and speech pathology majors, which meant that the classes were usually very large. Many other special education classes, however, were as large or even larger. He had commented about the class size to Stan several times. Historically, class sizes had always been large in the department. Everyone seemed to accept that packing students into every course was the norm. Stan was very supportive of Jim's area of expertise in teaching using the case method, but teaching cases was a problem in classes of 35 or 40 students. The ideal class size was between 12 and 15 students. Jim realized that such small classes were unrealistic at Alpha, but he discussed with Stan some ways of making the classes a little smaller in the interests of more effective instruction.

"Sure," Stan said, "I see your problem. You don't have to have unlimited enrollment, you know—it's not an absolutely rigid requirement. The dean is always encouraging us to reduce our student-professor ratio anyway. Why not close the class at about 25 students? If you close the class at 25, you'll have a much more manageable number of students, even if you decide to admit a few more on override."

Jim was relieved to get Stan's sanction and capped the class at 25 students for the winter quarter. Advising brought several distraught students who couldn't get into the class. Jim listened patiently to each story. There were several students who through no fault of their own needed to be in the class that quarter. Jim gladly signed override slips, which would admit them to the class in spite of the cap. He advised other students to sign up for the following quarter. As the students came and went, Jim was glad of Stan's support. It made him even more eager to teach cases to a smaller class. He had no idea that his optimism would be short lived.

One last student stopped by. He listened to the student's story carefully. She wanted to enroll simply to make her schedule more convenient. Jim decided that this was not a pressing enough reason for an override, so he told the student to be sure to sign up for the course later. The disappointed student, Jim was about to learn, was one of Rebecca's advisees.

Jim was in deep conversation with one of his own advisees when the outer door to his office suddenly opened. Rebecca came striding through the outer office where two other students were waiting to see Jim. They stopped their casual conversation in midsentence. Something was clearly wrong. Leaning through the inner office doorway, and completely ignoring Jim, Rebecca cut across their conversation. She spoke directly to the student.

"Could you please leave?" Her voice was clipped and icy. "I need to speak to Dr. Grady."

Jim was flabbergasted. The student, looking rather confused, quickly exited. Rebecca moved swiftly into his office and closed the door.

"Look Jim, what's this about not admitting my student to your research course?" Rebecca was quite agitated.

"Well . . . " Jim's short, yet awkward relationship with Rebecca flashed through his mind. "I've closed the class at 25, and your student didn't make the cut. Based on what she told me, I didn't see that she had a do-or-die need to be overridden into the class. I told her to sign up next quarter."

Rebecca was growing angry.

"This is ridiculous! We all teach classes here that are much larger than 25! If we all did what you're doing, this department would be in deep trouble!!"

Jim tried to keep his cool. "All I can tell you, Rebecca, is that I cleared this with Stan after I discussed with him the kinds of numbers I had in class this last quarter." Jim's quiet response seemed to calm Rebecca slightly. She retreated: "Well, it's this whole system—students get their coursework out of sync and then we have these kinds of problems. I still think it's unreasonable for you to turn students down, though."

Jim didn't respond, but his anger was rising. He resented being so rudely interrupted and having a faculty member throw a student out of his office. While he was trying to collect his thoughts for an appropriate response, the strangest thing happened. Rebecca marched over to his bookshelf. The shelf had a row of prepared articles that Jim had under review with scholarly journals. She picked up several articles and read their titles, selected one she apparently found interesting, tucked it under her arm, and left the office without a word.

Jim was baffled. First the outburst, which he at least understood. But what about the silent removal of his personal documents? As he continued to see students throughout the day, he became more and more convinced that it was Rebecca's way of telling him who was boss, whether he liked it or not.

Later in the day, Jim bumped into Rebecca at the faculty post boxes. She ignored his greeting. Just then, Stan appeared.

"Oh Stan," Rebecca's deliberately loud comment had a sarcastic edge, "I just wanted to let you know that I'm closing my morning class at 25 students. If any students have a problem with that, I'll just send them to you."

Jim knew it was going to be a long quarter.

For weeks Jim reflected on what had happened. Should he have insisted that the student remain in his office, seeing that she had a prior appointment? Should he have stepped out of his office and discussed the issue in front of other students waiting in the outer office? Should he have relented and signed Rebecca's student into the class? He wasn't sure. He was sure, though, that there was little excuse for rudeness and that without some kind of resolution things might get worse. He wrestled with all the alternatives for action and inaction that he could think of. He called several mentors and trusted friends. After a great deal of emotional wrangling, Jim decided to let the incident pass, promising himself that he would be prepared if it ever happened again.

He didn't have too long to wait.

Jim again limited the class to 25 students in the spring quarter. Anticipating that similar problems might arise with Rebecca, he tried to head off any conflict by circulating a faculty memorandum to remind them of the limit. Advising week soon arrived. Jim's advising schedule was full. In the middle of advising a student, a group of three students congregated at his office door. They remained there until Jim broke off his conversation with his advisee and gave them some attention: "Can I help you?" asked Jim.

"Yes," volunteered one student. "Dr. Stone sent us down to enroll in your research class."

Jim's heart skipped a beat.

"I'm sorry," Jim replied. "The course is limited to 25 students and I've already signed quite a few overrides. I simply can't accommodate any more students. However, the class is offered every quarter and the backup we've experienced this year should be cleared by then. In addition, we'll offer two sections of it in the new school year. I doubt you'll be left out then."

The students left and Jim resumed his conversation with his advisee.

The outer office door snapped open. It was Rebecca, obviously ready to do battle. Oh no, thought Jim, I don't believe this!

Striding to his office door, she spoke to the advisee seated in Jim's office. It was a breathtakingly accurate reproduction of what had happened the previous quarter: "Could you please leave for a minute? I need to speak to Dr. Grady."

The student left immediately. Jim was dumbfounded. His anger, though, was much more focused than it had been the first time around. As Rebecca closed the door, Jim spoke in a deliberately measured, quiet voice before Rebecca could launch into any kind of tirade: "Rebecca, I really don't appreciate the way you interrupt my meetings by asking students to leave without even consulting me . . . "

Rebecca was caught off guard. She had not expected any kind of opposition.

"Fine, OK, OK, have it your way!" Rebecca interrupted, feigning hurt and uncharacteristic cooperation. She stepped out of Jim's office and spoke to the nonplussed student standing outside.

"Oh, *please* go back in," she said in an overly sweet voice. Her biting sarcasm hung in the air long after she closed the outer door and disappeared down the hallway.

Jim finished his advising meeting with some difficulty. He was angry at Rebecca's repeat performance, and he was embarrassed at having to confront a senior member of the faculty within earshot of students.

Rebecca was angry, and Jim knew it. So was he. He knew enough to know that Rebecca would do her best to avoid him and to ignore him—it was her way of getting control. He had seen her do this to students and some members of staff in other departments. She would ignore them until it was unequivocally apparent that there was a serious problem. Invariably, both students and staff couldn't stand the tension and went to her cap in hand, apologizing even if they were obviously not in the wrong.

Jim knew that he had to carefully select a time that would allow a one-to-one interaction. He waited until Rebecca was working at her computer in her office. There were no students around, and she wasn't on the phone. Jim stuck his head through the outer office door. Rebecca appeared surprised.

"Hi," said Jim, "do you have a minute?"

Rebecca hesitated, but it was obvious that she did. She took a deep breath. Jim moved toward her office door.

"Sure," she said.

"Look, Rebecca, I'd like to talk with you about what happened yesterday. I think we need to resolve this."

Rebecca was silent. Her blue eyes seemed to stare right through him as she formulated her response. Her face took on a tired, haggardly hurt frown.

"I have to tell you, Jim, that I haven't been spoken to in such a patronizing way in the last ten or twelve years. Things are in sad shape when one professor can't talk to another during advising."

Jim knew this was going to be quite a conversation.

To Do or Not to Do

Chief Protagonists
HOWARD SUMMERS, teacher
STEWART PEACOCK, teacher
DOUG KING, principal

This was Howard Summers's first teaching job. Finally, he thought, I get to do what I worked so hard for! He had worked very hard, indeed. The year before, he had done his final teaching practicum at Jenson Elementary and had spent a great deal of extra time on all of his student teaching commitments. His crowning achievement had been in organizing the annual sports day. The whole day had been a great success. Howard's high visibility paid off. At the awards ceremony, Howard was singled out by the principal, Doug King, for his exemplary efforts. A day later, Doug King offered Howard a job for the following year.

Howard had had a good start to his first year. The icing on the cake was that Stewart Peacock, one of his best friends from college, joined him as another new member of the staff. They both liked teaching at Jenson Elementary. Their novice enthusiasm paid dividends from day one with the parents and the students. The staff was a different matter, however. Howard and Stewart often discussed the many tensions that seemed to run just beneath the surface. They couldn't quite figure it out, but they were certain that the tensions were long standing and that Doug King played a large part in the general discomfort of staff relations. Staff meetings, for example, were usually tense affairs with little discussion. Doug King, his head buried in copious notes and official-looking folders, would mumble through the latest round of official directives that had come down from the district administration. Nobody asked questions, nobody commented. There was a subtle but unmistakable sigh of relief when Doug formally ended the meetings and left.

Looking around the room in one of those interminable meetings, Howard wondered if some of the tension arose because of the peculiarities of the teachers. There were, after all, some interesting contrasts among his colleagues. Wendy Fine, the senior departmental chairperson, was fastidious and vastly experienced. She ruled her students with a rod of iron but was scrupulously fair and highly competent. Students often got anxious when they learned that they were to be in her class the following year, but they soon came to rely on her structure, teaching skill, and highly professional attitude. She commanded the highest respect among all of the faculty. School protocol required that Howard and Stewart turn in their lesson plans to her each Friday. She didn't like getting the plans late.

Ann Jordan was a year from retirement and seemed to be grimly hanging on. She ineffectively ruled her classes in a different way: worksheets, worksheets, worksheets. It seemed that over the years she had collected and filed away every piece of curriculum material she had ever used. Piles of papers lay everywhere. She was a firm believer in allowing her students to draw and color when they had completed their work. It didn't cross her mind that perhaps seventh graders might be capable of doing other things. Her classes were chaotic. The students only quieted down when Ann couldn't stand the racket any more and bellowed at the top of her voice for minutes on end. As much as the students respected Wendy, they saw Ann as some kind of living, breathing, joke. Most other teachers, Howard reflected, fell somewhere in between.

Doug King was a different matter, as Stewart often liked to say—in a category all by himself. He was a strange man in most senses of the word. A small, introverted individual, he had, years before, been "promoted" out of a teaching position to that of school librarian. It was common knowledge, even to the new teachers, that this honor resulted from his incompetence in the classroom. The library seemed to suit him better. His deep affection for order, rigid guidelines, and rules was nurtured in the hushed confines of the bookshelves. His interactions with the other members of staff were limited and controlling the students was much easier than it had been in his classroom days. Doug had bided his time for a few secure and happy years. Through several lucky bureaucratic breaks, he had assumed the principalship at Jenson Elementary six years before.

Doug was a play-it-by-the-book kind of administrator. His office was curiously neat—never a paper or file out of place. His desk gleamed in the morning sunshine as forms and reports moved via his gold fountain pen from his "in" box to his "out" box. The only sound was the ticking of the district-issued clock on his office wall. He would often break from his work to stare out of the window at the rose garden below his window. If Doug had a passion, it was surely roses. He would often spend time tending to them between appointments and meetings. He kept a pair of pruning shears in the bottom left drawer of his shiny desk, the same desk where he ate the same kind of sandwich every day, never seeming to drop a single crumb. He always carefully folded his brown paper lunch sack and took it home for the next day's meal. Doug recycled lunch sacks long before anyone knew what recycling was.

Doug rarely visited with his teachers and appeared to be uncomfortable with direct staff interactions. He would always offer a formal "Good morning" or "Good afternoon" but he generally avoided anything more intimate. Some staff who had worked with him over the years consistently deferred to his every wish. Others snickered behind his back. No one, though, ever attempted any kind of humor face to face with Doug King. It simply had no effect. Howard and Stewart had never seen anything approaching a smile cross his craggy face.

Doug didn't like dealing with parents either. If he had to meet with them, he invariably insisted that the classroom teacher be present. He would barely say a word and leave the teacher in charge of the meeting. Most parents learned quickly to bypass Doug and deal with John Abernathy, the vice principal.

Doug always dressed in a three-piece brown or black suit which, for some strange reason, seemed to accentuate his balding head and chiseled, drawn face. Howard admired the way Doug's spectacles never seemed to get smudged. Once Howard had stopped by to inquire about Doug's daughter, who had been diagnosed with multiple sclerosis the year before. Howard noted the pained look on Doug's face as he mumbled a quick reply before abruptly getting back to his perpetual paperwork.

Howard did feel some sympathy for Doug King, though. He was such a complete oddity. A popular staff tale illustrated how King, whose home language was not English, had embarrassed himself repeatedly to students in his teaching days. In one instance, the class Doug was teaching became quite rowdy while he was writing on the board. Turning swiftly toward the offending students, and momentarily forgetting his sometimes limited proficiency in English, he had yelled "What is this noise coming from my behind?" The stuff school legends are made of, Howard thought.

Howard had a tale to tell all of his own. It was the only time in his experience, he reflected, that Doug had made him laugh. One day Doug's pants had split while he was tending his roses. He was mortally embarrassed and waited in the men's room until Howard happened to wander in, whereupon, through the closed stall door, Doug communicated that he "had a predicament in his trousers."

Howard and Stewart were enjoying their newfound freedom. Their new paychecks firmly in hand, they had both bought large motorcycles. The children were delighted when the two novice teachers came roaring up each morning and parked their shiny machines side by side close to their classrooms. Howard and Stewart suspected that Doug didn't approve, but they never heard him say anything. They did know, however, that many afternoons as they rode home, passing Doug at the bus stop (he was too frugal to drive his car to school), he stared at them disapprovingly. It didn't help that they wore leather jackets.

As the year went on, Howard and Stewart threw themselves into their work. They loved what they were doing. They instituted an afternoon student film club and organized several educational outings. Howard, who coached the swim team, organized extra training sessions before school and on Saturdays. Both teachers were popular with the parents who often commented on the "breath of fresh air" they brought to Jenson Elementary.

Late in the school year, the issue of the annual school concert surfaced on the faculty meeting agenda. Jenson Elementary had a long history of accommodating every student in the concert—a formidable task with over 600 students in the school. The combination of being new to the school, along with their enthusiastic approach, led the staff to unanimously vote on placing the two new teachers in charge of the event. The general idea was that each teacher would prepare a class item for the concert. Howard and Stewart would coordinate the program, set up and operate the light and sound systems, and be responsible for the three evenings the concert would run. Soon they were spending all their spare time planning and trying out ideas they thought would allow them to put on the best show Jenson Elementary had ever seen.

Ticket sales were brisk. Word had spread that Howard and Stewart were putting together quite a show. As the concert got closer, they began to spend long hours sorting out the many details that needed to be taken care of if the evening was to be a success.

An incident the week before the concert should have alerted them to what was to come. Howard and Stewart had worked their lunch period trying to hook up the sound system. The school's equipment was sadly out of shape, and so they were using their personal stereo equipment. Finally, every part of the sound system seemed to be working except that they needed to check how much volume they had. All three shows were sold out. They knew that with an overflowing 1,000-seat auditorium, knowing how much volume they had would be important. They cranked up the sound as loud as it would go. The empty auditorium reverberated as the speakers blared. The noise didn't last more than a second or two and they quickly busied themselves with other adjustments. Howard and Stewart both forgot that Doug's office was in the same building.

They didn't realize Doug had entered the hall until they heard his clipped stride approaching out of the cavernous darkness. They looked up. Doug's eyes were bulging and the veins on his neck stood out. He was flushed.

"What in the *HELL* was that? What do you two think you are doing?" His voice echoed across the stage.

"Sorry, Doug, but we had to see how much volume we had . . . "

"Sorry be damned, you two had better watch your step—this rebellious behavior won't be tolerated!!" Doug yelled.

Rebellious behavior? Howard's pulse raced as he looked across at Stewart. This was a Doug they had never encountered before. Before either one of them could reply, Doug continued: "I expect no more nonsense like this *EVER* again. If I have any more trouble, I'll call off the concert." He turned on the heels of his highly polished shoes and left.

"Don't worry about it," said Howard. "He's probably mad at other things as well."

"I guess," Stewart responded, "but I think that was a little uncalled for. After all, we have to know what the system sounds like, and it was loud for no more than a moment. I don't understand his reaction." They turned back to their work.

The rest of the preparations went off without a hitch and eventually the first night of the concert arrived. Howard and Stewart were confident that the evening would be successful. They had spent the two days prior to the concert working out the complicated schedule of getting each class called, on stage, and back off again with military precision. They saw this as their biggest job because access to the stage was very limited. Their plans were complicated further because most classes had devised bulky props. Howard and Stewart carefully devised a plan that let the students enter through a large outer door at the rear of the stage, perform their number, and move out of the hall through a tiny side door. Each teacher had studied their route maps and knew how to get their students in position. There was no sign of the impending potential for disaster.

"Perfect!" Howard had said, looking at the routing plan. "This means that we won't have kids going through that small side door in both directions!"

"That's just as well," Stewart retorted. "With all the props some of those classes have, and the number of kids, we'd never manage smooth scene changes otherwise."

By the final concert, Howard and Stewart had relaxed a little. All the hard work that they and the staff had done seemed to be paying off. Stewart peered through the curtain.

"We've got a full house again tonight. How long to show time?"

Howard looked at his watch.

"About 15 minutes" he replied. "Are we all set?"

"I think so, but you stay here while I take a swing over everything."

Five minutes later, Stewart was back, several shades paler than when he left.

"What's up?"

"The big outer stage door—it's locked."

"So, go open it!" laughed Howard.

"I can't—Doug took the master key with him this afternoon, and he won't be here this evening. I thought about calling him, but even if he left right away, he'd take an hour to get here. I tried to raise the custodian at home, but he's out shopping. None of the teachers who are here have a key, either."

Now it was Howard's turn to panic. "Are you sure there's no key available? Let me check the office."

Howard raced down to the office and furiously searched every possible place where duplicate keys might be. There were none, and the concert was ten minutes away. On his way back to the auditorium Howard saw the first class walking to their position outside the locked outer stage door. His stomach tightened.

"I've got an idea," ventured Stewart, "but I think it might get us in trouble."

"Let's hear it, this isn't exactly an ideal situation."

"Well, we could break the lock off the door," said Stewart, "that would get it open, but we'll damage the door quite a bit—that's a heavy lock and a sturdy door."

"Look, we either get that door open or we're sunk. We've only got about five minutes to curtain. To reroute all the classes at this point would create a mess. It would also mean we'd have at least five to ten minutes between acts so that we could get everyone back and forth through the small side door."

They jumped up, hammers, drill, and pliers in hand, and dashed for the locked door. The class waiting to enter stared incredulously as the two teachers went to work. They quickly unscrewed the outer handles and dropped them to the ground. The lock was solid. There was no possible way of accessing the bolt. It was show time in more ways than one.

"What do you think?" asked Howard.

"The only option I can see," ventured Stewart, "is to cut around the lock and yank it out."

"My thought exactly."

Having made the decision, Howard and Stewart attacked the door with all their strength. They drilled and hammered through the door as fast as they could. Some of the students began to cheer them on. Ten minutes later, the lock broke off and the first class was on stage delivering a slightly off-key version of "Danny Boy."

The following morning, Howard and Stewart rode to school as usual. They had remained at the school late the night before to clean up and get their equipment home. They had secured the damaged door as best they could. Once they had parked their motorcycles, they both headed down the hallway towards Doug's office. They tried to walk as fast as they could while dodging the sea of students who were on their way to homeroom.

They never reached Doug's office. He strode toward them through the mass of children. They'd seen that look before. Doug was so angry he was shaking. He was clearly struggling to maintain control.

"Good morning . . . "

"What happened last night?" Doug snapped.

"Well, we had a problem just before show time . . . " Stewart started.

"We did," Howard added. "We discovered that the door to the stage was locked. We tried to call the custodian, but he wasn't home. You had the other set of master keys, and we knew that you live across town and couldn't have gotten here for at least an hour. None of the other teachers had a key and we couldn't find one in the office. We had to make the decision—get the door open or create mass confusion. We decided to break open the door."

With such an admission of guilt, Doug couldn't restrain himself any longer.

"JUST WHO DO YOU THINK YOU ARE?" Doug shouted. Dozens of children stopped dead in their tracks to listen. "You'd better get the picture that *I'M* the principal here, *NOT* you!! How dare you make such a decision? Who is going to pay for this damage? Do you realize it's a serious offense to damage school property? What kind of example are you setting for the children? Do you realize how much auditorium equipment could have been stolen through that unlocked door during the night?"

Howard and Stewart didn't answer. They were in the wrong, and there wasn't much more to be said about it. Doug's final comment, communicated in his unique brand of English as he turned and stormed back to his office, left an ominous ring in their ears:

"I've got a good mind to charge you two with breaking and entering—even *burgelry!*"

Nature versus Nurture

Chief Protagonists
ALICE SWENSON, teacher
PENNY and MOLLY JOINER, sisters
RUTH JOINER, their mother

Alice Swenson is in her third year of teaching. This is the first year that Penny and Molly have attended Maple Elementary in Forest Bend, a small, booming city in the Northwest. Forest Bend, and its twin city, Myrtletown, are in different states separated by the Snake River, which forms the natural state line. Prior to the beginning of this school year, the girls had attended school in Myrtletown, across the river. Both children have experienced and continue to experience significant problems in school. Alice Swenson, Penny's teacher this past year, takes up the story:

Of all the kids I've taught in these last three years, perhaps the most perplexing are the Joiner sisters, Penny and Molly. There are so many problems that it's difficult to know where to begin.

Penny

Penny is a mixed-race child. Her mother, Ruth, is Caucasian, and we think dad was Native American, although nobody seems to know where he is. No one is sure whether Molly, Penny's younger sister, has the same dad. There are two other, older siblings, both in high school. The younger of the two, Nelly, lives in a foster home, and her slightly elder sister, Nora, lives with her boyfriend although she lived at home with Ruth and the two younger girls for a while this year. We don't know if Nelly and Nora have the same or different fathers. We do know, however, that the older set and the younger set have different dads.

Penny, in fifth grade, is mainstreamed only for music, gym, lunch, those kinds of things. The rest of the time she, well, she *sits*. She *sits* in health and hardly does any work. She *sits* in Science and Social Studies. She *sits* in English, Reading, Spelling, Math. *Sitting* is her standard behavior! Then, of course, there are the frequent "shut-downs," and when she shuts down, she shuts down for a long time—she'll often literally do nothing for an entire day. She sits in her chair with her hands in her lap and her head completely down. She will not look at you, and her body is completely rigid. Even if you touch her, she doesn't move. She will not look at you, she will not speak to you, she will just *sit* there. There's nothing there—not a glimmer, not a shine, she's just blank. She has done this with my student teacher and the speech teacher a couple of times. Penny and the speech teacher have a personality conflict. And so when the speech teacher asks her to answer a question, whether Penny does not understand it or understands it and just won't answer, we don't know; but she won't talk, she won't communicate. The speech teacher gets upset, and Penny shuts down even more.

The last time Penny shut down, it lasted from 10:30 until 3:00. At 3:00, she realized it was time to go home, and I'd stipulated that she wasn't going home until she answered the math question I'd asked at 10:30. She suddenly said, "Oh, I know the answer."

Penny's cumulative records reflected that the school in Myrtletown had no idea of exactly what her problems were. I recall a report that listed several labels, including "emotionally disturbed," "speech impaired," "mentally re-tarded," and "learning disabled" followed by a question mark! We've tried to get an outside evaluation done for several months now. However, I'm not sure if Ruth has followed through with that yet. We really want Penny's evaluation done carefully so that we can see where we are and to determine appropriate placement. Socially, Penny's immature. Academically, she's at the first grade level.

Molly

Molly, Penny's little sister, is in second grade. She's very, very aggressive. She has more of a dissociated look to her, but she's more of a fighter than Penny.

Just before Christmas, Molly was admitted to Chambers Hospital's psychiatric unit because she assaulted Ruth. Ruth brought her to the hospital because she said she couldn't control Molly, she didn't want her, and didn't love Molly any more. Molly told me that Ruth had said, "I'm not coming back to get you. I don't want you." Apparently another reason for the hospital admission was that Ruth had also told Molly that Molly was the devil and needed to be prayed over. She told Molly that the church would take the demons out of her. Ruth would also spend time at home praying over her. In fact, in passing, Molly once said to me, "My mom thinks I am the devil, so she prays for me. She prays funny."

Chambers Hospital kept Molly for about a month and a half. Subsequently, for another two weeks Molly went to Chambers just for school hours and was at home at night. Then Chambers started to transition Molly back here into school, first every other day, then to consecutive half days, and then back here full time. I think they did this primarily because they wanted to keep some kind of contact with Ruth and Molly. All that the final report from Chambers said was that Molly was "psychologically impaired."

Ruth

Ruth is strange—I don't know how to describe her!! She sometimes comes across as knowing what she's talking about, but in other instances, she gets very confused. For example, she'll talk about Molly when we're talking about Penny, and vice versa. Ruth also has some strange ways of describing things. For example, she told a colleague that the reason that Molly and Penny are like they are is because their dad had alcohol in his semen. She does not work—just kind of hangs out at home.

When we've met with Ruth, there's usually the principal, the speech therapist, the general education teachers, and me. I must admit that we spend a lot of time in these meetings trying not to let our mouths drop to the floor! In every meeting we can't get a word in edgewise. Ruth talks the entire time—anything and everything that comes to her mind. It's very unfocused. We've tried redirecting her, but it doesn't work, so we let her ramble on and, in the end, interject where we can.

We've also tried other forms of communication with Ruth. We used to call home, but she disconnected her phone because she didn't want us to call her. We sent notes home, but she tore them up. She said she doesn't want communication with the school because she doesn't want us to know any of her business. They had the same problem in Myrtletown, too. In Myrtletown, the social services started to put the pressure on her to get to the bottom of all this so Ruth moved across the river to Forest Bend—it takes forever to get started all over again with social services in a different state.

The other teachers get very angry at Ruth. They are also angry at the school and social systems for allowing the girls to remain in the home. Ruth doesn't know the name of most of the teachers, including me. For example, she came in the other day to get the girls for early dismissal. I took Penny and Molly downstairs to the office where I began to explain their homework to Ruth. She said, "You're not that Mrs. Fry, are you?" And I said, "No," and the girls said, "No, this is Mrs. Swenson." And she said, "Well, um, the speech teacher was grabbing . . . Penny . . . Molly . . . no, Penny said that the speech teacher was grabbing and holding her tightly, and throwing papers at her." Well, this is not true. The speech therapist is firm and will try to pull Penny's chin up or will put her hands on her shoulders as part of the speech therapy, but she's not "grabbing her."

The Home

Things at home are poor. For example, Molly ran away from school a couple of weeks ago. She got as far as school here, and dropped her bike off. She then walked right across town to her old school. We missed her at roll call and contacted Ruth, whose only response was, "You lost her, you find her. I don't care where she is." We got a call around noon from her old school—Molly said she had gone over there to see the pet hamster in her old class. It seems she frequently runs away from home on Saturday mornings. She'll get up at 5:30 or 6:00, and walk to downtown Forest Bend, hanging out around all the seedy bars. Ruth doesn't go looking for Molly and makes it quite clear that if it were Penny, she'd be out looking for her because "Penny's always the good one."

School records hint at the question of some sexual inappropriateness by Ruth's numerous boyfriends. I think the current boyfriend is the fourth she has had living in the house this year. The girls see a lot of men come and go. The other day Molly said, "Dad's back." And I said, "He is?" She's never called anyone Dad before. And she said, "Yeah, Dad's here, you know, Roger—he went back to his wife for awhile but he came back to us." We have had no contacts with any of the boyfriends other than Ruth saying, "Oh, no this isn't Roger. I'm not seeing Roger anymore, I'm seeing Rick."

Other things make me uneasy. For instance, Penny hasn't had a male teacher this year until John, my student teacher arrived. Penny shut down a couple of times on him. I think she also rubbed up against him in an inappropriate way and said to him, "Oh, I like sitting by you," or some similar inappropriate comment. John handled it really well—he said, "That's not appropriate, you need to just sit in your chair," and he scooted her back to work.

I think social services should be more involved, but I think in the end it's really difficult for us to do anything. We've reported what the children have said. The problem is that the kids usually get to school on time, they're clean, they're dressed appropriately, and they seem to be fed—somewhat. I feel that we're not making any headway, but where do we go from here?

The Broken Bond

Chief Protagonists
RICK LEYLAND, science teacher
PETE CARRIER, science department chairperson
LYLE BLACK, teacher

Rick Leyland had enjoyed his first semester teaching at Moore High. It had been hectic, but, he thought, exhilarating fun. As he sat alone in his classroom that Friday afternoon, he recalled how much he had learned in such a very short time in his chosen profession.

Moore High was a new suburban high school in Red Ridge, a midsize northeastern city. The region was largely agricultural with Red Ridge serving as the economic and cultural center of a tristate area. Unemployment was low, businesses were booming, and the combination of farming and commercial development made for ideal recreational opportunities and an excellent quality of life.

Rick had pondered his future deeply in his last year of college and had decided he needed a change of scenery from his southwestern roots. He had applied for jobs in four states and had taken the time to interview for several attractive teaching positions. He knew that with his specialty—teaching chemistry—and his excellent academic record, he would be able to choose among a range of viable teaching positions. He liked Moore High from the moment he walked through the door for his interview. The search committee had been very supportive, the district personnel had gone out of their way to accommodate his visit, and he did not detect any subtle undertone of problems either with the school or the faculty.

When the call came from the principal, Irene Dean, Rick didn't hesitate, accepting the position over the phone. Over the summer he moved to Red Ridge, settled into a very comfortable apartment, and busied himself preparing for his first year in teaching. He wondered how his working relationships would develop and reminded himself that he would be the most junior member of staff. He was acutely aware of the need to be cooperative, willing to learn, and fully expected to do more than his fair share as a way of adjusting to school life.

The week before school began, Rick's apartment phone jangled noisily. It was Pete Carrier, chairperson of the science department:

Rick: Hello?

Pete: Rick, it's Pete, how are you settling in?

Rick: Hi, Pete. Very well. I was just sitting here going over some of the finer details of the chemistry curriculum. I think I've got things just about ready for next week, although I'm sure there are tons of things I haven't anticipated!

Pete: Well, I'm sure things will be fine. I was wondering if you'd like to join us for dinner tomorrow evening. It would give you a chance to meet Louise, my wife, and Tim and Carey, our children.

Rick: That'd be great—I haven't had time to do much aside from moving in and trying to get prepared. A break would be most welcome!

Pete: OK. We'll see you at 6:30 then!

After a friendly evening, Rick pondered several instances during the conversation that were quite baffling. He was especially perturbed by Pete's comments about other faculty members in other teaching departments:

Pete: Well, it'll take time to settle in all right. I think you'll like it, though. We have a great science department—best department in the school. To be honest, though, I think there are some serious problems in English and social sciences. You haven't met Barbara Bellamy, yet, but you will. Oh, boy, what an idiot—I could tell you some stories about her!! Remind me some time, I'll tell you the wacky way she got tenure!! And then, of course, there's Dick Arrow who chairs social sciences—unbelievable!! He's been screwing things up for fifteen years. Just wait and see—you're sure to run into him on a committee, and then you'll see I'm right.

Why was this information coming his way? Rick wondered. He had done his best to be polite, but didn't follow up on Pete's comments. He thought it best to let it go. Sitting in his classroom, however, he recalled that Pete's comments were the beginning of a long line of problems.

Soon after the beginning of the first semester, Rick and Pete met at the faculty lounge coffee pot:

Pete: Hey, I'm glad I bumped into you! Are you a professional football fan?

Rick: Well, yes, I follow the NFL quite a bit. . .

Pete: Great! Look, there are several of us who get together on Monday evenings to watch football. We have a great time. I think you know Steve Grantley and Lyle Black over in phys. ed.—they wouldn't miss the games for anything! It's nothing fancy—have a couple of beers and some snacks. It's a good break from all the stuff that goes on here at school.

Rick: Thanks, Pete, I'll let you know.

Rick wanted to remain uncommitted. The dinner the week before had left him with some uneasy feelings. After mulling the invitation for a few days, he resolved not to go.

Pete's negative comments and perceptions kept coming. Rick recalled several departmental meetings where Pete had taken every opportunity, no matter how tangential, to speak negatively of other members of the staff. It was clear that Pete had a history of conflict with many people on Moore High's faculty, and Rick had no idea whether Pete's animus was justified or not. Pete was experienced, knowledgeable, and had many innovative ideas that had made the department function quite well. What Rick did know, though, was that these relentless tirades derailed meetings from other very important issues. Rick recalled one particular meeting that left him discouraged and angry. The science department was discussing how to divide up the science courses for the following year. The discussion was animated and quite productive, at least until Pete began dominating the conversation:

Pete: Well, at least we're making some good progress here—unlike Dick and Barbara. That whole department couldn't decide anything if their lives depended on it! I've heard that the higher-ups are really going to get on their case in the near future. In fact, we were all in a head of departments meeting last week. I really got in my licks! They just sat there and took it—I mean, they just couldn't answer what I was saying! Now I know Irene thinks they're hot stuff, but I slammed her pretty good, too! It was great! If they want to see how a department should work, they should look at us!

Rick was even more intrigued at the reaction of the other members of the science department. Pete's customary harangues drew little protest. It seemed as if everyone was either used to it or didn't notice it. Rick didn't know enough about the people Pete consistently demeaned to know how accurate his perceptions were. What he did know, however, was that true or not, the constant barrage was irritating and showed that Pete had agendas other than the science department and its students.

It was in this context that Rick, midway through the second semester, had to discuss an important issue with Pete. There had been serious discussions at the district level about consolidating the science departments of Moore High and the other high schools in town. There was also talk of some teachers being let go if the consolidation actually took place. Rick knew that he would be the first to go. He was new and didn't have tenure in the system. His situation was complicated by the fact that he was about to marry. His future wife and stepchildren were to move from the Southwest to join him in Red Ridge, and plans for the move were already quite advanced. Rick had a dilemma: Should he continue making plans for their move if it turned out that he would soon lose his job? Clearly, that would be unfair. His future stepdaughters were settled and happy in their schools, and there was no other job in Red Ridge or the surrounding area that would allow him to move to another school. Rick felt vulnerable and needed to talk to somebody who would know more about what was likely to happen than he. He was resolved that if it was more than likely that he would be let go, that he would return to the Southwest rather than move his future family. As far as he could tell, Pete was the only person who might have the information he needed.

Rick arranged to meet with Pete after school.

Pete: Come on in, Rick, what's the problem?

Rick was careful to close Pete's office door.

Rick: Well, Pete, what I'm about to say needs to remain confidential between you and me. I have to talk to you about this issue, but I don't want anyone else to know, at least not at this point . . .

Pete: Of course, what's going on?

Rick related his dilemma to Pete. Pete listened carefully as Rick outlined what he saw as the problem.

Pete: Well, I've been at all the district-level meetings and I'm sure that they're going to keep you on. They will cut some positions, but they're going to offer early retirement packages to three teachers at Pine High and another two at River Central. I wouldn't worry. I hope that makes you feel better.

Rick: Thanks, Pete, that helps in my decision. Again, please keep this between you and me. The privacy of my life outside of my job is very important to me . . .

Pete: Absolutely! Have a good weekend!!

Three weeks later, Rick had worked long and hard on his preparation for the following week. It was close to eight o'clock on that Friday evening before he was done. He opened the refrigerator but didn't find anything too appetizing. Heading out for a restaurant meal seemed much more attractive. As Rick was being escorted to his table, he heard a familiar voice:

Pete: Hey, Rick! Come over and join us!

Seated at a side table were Pete, Louise, and Lyle. Rick felt that he couldn't refuse, although he had hoped for a quiet meal alone. He walked over and slid into the booth next to Lyle:

Rick: Hi! Sorry I didn't see you on my way in! How are things?

Lyle: Great! Hey, I hear you're getting married—congratulations! Tell me all about your soon-to-be-family!

Rick, for once in his life, was speechless—and furious. He managed to recover well enough to quickly change the subject. He ate as quickly as he could and feigned tiredness to excuse himself.

For several weeks, Rick fumed about the betrayal of his trust. He knew well that nobody else knew about his personal plans and that the only way Lyle could have known was through Pete. Rick wrestled with whether he should confront Pete over the breach of confidentiality. As it turned out, the matter was decided for him. Rick had misread his new meeting schedule and missed an important departmental meeting. Pete stormed into his office, waving the schedule that Rick had misread:

Pete: You missed the meeting—this will not stand! What the hell happened?

The vehemence of Pete's rebuke had taken Rick by surprise, and it brought his own resentment to the surface:

Rick: Pete, I'm sorry. I misread the schedule and thought the meeting was the following day. I'll certainly be more careful next time. While you're here, *I* have something on my mind: I made it really clear to you when I met with you a couple of weeks ago that the decisions I was making in my personal life were to be kept strictly between you and me. I resent your breaking that confidence by telling Lyle . . .

Pete: I didn't tell Lyle—he must have heard it from someone else.

Rick felt his face redden in anger.

Rick: No one else in this whole community knew but you, Pete. You deliberately told Lyle after I'd made it clear that this was a matter between one of your faculty and you as chair.

The silence was deafening. Pete shifted in his seat. He knew there was no other explanation.

Pete: Well, perhaps I mentioned it in passing . . . I didn't mean any harm by it . . .

Rick wondered how he was going to be able to work effectively with Pete in the future.

The Rising Storm

Chief Protagonists
JUDITH JUDD, principal
JOYCE HILTON, teacher
JANE LEECH, music teacher
ELLEN RICH, school secretary

The following excerpts are from the files of Judith Judd, principal of Willow Falls Elementary School. They document Judith's struggle with a fourth grade teacher, Joyce Hilton.

May 15, 1995

Decided to get teachers to evaluate their own performance seeing that I have been in this job less than a month. Didn't feel it was fair for me to evaluate them seeing that I am so new to the school. Memo to each teacher's personal file read as follows:

> The attached performance appraisal was for each teacher to evaluate their own performance. The appraisal was discussed with the teachers after my observational visit to their class. I accept these self-evaluations as valid and have attached my signature to that effect. I feel that a detailed, critical evaluation by me would be premature given the short time I have been at Willow Falls Elementary.

June 18, 1995

Mailed contract to all teachers, including Joyce Hilton. Includes cover letter welcoming Joyce to the new school year. She will teach fourth grade again in the fall.

September 5, 1995

Sent letter of appreciation to Joyce for her hard work on the annual school open house.

October 6, 1995

Prepared for teacher evaluations. Reviewed past teaching evaluations done by my predecessor and teachers' self-evaluations from the end of last year. Joyce's file documents evaluations for previous four years. Evaluations show Joyce to be producing satisfactory teaching performance in all areas and several significant strengths. No weaknesses documented. Is this possible? Joyce's file also includes two letters from parents commending her efforts with their children.

October 8, 1995

Met with Joyce for pre-observation conference. Joyce indicated that she would conduct a reading lesson.

October 14, 1995

Observed lesson. Joyce is obviously an experienced teacher. Her classroom management skills are excellent and she displays all the skills expected of an experienced teacher. Only noted a few very minor points in the lesson that could have been improved. Overall rating: highly competent.

November 6, 1995

Informal observation of math lesson. Teaching was logical, effective, meaningful. However:

Issue 1: Joyce very sarcastic with children. Some comments questionable, but others quite hurtful (e.g., "So you finally figured out the answer, maybe you'll get out of fourth grade one of these days!").
Issue 2: Minor documentation problems: No "emergency kit" for emergency substitutions, gradebook not up to date, students' medications in classroom rather than in office.

November 7, 1995

Met with Joyce and discussed lesson. She was quite angry about the two issues that concerned me. Said she thought I was picking on her. I emphasized that all the staff were having similar visits from me and that the point of my observation was to help, not hinder. I'm not sure we resolved the matter.

November 8, 1995

Asked Joyce a question in faculty meeting. She ignored me and instead made sarcastic comment to colleague sitting next to her (I did not hear exactly what she said).

November 11, 1995

Jane Leech, music teacher, became suddenly ill halfway through her music lesson with Joyce's class. Jane informed me of her sudden illness, and I suggested she take the rest of the day off. I sent Joyce's class back to her and requested that she take up the slack (she would have her class for approximately the last 30 minutes they should have been in music). In front of the class, Joyce became very angry and complained loudly to me about having to "babysit" her class. She informed me that this wasn't her problem, but rather mine and Jane's. I left the class without responding in the hopes that I could deal with the matter a little later in a private conference when Joyce had calmed down. Tried to contact Joyce immediately after school to settle the issue but she had already left for the day.

November 12, 1995

Met with Joyce regarding yesterday's incident. She was still angry and insisted that she was right. Added that she also thought I had treated John Slater, third grade teacher, unfairly when I had declined him leave several weeks ago. I reminded her that I could not discuss other teachers' issues with her. Joyce gave notice that she would not help out in future as it was my responsibility to find a substitute if a teacher was ill. Joyce ignored my explanations that Jane's case was a quasi-emergency and that I expected some support in those kinds of situations.

November 16, 1995

Jane Leech met with me after school today because she was concerned that Joyce had kept several students out of her music class to finish some written work. Jane had tactfully suggested to Joyce that it was unfair to keep these children from the music class, especially seeing that they had important parts in the annual Christmas concert. According to Jane, Joyce's response was "So what, they're not going to make a career in Christmas concerts when they leave school."

November 17, 1995

Met with Ellen Rich, school secretary, before school. Ellen was concerned that Joyce is making derogatory comments about me to other members of the faculty and to several parents. According to Ellen, Joyce is asserting that I am incompetent, that I expect more from some teachers than others, and that I am treating her unfairly. Met with Joyce and discussed Jane's concern. Joyce was noncommunicative and would literally not respond to any of the questions I raised. However, when I asked her if there was anything else we needed to discuss, Joyce alleged the following:

1. That I had been rude to Patty Jones, second grade teacher, in a faculty meeting a month before. I did not recall being rude to anyone, and told Joyce so. I also was sure to tell Joyce that if Patty felt wronged, that I would be more than happy to sort out the problem with Patty.
2. Joyce asserted that I spent too much time in the secretaries' area of the administrative office rather than in my own, and that she felt that this was because I clearly did not have enough to do.

Joyce finally admitted that she was angry because I had not gotten someone else to take over her class the day Jane had left suddenly due to illness. I attempted to compromise a solution that would alleviate this problem between us but to no avail. Several minutes later, Joyce unexpectedly left my office.

November 19, 1995

I was out of the school building for approximately one hour between 8:30 and 9:30 this morning at a district administrators' meeting. When I returned, Ellen Rich informed me that Joyce had been into the office several times (leaving her class unattended) asking to see me. Ellen told her that I would not be available until approximately 10 a.m. Joyce became angry and made several derogatory comments about me to Ellen. Joyce was especially upset that the four special education students in her class would have to remain with her for the day because the special education teacher was absent. Ellen also reported that Joyce continued making derogatory remarks about me to several other staff members who happened to come into the office while Joyce was there. The other staff members did not respond, according to Ellen Rich.

Shortly after I returned to my office, Joyce entered and vehemently questioned me as to why I had not gotten a substitute for the special education teacher. She felt having the special education students in her class was detrimental to the learning of her other students. Joyce was clearly very angry. I calmly began responding to her complaint but never finished. Joyce suddenly rose and left my office, slamming the door behind her.

At 10:30 I contacted the district personnel director and informed him of Joyce's actions, and that I felt some form of formal reprimand was warranted. He agreed. He suggested that I document the disciplinary meeting as a formal reprimand.

I met with Joyce at 2 p.m. and informed her that:

1. The meeting was a formal disciplinary meeting because of the seriousness of her cumulative actions over the past several months.
2. I had reviewed all the prior problematic instances that I had witnessed and had been told of by other staff members, and that I felt she was being insubordinate.
3. Her ongoing belligerence was unacceptable and that if it did not cease immediately further disciplinary action would be taken.
4. In future she should encourage teachers who had problems to speak to me directly rather than through her.
5. If she had any problems with me in future, they should be addressed to me directly and not shared with anyone else.

December 3, 1995

Just before the start of school, Betsy Gillen, a regular substitute teacher at the school, stopped by my office and told me that she would be substituting for Joyce. Joyce, contrary to established school policy, did not inform me or Ellen Rich that she would not be at school. In the light of our previous problems, I was extremely concerned. I called Joyce at home, but there was no reply.

December 4, 1995

Joyce voluntarily gave up her ordered pizza lunch to a student who had forgotten to order his own. Joyce, in my presence, but addressing her remarks generally to several other people in the room, then announced

"I'm going out to get some lunch as I don't have any here. If I'm not back by 1 [p.m.], someone will have to take my class."

December 6, 1995

Joyce's husband called at midmorning to say that he had locked his keys in his car and wondered whether he could speak to Joyce. I called her to the phone from class and returned to my office. Shortly thereafter, Joyce left the building, presumably to take her husband a spare set of keys. Joyce did not ask me for permission to leave or tell me that she was leaving. She had also not asked me whether it was permissible to get another teacher to watch her class while she was away. Joyce did not let me know when she arrived back in the building . . .

Carmela's Predicament

Chief Protagonists
ROYCE BURROWS, student
MONICA LAKE, Royce's mother
LARRY LAKE, Royce's stepfather
JEREMY LYONS, assistant principal
CARMELA HINES, special education teacher

Royce Burrows is a sixteen year old who comes from a troubled family. He lives in a small rural town in a largely agricultural state with his mother, Monica Lake, his stepfather, Larry Lake, his brother, Mike Burrows, and a younger half brother, George Lake. Royce also has two older sisters. Karen Burrows, seventeen, lives in permanent foster care and has a history of suicide attempts. Prior to her permanent foster care arrangement, Karen had been placed in temporary foster care three times during her adolescence. Janice Burrows, the oldest sister, lives on her own in another part of the state and rarely has any contact with the family. Larry Lake is self-employed and has a long history of alcohol and other substance abuse. Larry and Royce are careful to avoid each other at home, and when they don't, bitter fighting ensues. John Peavy, the school counselor, reports that:

> Larry is self-employed so he is home at odd times during the day if he happens to be working in the area. He's in and out a lot, and there's generally friction when he and Royce are home together. Royce will usually

go to his room and stay there and will not come out as long as Larry is in the house.

Monica Lake, Royce's mother, appears to revel in her role as the family advocate to the school system, especially when Royce is involved. She has a reputation in the county for being aggressive, persistent, and threatening. Monica worked hard to obtain an education degree although she did not choose to obtain a teaching license. Jeremy Lyons, an assistant principal, recalls that Monica:

> knows all about education and special education law. She knows all kinds of things that the normal run-of-the-mill parent usually has to be told by teachers or the county. Monica certainly doesn't have to be told! She's very involved with every advocacy program and committee in the county and several at the state level.

Royce attends Willow High where he has just completed tenth grade. His school records report long-term learning and motivational problems. The domestic turbulence is reflected in his school attendance. Carmela Hines, the special education teacher, takes up the story:

> The family has gone through school districts like water. I think they get tired of fighting battles in one district so they move on. I think Royce was failing in the other schools, and the schools were after her to get Royce help. That's their history. Royce has been in our school district for three years. During Royce's first year, he spent most of his school time at a day treatment center because of what had happened the previous year at his old school. Apparently, he would not go to class and would run away and hide under the bleachers. He also assaulted a teacher. The previous district supplied a one-on-one teacher for Royce for a while, but when that didn't work they put him in day treatment with more structure. It was only in April of his first year here that he started to be reintegrated back into our school. Since then, we've all worked hard with Royce and done our best to cope with Monica. Royce's behavior isn't unmanageable, but he does nothing, just nothing—he's oppositionally defiant. He also has an anxiety disorder, so he is very nervous—new unpredictable situations are quite problematic for him. For a while, things seemed to be pretty stable.
> Our even keel didn't last long. Monica thinks he's good with his hands (he's not) so she wanted him to take a bunch of vocational classes. When we asked him if he wanted to do a metal class, because he's Royce, naturally, he said "Yes, I'll try it, whatever."

Soon he started having problems with the vocational teacher. Unless the teacher stood right over him, Royce did nothing. Finally Royce told me that he was afraid of the welder: "I'm afraid I'm going to get burned," he said, "Or I'm going to do something wrong and I'm going to burn somebody else." So I went and talked to the vocational teacher and got that straightened out. Things seemed to be better, and then "vacation" came along. Monica pulled all the kids out of school for three weeks for a family vacation. That changed everything.

When Royce got back to school he was hell on wheels. He wouldn't go to class, and he refused to do any of his makeup work even though it was right at the end of the quarter. Nothing that we did worked, so we had to almost start over again with him to get him going to classes again. He ran away from school twice. We decided that we were getting nowhere fast and decided to have a team meeting. Monica was there, of course (Larry never attends). I was there, as well as the welding teacher, another vocational education teacher with whom Royce had a class, his social service manager from the day treatment center, the paraprofessional, and Jeremy, the assistant principal.

Throughout the meeting Royce would not talk directly to Monica. Instead, he talked through me. Keeping him in the meeting was difficult, though. He'd start out quite well and then he would get frustrated as Monica attacked him. She kept at him right from the beginning of the meeting, especially about being in the welding class: "Royce, you can do this, this is what you have to do, you are seventeen years old, it's either this or you're out." It went on and on: "You have to do this work, you need to be in this class, you're going to work with your hands, you can do that, I'll help you, your stepfather will help, you have to do this." She'd say all this while half-turned away from him. His body language was very tense and tight as he listened. I tried to stem the flow by pointing out that Royce really didn't like the welding class and that there were several alternatives that might be less threatening. She just went right on. She wanted him to stay in the class no matter what.

While this barrage was going on, Royce left the room several times. I would go out after him and talk him into coming back in. I remember saying to him: "Royce, tell me what you want and I'll tell them. If you feel like coming back, come back." When he did, Monica would weigh right in again. He just couldn't handle that kind of pressure.

Monica finally agreed that he should quit the welding class, but she stipulated that he had to fail it. The welding teacher was willing to give Royce the option of making up the work after school but she wouldn't hear of it. Instead, she said "No, he can fail the class—he needs to fail." It almost seemed her way of proving a point—that if we were going to say he didn't need to do this class then he should fail it, which he eventually did.

The following quarter, out of the welding class, there was a general improvement in Royce's performance and attitude. He didn't have to face that class anymore. He liked the teacher in his new vocational class. He took the tests independently, he did the work, and, in fact, ended up with a B at the end of the semester. His other classes were also coming along, although English was very difficult for him, mainly because he could not write cursively at all and because his grammar skills were very poor.

But it wasn't all bad. I remember that in English they did a unit on Julius Caesar. You would have thought any kid would have said "yuck!" Not Royce. He took my audiotaped version of the play home and listened to it day after day. He would go to English fully prepared and participate in class. The English teacher came over and said, "You're not going to believe this!" This was the same kid who previously wouldn't participate even when he knew the answer. He ended up with a B in English—quite phenomenal for Royce.

We finally had Royce back on track. Everything was going along just fine until just before the end of school when Royce told me that Monica was insisting that he apply for a summer job in our county job training program, Job Success (JS). JS is a real job training program for adolescents and adults who qualify either because they have disabilities or are below the poverty line. Royce had been part of the JS program the previous summer for two weeks and then quit because he "didn't like it." We suspected Monica's renewed insistence that he try JS again had more to do with keeping him out of the house for the summer rather than any good JS might be able to do for him. Monica knew that having Royce at home in the summer just doing nothing created problems—especially with Larry.

Suddenly, during the last week of school, Monica called and insisted that Royce needed to have an extended school year through the summer. "He's going to regress," she said. "He's going to be terrible—he's not going to want to go back to school in the fall if we don't do the extended school year—you have to do it!"

I was completely floored. I made a couple of phone calls and discovered the reason for Monica's urgency—the Department of Rehabilitation and JS didn't have any vacancies for Royce. Apparently Monica had been calling everyone on the face of the earth trying to get Royce accepted, but given his poor performance in JS in the past and her belligerence, she ran into a stone wall. The extended school year seemed like a last resort.

The district coordinator assured me that the extended school year idea was inappropriate. I called Monica on the last day of school to let her know. She was angry, to say the least. I tried to deflect some of her anger by offering to have the team meet with her to discuss the matter. "Please call me if you are willing to have this meeting," I said. "We need to have it at nine o'clock on Friday morning, which is my last duty day for the year." She never responded, so I thought that she'd given up on that idea, too.

Three weeks later, I got a call from Jeremy saying that Monica had called him and demanded a meeting to discuss the extended school idea again. By this point, we were getting beaten down. School was over for the year and both of us were busy with other things. We discussed it for a while. Eventually I said, "Jeremy, let's just do it. It will take two hours out of our day. So what? Perhaps we'll make her happy and perhaps we can go from there . . . " I knew that Jeremy was reluctant to meet with Monica. They have a history of conflict, mostly at Monica's instigation. I knew, for example, that Monica had accosted Jeremy out in public a couple of times insisting that he discuss some problem or the other, right there in public.

Jeremy set up a meeting for that Thursday morning, two days later, at ten o'clock. He called everybody else on the team, but with little success. The case manager was away at a conference, none of Royce's other teachers were available, and the district coordinator was out of town. By the time I arrived for the meeting, Jeremy was furious. Monica had called him half an hour before the meeting and said she just couldn't make the meeting at ten. Jeremy managed to hold firm and explained that I was already on my way and that the meeting would proceed whether she was there or not.

When I arrived for the meeting, I realized that we didn't have a general education teacher there, and we needed one in order for the meeting to be legal. Two teachers just happened to be in the building at that time, both of whom knew Royce quite well. We begged them to help us out. They agreed.

Monica finally showed up a little after ten, and I decided that we needed to really emphasize that the extended school year idea was not appropriate for Royce. I knew that what Monica really wanted was day care. Monica was her usual self, but Jerry and I were persistent and focused. As soon as she realized that we weren't going to budge, she appealed to the two commandeered teachers, but they knew Royce well enough to know that Jeremy and I were right. I could see Monica getting nervous, and she soon switched tactics: "Well, if we can't do extended school year then I want Royce in summer school because he failed the welding class," she said. We nixed that idea, too. Monica, however, was relentless, and her next remark pushed Jerry over the edge.

"Well," she said, "we have to do something. You people aren't being any help. I wanted something done about this and you won't do anything." I tried to head Jeremy off by interrupting Monica and going through my record book, reciting all of the meetings, phone calls, discussions, and other efforts we had made through the year. Jeremy was livid. His face reddened even further when she said, "Well, obviously you're not going to help me. I'll just have to do this on my own." Monica rose abruptly and left the room. We all just sat there looking at each other.

Jerry was the first to speak: "I'm sorry. I probably shouldn't have gotten so mad, but it just makes me angry that we have bent over backwards for her all year but as soon as she doesn't get what she wants, then we're the bad guys."

Before any of us could respond, Monica reentered the room and started right in with her "poor me" theme. We tried our best to brainstorm some alternatives but Monica kept coming back to the extended school year, and we kept rebuffing it. By this point, Jeremy was a little ashamed of letting Monica get the better of him. He tried his level best to make up for it with a number of viable suggestions, but to no avail. She had excuses for everything he suggested:

"How about an in-home family therapist?"

"We're on a waiting list."

"A support group for parents of children with oppositional defiance?"

"I already started one."

"How about letting Royce work at odd jobs around the neighborhood?"

"There are none."

Suddenly, Monica showed her hand: "You're just not going to help me—I can see that. What am I supposed to do when Larry comes home and yells at Royce because Royce has been lying around all day doing nothing?"

With that, she left, slamming the door behind her.

That was a month ago. I stopped at my usual convenience store last week and there was Monica, working behind the counter. She was quite friendly, although our pleasantries studiously avoided any talk of Royce. I'll bet she solved the summer problem with Royce by getting herself out of the house instead.

A Question of Color

Chief Protagonists
BOB DANIELS, head of recruiting
JUANITA SANTISTA, SHELLEY ARNE, and
TERRY SIBLEY, recruiters

Grimes Academy, established in 1967, is a private school located in Center Point, a picturesque large town in a southern state. The school, proud of its African American heritage, is situated amidst large tracts of well-manicured farmland. The school has a national reputation for graduating students who excel in all walks of life. Among its alumni are prominent political figures, artists and entertainers, scholars, and activists. Fund-raising events for the school's ever-growing endowment are always celebrity-studded occasions that draw national media attention. Grimes, however, has more than money and prestige. Entrance requirements are extraordinarily high, beginning with rigorous admission evaluations even for first graders. The screening process ensures a steady stream of academically talented pupils from the 2,000 strong student body who routinely win local, state, national, and international awards.

Coupled with its stellar reputation, Grimes Academy has developed the Student for Tomorrow project (SFT), a nationally recognized model for student recruitment. Project SFT is a high-priority budget item at Grimes with its own staff. The efforts of the SFT team are seen as vital for the maintenance of

Grimes's high standards and for future expansion of the school. SFT efforts have resulted in extensive waiting lists for admission. In many cases, students are placed on the waiting list the day they are born.

An ongoing concern at Grimes in recent years has been the lack of diversity among the student body. School records indicate that the school is 96 percent African American, 3 percent Caucasian American, and 1 percent Asian American. A special task force had previously identified the need to increase efforts by SFT recruiters to attract Caucasian, Asian American, and Hispanic students. SFT responded to the report by establishing a minority recruitment division, headed by Bob Daniels, a dynamic member of the counseling faculty who had been at Grimes for twelve years. Consistent with Grimes's priority for the division, Bob was given authority to hire several recruiters to get the program under way. The recruiting positions were to be choice appointments with disproportionately large salaries and opportunities for national and international recruitment travel.

The Recruitment Counselors

Bob Daniels, with the mission for diversity and excellence as his central compass, hired three new recruiting counselors over the summer of 1993. The recruiters had one thing in common: they were all recent graduates of private universities who had graduated at or near the top of their class. They were obviously bright and almost overwhelmingly enthusiastic.

Juanita, Shelley, and Terry came from three very different backgrounds. Their contrasting perspectives on life soon meant that as they settled into their new job, they became firm friends. They could laugh, joke, and make good-natured fun of the stereotypical quirks of each other's upbringing. Underneath it all, though, they were acutely aware that they were products of those environments.

Juanita

Juanita Santista, an attractive, outgoing, and personable twenty-two-year-old Hispanic woman, was raised in a life of luxury. She grew up in a large metropolitan city and found working in Center Point a pleasant change. In spite of what most people would consider a fairy-tale childhood, she realized the value of hard work and by the end of her first year was one of Grimes's most valuable recruiters. She also had an uncanny ability to get what she wanted from her colleagues and the administration. She saw her work at Grimes as excellent preparation for advancement to becoming a university recruiter later in her career. Juanita's combination of wealth and hard work meant that she had rarely not gotten what she wanted. She took pride in recounting that she had chosen her exclusive private college education un- fettered by concerns of cost. College had been easy for her, and she had made good use of her ability to influence others, including her instructors. She applied for and was offered three jobs the month after graduation and was clearly under no pressure to choose Grimes Academy. It sometimes seemed, as Terry once said, that "She'd never been told, 'Sorry, there is someone better than you we would like to select.' "

Shelley

Shelley Arne, also twenty-two, was raised in a very small, almost exclusively Caucasian rural town in the Midwest where agriculture was the main economy. Shelley, however, was neither Caucasian nor remotely interested in agriculture. Her Caucasian parents had adopted her at birth from a Chinese family and had raised her on their farm. Shelley was, without a doubt, the most knowledgeable recruiter of the three. She had worked all four of her undergraduate years in the admissions office of a small state university and stepped easily into her position at Grimes. Shelley saw her position at Grimes as an opportunity to assist Asian as well as other students to find a home at Grimes. While Shelley was from a small rural town, she had no aspirations of returning to the farm. Shelley wanted very badly to get out of Center Point for bigger and brighter lights.

On many occasions, Shelley had confided to Terry her discomfort at being Asian with an American name and having been raised in a predominantly Caucasian region of the country. She had, she told Terry, "Dreamt many times about unzipping her Asian skin and stepping out as a blonde-haired, blue-eyed all-American girl." Not surprisingly, many people knew that Shelley was ultra- sensitive about racial issues.

Terry

Unlike Shelley and Juanita, Terry Sibley very much liked living in Center Point. A lanky twenty-three-year-old Caucasian, Terry loved his new job at Grimes and had aspirations of growing into more responsibilities, hopefully with several promotions, at the school. Shelley and Juanita were Terry's closest friends.

The Friendship

In a very short time, the friendship between Juanita, Shelley, and Terry deepened. They worked very well in the division and were firm companions after hours. They spent a great deal of time in each other's company and shared many details of their personal lives with each other. There seemed to be nothing about each other that they didn't know. Relationships, intimate concerns, future career goals, and everything in between were shared. They thought they knew each other very well indeed. Bob Daniels often bragged that he had the most cohesive staff in a five-state region.

The Problem

By the second year of the division project, Bob was ready to expand minority recruiting further afield than the surrounding counties. Things among the three friends had also changed. Terry had married the local judge's daughter and was more firmly implanted in Center Point than ever. Juanita and Shelley, however, were impatient to expand their job activities. They had both accumulated excellent work performances since arriving at Grimes and both felt strongly that they needed the experience that the extended recruiting would provide. Independently, they both told Terry they wanted to travel as part of their jobs. Juanita had even suggested to Bob Daniels that it might be in Grimes's best interests to relocate one of them to Atlanta, long seen as a primary recruiting area for Grimes, but which, until now, had largely remained untouched. Terry also knew that they both appeared to have tired of the limits of Center Point and were looking for the lights of bigger, brighter cities.

In the fall, the Grimes Board of Trustees flanked Bob Daniels on local television as he announced the school's intention of establishing a permanent recruiting office in Atlanta with the specific goal of attracting a more diverse student body. The announcement attracted several national news reporters and a short clip of the event was even carried on the network news. The announcement made two facts immediately clear: Terry didn't want to move, so that meant the recruiting job would logically be given to either Juanita or Shelley.

Initially, Juanita and Shelley firmly reiterated to Terry and each other that this new twist would not affect their friendships. They were content to mouth platitudes that the best person for the job would be selected and the other would have to live with that decision. However, each woman had strong reasons for wanting the Atlanta job. Juanita had grown up in a similar metropolitan area and felt she could most successfully relate to students and families from those schools. Shelley's claim was also strong. Atlanta had a large concentration of Asian families, and she naturally felt her efforts would net many students for Grimes.

Very quickly, Terry found himself in the middle. While Juanita and Shelley maintained their outward geniality, they both spent growing amounts of time talking privately with Terry about why they should get the job. Terry soon learned that, in spite of promises to the contrary, neither was prepared to accept the other being chosen for the position. It seemed to Terry that both Juanita and Shelley were prepared to do everything in their power to get the transfer. He knew, for example, that on several occasions Shelley met with Bob Daniels to argue why she was the best person for the job. Likewise, Juanita had met with Bob and made it very clear she would leave Grimes if she didn't get the Atlanta position. While all of the politicking was done behind closed doors, everyone at Grimes knew what was in the air. The tension in the division and throughout the SFT staff was palpable.

The Confrontation

One night Shelley and Juanita decided to meet over dinner to discuss what was quickly becoming an unbearably tense situation. They were tired of avoiding each other and from hearing vague whisperings among their colleagues. They agreed that it was time for the truth, and that whatever they said would remain between them. As the conversation developed and the wine flowed, Juanita finally confided, angrily, that she felt she would not get the job. Shelley was equally honest in her feelings about the situation. Soon, Juanita dropped the bombshell: "Well, Shelley, seeing that we're being so honest here, I'll be as frank as I know how: You're going to get the job in Atlanta because you're Asian. It wouldn't be the first time, as far as I can tell, that you've gotten preferential treatment because of your skin rather than your ability. Let's face it, Shelley, we're not exactly 'Diversity Central' at Grimes—you're the token, don't you see that?"

The Aftermath

Shelley spent the next several weeks simmering over Juanita's harsh words. Finally, she decided to remain silent no longer. In the next staff meeting, with Juanita out of town on other school business, Shelley tearfully related their conversation. By the time Juanita returned to Grimes a week later, Shelley had met individually with everyone in the division, explaining that she saw Juanita's remark as blatant racism. Juanita quickly denied Shelley's claims, but Juanita suddenly no longer communicated, unless it was absolutely necessary, with anyone, including Bob Daniels.

Two weeks later, Bob Daniels sat pensively alone in his office. The decision for the Atlanta job had to be made in the next twenty-four hours. He had no idea of how to proceed.

James's Uncertain Future

Chief Protagonists
JAMES JUDSON, student
ANNA JUDSON, James's mother

James Judson was enrolled in my third grade special education class from the beginning of the school year. James lived with his mother and an older brother, Kenny. Kenny was a tenth-grade, straight A student and an athlete—an all out, good kid. I was not surprised that James idolized Kenny. As was so often the case with my students, Kenny took the place of James's father. James knew where his father lived, but hadn't had any contact with him for about a year.

James's mother, Anna, did her best to support the family but had a history of frequently changing jobs. She was very big and tall, an intimidating woman just by her bearing and aggressive attitude. She had a very deep, raspy voice, and when she talked her comments were so pointed and harsh that they often left me breathless. In our many interactions over the year, she often appeared angry and usually claimed that everyone was picking on James or on her parenting skills. Anna was, however, highly verbal and always seemed very interested in James's academic progress. If he took work home, she usually tried to help him.

The family lived in a run-down part of town comprised mostly of Mexican and African American low-SES families. The area had a reputation for gang activity, and children commonly witnessed violence in the neighborhood. The school reflected the neighborhood. West Side Elementary housed 1,200 students with multiple classes for each grade. Official school statistics reported the ethnic mix as 50 percent Hispanic, 45 percent African American, and 5 percent Caucasian and Asian.

When I first met James, he seemed nice enough. However, I didn't see James every day—he would only come to me for extra help or reteaching as needed. At first, James would come to my class only once in a while. Even in those early days, he was very distractable and talked out of turn all the time. If the class were answering questions from the textbook, for example, he would burst out with "Oh, Oh, Oh, I know that. Oh, Oh, Oh," and then, nine times out of ten, he'd give the wrong answer.

What I was seeing in my classroom was soon mirrored by what Jill was experiencing in hers. James had begun picking on other students. He'd been hitting, pinching, scratching, kicking, tripping. Students would walk by to go to the sharpener and James would whack them on the back of the head. Soon Jill started sending James to me much more often—more for his inappropriate behavior than his schoolwork, I thought. Although he was labeled learning disabled, James was academically up to par. If his inappropriate behaviors hadn't been so obvious, he never would have been in my room. Everyone knew James's behavior was the problem. Even his mother acknowledged that by saying, "Well, he's active, that's all there is to it." His activity, however, wore people out. Jill would go home crying almost every day. He just overwhelmed her.

By midyear, James was acting out all the time. We tried a wide variety of behavioral approaches, but none of them worked. The school psychologist tried, the general education teachers tried, the learning disabilities teachers tried, and the principal had ideas that she tried, all to no avail. By the middle of the year, we had had four conferences with Anna. In spite of our strenuous urging, Anna would only help with homework, and not much else.

In the fifth conference, we repeated the now-growing litany of problem behaviors to Anna. She refused to believe that James was misbehaving in class. "He's not really doing that," she said. By this point, we had all had enough, so we invited Anna to see for herself. We put up some dark paper on my windows with smaller viewing slits into the classroom so that Anna could observe James in my class without being seen. After witnessing James's behavior several times over a two-week period, Anna seemed completely overwhelmed.

At our next meeting, we saw a different Anna. She broke down, saying she couldn't believe this was her James. We were all touched by her outpouring of frustration as she told us how hard it was for her to hold the family together, her helplessness at not being better able to provide for her children, and her bewilderment that James was "not more like Kenny." I was concerned, though, that she seemed to leave the meeting with a fiercely determined look on her face. Her parting comment that she'd "take care of things" didn't help matters either.

Whatever Anna had meant by "taking care of things" appeared to work. James was quiet and compliant for about a week after the meeting and actually attended to academic tasks. We soon realized, though, that this was not necessarily progress when, one day, he came to school but couldn't sit down in his desk in Jill's class. Jill insisted he explain what the problem was. James reluctantly showed her switch marks from the middle of his back to the middle of his thigh where Anna had taken a switch and "whipped" him. James couldn't sit down at all and he was scared to go home without having done his work. His fear didn't last long, though. Anna was soon "whipping" him at night quite regularly, but the effect wore off swiftly, and the misbehavior reappeared as troublesome as it had been before.

The county child protective services intervened quickly. When they spoke with Anna, she was defensive. Her only explanation was that "This is my child and he gets a spanking." That's all that ever came out of it. Inexplicably, child protective services never followed up on the incident. I think James slipped through the cracks, or the report was simply put under a pile of others somewhere and forgotten. This episode didn't exactly endear us to Anna. Her growing suspicion that we were all conspiring against her only intensified.

In desperation, I reviewed James's records carefully once more and found that he had been diagnosed as severely ADHD almost eighteen months previously. In spite of the physician's recommendation that James receive medication for his disorder, no further action was noted in the record. I began to wonder. Why hadn't James received the recommended medication? I raised the issue with Jill, and learned another piece of the puzzle.

Outside of school, James spent a great deal of time at church—after school and over the weekends. Anna was a devout follower of her faith, part of which frowned upon reliance on medical science, including any medication for James's hyperactivity. Any mention of medication drew vehement protests from Anna.

With this additional information, I called yet another meeting with Anna and insisted that James be retested for ADHD. Reluctantly, she agreed. The physician's report was the same as it was before. James was severely ADHD, but Anna refused to allow medication. She would not budge. Anna's perception that we were all ganging up on her increased to the point that she demanded the appointment of a mediator to serve as a buffer between her and the school. In the last two months of the school year, Anna would only communicate with the mediator, so all our recommendations had to be relayed through him. We were desperate. Medication was not an option and nothing had worked with James except, for a while, Anna's intimidation.

Eventually, Anna suggested that she spend a great deal of time each day at the school in the hopes that her presence would keep James on track. She began appearing at school for several hours each day. James only knew that she was physically somewhere in the building. Sometimes she would be watching through the peephole, while at other times she helped out in the office or walked around the playground. James's behavior improved, but as with the beatings he received at home, the effect of Anna's presence soon wore off. By the last month of school, Anna's appearances dwindled, although she remained available by phone. Probably three days out of five we would call Anna to come and get James by noon. It was the only strategy we had left—to get him out of the way. It stayed that way until the end of school.

The following year James's home was rezoned for a newly constructed school several blocks away. I heard that Anna was very excited that he was going to a new school. She thought he would get a fresh start.

I saw James at the mall yesterday. Still energetic, still impulsive, still unmedicated. My thoughts were not positive. He's going to get into trouble not only with authority figures, but also with his peers, who will understand even less about him than we did. Soon he'll get to high school where there are more guns, knives, and aggressive behavior. He's going to upset someone and that'll be the end. As I tried to look on the sunny side, I couldn't help but remember Anna's parting words to me the year before: "I don't want the teachers spanking, and I'm tired of having to get James from school when he misbehaves. I'll just have to take care of his sorry attitude at home."

Help for Jay

Chief Protagonists
JAY RAMIREZ, student
ADA DOMINGO, Jay's grandmother
GINA CARRERAS, Jay's mother
MARY PENNY, teacher

Jay's School Life

I work as an elementary school teacher in a rural area of my state. I first came to know Jay when his fifth grade teacher, Mary, asked me if he could move to my class. Mary felt that she was getting too emotionally involved in his case, and her objectivity was slipping. Mary was starting to let Jay get away with quite a lot of misbehavior, and she felt that she needed to be removed from the situation.

When Jay arrived in my classroom, I knew I had a student who wasn't used to consequences for his misbehavior. He would leave the classroom whenever he wanted to (other teachers called it a "walk-about") to wander around the school. Many times he couldn't be coerced back to class, and someone from the office would just take him home. Jay also had problems with aggression as well as a history of sniffing gasoline and of other substance abuse. Academically, he read at an early second grade level and mathematically he was a little stronger. Jay was only able to construct and write a complete sentence with an enormous amount of prodding, and even at his best would quickly become frustrated and noncompliant.

I did my best not to allow Jay to wander from class. In Mary's class, he usually did not do any work, so I immediately set up a simple behavior modification system whereby he had to do some work in order to earn a reward. The system seemed to improve his behavior. Over the winter quarter, Jay did quite a bit of work for me. In addition, his "walk-abouts" lessened, and he generally did quite well.

Jay's Home Life

Jay lived with his grandmother, Ada, and one of his brothers, Harry, in a very poor county notorious for its very high rate of alcoholism and drug use. The rate of fetal alcohol syndrome in this county is the highest in the state. In addition, many of the students in this area come from abusive homes or highly dysfunctional families. Jay, Harry, and Ada lived in an old house at the end of a long, isolated driveway. The boys had been with Ada for several years.

Jay and Harry had previously lived with their mom, Gina. Gina's serious problems with alcohol and gambling eventually resulted in the brothers moving in with Ada. Since the move, Jay had seen Gina infrequently, even though she lived only an hour away. Many times Gina had promised to visit but she never arrived. In one instance, Jay had stayed up all night waiting for Gina, to no avail. On another occasion, she showed up at four in the morning after telling Jay that she would be there at eight the evening before. In spite of this kind of treatment, Jay still hoped that he'd go to live with her. It's been difficult to establish the details of the rest of the family, but other teachers have told me that there are several other siblings who are in foster homes. I'm not sure how many there are but at least three or four others, both older and younger.

There are problems in Jay and Harry's living with Ada, too. Although Ada is listed as Jay's legal guardian in our school records, her participation is pretty spotty. For example, Jay is supposed to receive weekly counseling in a neighboring town, but he has only been to two sessions this year. Supposedly, there is always a problem—car doesn't run, or there's a flat tire, or the roads are too bad in the winter, and so on.

Ada is quite a striking woman who's lived a rough life. There are several scars on her face that look as if they've come from being struck in the head. Ada seems to be in her fifties, although she may be a lot younger. She appears to be partially paralyzed around the left side of her mouth. She also seems to be very lethargic at times as if she is heavily medicated or very depressed.

The boys are not well cared for, either. Soon after school started, Jay complained that his feet were hurting to the point that he was having a hard time concentrating. I took him to the office and had him pull his shoes and socks off. The smell from his feet was overwhelming. His feet were completely raw, bleeding, and infected. It was obvious that he hadn't washed or tended to his feet in quite a while. We got him to the school clinic right away, but Ada refused to take him back for follow-up visits because at the initial visit the clinic had filed a report of child neglect. There have been other instances of neglect. Jay always wears very dirty clothes and obviously doesn't get much sleep.

There are other problems with Jay. He has several medical and psychological problems—especially self-inflicted injury. I've seen Jay pull out handfuls of hair, bang his head with a book, and run his head into a pile of boxes. Once I saw that he had a laceration across his wrist. It looked to me like a rope burn and it probably was, because I had previously seen him tying string around his wrist and pulling it tighter and tighter. Jay told another teacher that it was frostbite from riding his snowmobile, but I wasn't convinced.

Jay's Relationships

Jay doesn't have any really close friends. Sometimes he eats lunch with some of his classmates but he's not really good friends with anyone. However, he did show a different side to his personality one weekend when he and another student came over to my house to ride our horses. I think that helped my relationship with Jay because he was invited someplace. I'm not sure he has much opportunity to go out at all. He asked if he could call me by my first name, although it was clear that he wasn't trying to be disrespectful. He was inquisitive and very curious about the horses. I have to admit I was very nervous about having Jay at my house—I was more than a little skittish.

Jay was unable to ride the horse because he's very heavy. He was not physically able to do it. Even although he didn't ride, he enjoyed himself. I thought it was telling that at about eleven o'clock in the morning, he said he was hungry because he'd gotten up at six that morning, and he hadn't had any breakfast at all before he came over. So I fed him. Jay was very polite. He cleared off his own plate and brought it over to the table. I'm quite sure that if it weren't for breakfast and lunch at school, he probably wouldn't eat any regular meals at all.

Jay also seemed starved for physical affection. So often we're warned as teachers not to touch our students. At Aspen Elementary many of the students seem in need of some small sign of physical affection. They often come up and give the staff a hug. Jay will sometimes come up to me after a real tough day and when I have helped him through it, he'll put his arm around me and say "Thanks, Mrs. Penny" or he'll just say "See you tomorrow, Mrs. Penny." It's just another part of him that I don't think he always shows. I think it's experiences like that which make me so attached to Jay. I watch myself and I try to be as objective as possible in the decisions I make. Perhaps part of why Jay is so special to me is because I know his background but a lot of those other kids have had rotten backgrounds, too. I think part of it is because I've taken the time to see what's underneath the surface.

I don't think I've done enough to help Jay. It's time to turn more resources and people loose on this poor child. I just wish I knew how.

Requiem for Amy

Chief Protagonists
AL RILEY, conflict mediator
AMY CALLAHAN, teacher
PATTI HAWKINS, teacher
JUDY WEILL, principal

Al Riley is a mediator for a rural school district in a western state. The following transcript is of an interview with Amy Callahan, a fifth grade special education teacher. Amy's principal, Judy Weill, had requested the meeting between Amy and Al after a heated discussion between Amy and Judy the week before. Amy was one of Judy's best teachers whose only professional weakness seemed to be her sometimes abrasive directness. However, Judy reflected, even though Amy could be brutally honest, she was usually right.

Their discussion had centered on the other special education teacher, Patti Hawkins, who taught sixth grade students with emotional and behavioral problems. Judy was well aware of Patti's problems, and also of Patti's intractable position—she had had tenure for several years and was a prominent member of the local and national teachers' union. In fact, Patti had won tenure after a nasty fight between the school district and the union. Judy had not recommended tenure based on Patti's chronic poor performance, but the union had filed suit, and after a protracted and very public fracas, the district had granted Patti tenure anyway. Patti never missed an opportunity to remind all who would listen that she had won tenure in spite of "Judy the Nazi, who tried to do everything to destroy my career."

Judy had met with Patti several times regarding the way she ran her class in the hopes of avoiding complaints from other teachers and parents. For the most part, Judy's strategy had succeeded if for no other reason than that many teachers remembered the tenure fight and found it easier to avoid Patti than complain. Amy, however, was the first teacher to openly question Patti's behavior. By bringing in Al, Judy hoped to avoid any hostile escalation of the situation while simultaneously removing herself from the line of fire.

After exchanging pleasantries, Al and Amy got down to business:

Al: Well, Amy, let's see if you can fill me in. Tell me about your work situation.

Amy: Well, I teach in a separate building from the rest of the school. The only other rooms in the building are the gym and another self-contained sixth grade class for emotionally disturbed kids next door. I do love my job, even though many general education teachers don't know how I do it—it's quite funny, actually, because they're always appalled that I chose work with the "crazy" kids. Most of them will say "I couldn't do what you do," which always makes me ask *myself,* you know, how can I do it and like it? But, I think I have a very good reputation as being a good disciplinarian, because my kids act much like general education kids, which surprises many of my colleagues.

It seems that the way I run my classroom has not always been the rule. I understand that my predecessor was not rehired, at least in part, because he did not have an organized and orderly room. I feel structure is important since most of these children live highly disorganized lives. Most of the students were a little surprised at my style, but they were pleased, I think, that they were going to be using the same books as their general education peers this year. They told me that my predecessor had not used a single textbook the whole year!!

I started the first day with a schedule of academic work listed on the board. The students have all morning to complete their work and then to have lunch and recess. After recess, they have one additional period of academic work and then they leave for either art or music. PE is the last period of the day. The students know what is expected of them academically and behaviorally. We have the class rules and consequences posted on the bulletin board. As a class, we discussed the rules and consequences and their importance on the first day. Their behavior, overall, has been relatively good. There have been instances where they have not completed their work, some name calling, and a few scuffles, but the biggest problem is their bad language. In fact, it could be a new classroom theory—the number of times you hear the F-word is directly proportionate to the level of management success for the week!!

I think other teachers have noticed my style, too. For instance, Jody, the librarian, is always very impressed with structure. She and I had a real time of it last year because she treated these kids very much like the general education students—she would have a lot of unstructured time in the library, which my kids couldn't handle. Jody and I went round and round about it until I put my foot down and said "If we're going to come to the library, I have to have a structured program from you for my class." At first I think she didn't like it, but she was tired of all the hassles they caused in the unstructured time. This year, she spends most of the period reading them a story and then they have about seven minutes to pick out a book—then we leave, quickly, before any trouble can start!! It's perfect, and she's always complimenting the class. I'm sure to remind her about what made the difference—there's no time for them to wander, to get into anything. So, I think my colleagues think I do a good job.

Al: What about the other special education teachers?

Amy: I don't have a lot of contact with the other special education teachers. I'm especially careful to avoid Patti, the only other EBD teacher. She's very unstructured—totally my opposite, and I hate what it's done to those poor kids in her class. She's quite the "If-it-feels-good-do-it" type. Her class is an unmitigated disaster—I don't think there's any doubt about that. It's hard not to notice because our classes are side by side. I think they were originally one large room, and now we have some thin wallboard in between. My kids complain all the time about the noise from next door. Patti's kids, from what I see, produce very little, which I think is why she has as many discipline problems in the room and why the noise level is so high. She is getting very burned out.

Al: So you see Patti as more detrimental than helpful in getting her students what they need?

Amy: How else could it be when the teacher is into this wacky philosophy of "If you feel like it, do it, and if you don't feel like it, don't bother, I don't want to hurt your self-esteem?" Of course, the situation isn't helped any by the good old rug area where her kids can go at any time they feel they "need a break" and lay on the bean bag chair and watch the small TV she brought to school this year. I know for a fact that a lot of those kids watch some of the daytime soaps and talk shows. She justifies it all with some nutty "Teaching them about the real world" nonsense that I have given up trying to under-stand. In my mind, it's not justifiable. Yes, these kids have atrocious home lives, but TV is not something that they are deprived of outside of school. Everybody has a TV. Everybody watches it all the time at home, and I don't see the point in them watching it at school, too.

It's not only in the class that problems surface. Patti also tried a really ditzy idea that embarrassed the whole school. She decided that her class should have a yard sale. She justified it in a staff meeting by saying they'd be learning how to make change and how to price items. It was a disaster because the kids could not behave, and some of the customers from the general public who stopped by were appalled at the kid's behavior. I think, though, that Patti has a very deep need to be liked by her kids. It seems more important to her than being liked or respected by any of us. She is afraid to discipline. She is afraid to structure the class for fear that the kids won't like her.

Al: Do the kids like Patti?

Amy: Well, she keeps the kids for two years. She had these kids as fifth graders and now as sixth graders. There are significant problems. The class does not use general education textbooks, so I don't know how she thinks they'll ever get back into the mainstream class. She uses lots of photocopied sheets—almost all the time. I use worksheets every now and again, but I don't rely on them exclusively. That's what I think happens in there. Some of her kids—including some of her worst behavior problems—often come over to my class and say "I hope we have you next year"!! I think they saw and liked the structure in my class—desks in a row, teacher's desk, assistant's desk, everybody in their seat doing work—that's what they would see most of the time. To them, that represents what school is, what school should be. That's what they see on TV, for heaven's sake.

Al: So, this class is such a contrast that even the kids notice?

Amy: The kids notice.

Al: Now, do you get any feedback from anyone else, any of your colleagues, that tells you there is a difference?

Amy: Yes. Because other people notice. Other people see that the behavior of Patti's class is what one stereotypically expects of kids with behavioral problems. Even Sara, the school psychologist sees it. She and I have gotten to be pretty good colleagues. Sara's caseload is exclusively made up of kids from my class and Patti's class. Sara constantly reminds me that these kids thrive on the structure that I provide for them. Sara firmly believes that most of my kids don't look or act behaviorally disturbed. Sara's also quite open about how Patti's kids don't do as well because of the lack of structure.

Al: What about the administrators? The principal, the district coordinators?

Amy: I think perhaps the principal and the assistant principal have seen the difference in how the classes are run and what is happening because they asked me very early this year what grade preference I had for next year.

Having to deal with Patti and the administrators is also problematic when placement decisions need to be made. This example is one of quite a few that have happened this year: One of the kids that was placed in my class, Rudy, is a sixth grader who was returning to us after discharge from a day treatment center. It soon became clear that the administration didn't want to put him in Patti's class because of all the behavior problems that happen regularly over there. I think the office knows more than what they let on, sometimes. The only other place to put Rudy was in my fifth grade class. It didn't make me happy, I can tell you! Initially, it didn't make Rudy happy either. When I pressed the point about the move, Jill, the assistant principal, flat out told me that it was because of the problems in Patti's classroom—the lack of structure, the inconsistency, the chaos that seems to be a way of life with Patti. On the other hand, for Rudy, the administration needed this child in a room, with a predictable, consistent structure. Now, unfortunately, he's doing wonderfully, and so I know I'll never get rid of him!! He's a sixth grader, but he'll be with me in fifth grade for the rest of the year!! Rudy's happy. He's thriving on what's there. He's thriving on the attention he's getting from me and from my aide. He's beginning to feel really good about school, I think. He shows up daily, which certainly hadn't been happening before he went to the day treatment center. I'm convinced a large part of the improvement comes from him knowing what's expected, that he's accepted, and that we like him. Why not come to a place six hours a day and feel pretty good about yourself?

Al: How supportive is the administration of what you do?

Amy: Ninety percent of the time, the principal and vice principals are really supportive, even although I have to remind them every year that I need their help! This year we have a new assistant principal in charge of all the discipline problems in the school. I had to remind him that you don't "talk" to these kids. For example one of my kids gave a general education teacher a lot of "lip service" and the teacher wrote a referral to the assistant principal. Well, nothing happened and pretty soon the kid was mouthing off, saying "See, I told you nothing would." I had to go to the assistant principal and say, "You know, what you're doing is setting a precedent that teaches these kids to think 'I can say what I want to anybody else and get away with it.' The kids won't do it to me because I'll *do* something. You can't let it slide. They don't operate on the 'Let's talk about it' level—there has to be consequence." So, he did. He called the kid back. He said "You can't do this," and the kid got two days in-school suspension. The administrators know that by the time I send the kid to the office that I've done everything that can be done: I've tried ten ways to contact the parents if they don't have a phone or if they don't return my calls. I have taken away recess. I have talked to the child. In all, it's time for their "office vacation."

Al: I think this gives me a solid background of how things are. Now, Amy, what is it that you need me to help you with?

Amy: Well, I just can't stand that upheaval next door any more. It's affecting all of us. I'm even having a hard time being civil to Patti on those few occasions I can't avoid her. I'm seriously considering a transfer. I'm fast getting to the point that if I don't do something, I might end up in a really nasty all-out confrontation. That won't do me any good, and there's a fair chance it'll blow things wide open, because I've been diligent about documenting every instance of incompetence I've witnessed or heard about. Perhaps it's time to turn it all over to Judy . . .

Frozen at the Precipice

Chief Protagonists
SHARON HILL, student teacher
MATT JOHNSON, Sharon's friend and a teacher
EILEEN SINGER, supervising teacher

Sharon Hill was nearing the end of her second field experience in the Glade County schools. Nestling in the forested hills of a midwestern state, Glade City is a small, dynamic city well known for its upper middle-class citizens, excellent public schools, and its central location to several much larger metropolitan areas. Sharon had not decided to become a teacher immediately after high school. After obtaining a degree in marketing, she had worked for several years as a sales associate for a large computer software company. She soon tired of the constant travel and high-pressure sales quotas. At the age of twenty-six, she returned to Central State University to pursue a degree in elementary education.

Central State is the state's flagship teacher-training institution with a strong national reputation. The faculty were nationally and internationally known teacher educators. The elementary education program covered five years of intensive coursework leading to a master's degree in education. Many students in the program reported feeling under pressure to complete their studies successfully, because if the master's degree was not awarded, no bachelor degree was awarded either.

Sharon was under even more pressure. She was not doing as well as she wanted or as was expected. Her academic work was above average, but actually working with students and teachers somehow left her frozen. In the last several weeks, she had distinct feelings of panic about how her student teaching would turn out. It seemed that no matter what she tried, things didn't improve.

In desperation, she called Matt Johnson, a friend since childhood and a successful educator.

Matt: Hello?

Sharon: Hey, Matt, hi! It's Sharon!

Matt: Hi, Sharon, I haven't heard from you in a while! How are things going?

Sharon: Well, that's why I called . . . . Do you have a few minutes for me to discuss some things with you?

Matt: Sure—fire away.

Sharon: Well, as you know, this is my second teaching field experience. Last semester I was at Bream Elementary, where I had a third grade class, and right now I'm at Valley View Elementary teaching a fifth grade class with Eileen Singer. This time I have twenty-three kids. I'm getting pretty despondent. Last semester my university supervisor didn't think I did too well, although I managed to pass the practicum. I don't quite remember what her evaluation said, but I just feel like everything isn't right.

I've wanted to be a teacher for so long, but I guess I'm doing a lot of things wrong. I'm very concerned I might fail this practicum, and you know what that means—goodbye to any hopes of getting a teaching degree.

Matt: What seems to be the biggest problem?

Sharon: Well, I would have to say I've never been in a job or a situation where I've had to make so many decisions so quickly throughout the whole day. I think part of it is because I'm a student teacher. Eileen seems to have every-thing planned out and the kids come to me and expect me to know what's going on, so I get a lot of questions that I don't know how to answer, and it's not only about the lesson content—I get incessant questions about class logistics that I haven't thought through. For example, what is the routine for where completed assignments are collected and stored? There are so many details to this job I can't believe it . . .

Matt: So you're getting confused by some tough teaching *and* organizational questions . . .

Sharon: Yes. I just seem to be way out of it because I'm teaching half of the subjects right now and Eileen is teaching the others. Naturally, the kids don't remember who is teaching what, so they sometimes ask me about Eileen's projects. I feel so dumb when this happens because I can't necessarily answer their questions or even key in to what they are talking about.

Matt: OK . . .

Sharon: I guess it's because I haven't thought through everything. I'm sure if I planned out everything, I would be able to answer their questions . . .

Matt: Well, why don't you do that?

Sharon: Because Eileen hasn't shared it all with me. It would take forever for her to remember all those things and then tell them to me. I guess I could just ask her when the kids ask me, but if she's not around, if she has to step out of the room or something, that's the time when everyone will come to me and ask me questions that I can't answer.

Matt: Give me an example . . .

Sharon: Well, several kids have assigned chores in the room, and if Eileen isn't there, I'm not sure whose responsibility it is. I'm just hesitant to go ahead and give them permission to do things. Today, they wanted to stay with me for their fifth period science class, which they have down the hall. I don't know why, but they just decided they wanted to stay with me. I wasn't sure if Mrs. Devers, their science teacher, wanted that. Now that I think about it, whether they went or not probably didn't matter . . . . I guess that with little things like that I'm not sure how consequential these things are.

Matt: It seems to me as if you're being really careful about setting something in motion that might come back to haunt you later.

Sharon: Right!!

Matt: Did anything similar come up last semester in the third grade class?

Sharon: Let me think . . . . Yes, I guess. I think I had trouble in the third grade class relating to the kids. I wasn't used to being around such small children, I guess. I had a really hard time communicating with them. My vocabulary was too sophisticated. I gave them concepts that were too abstract. I had to keep reminding myself that then, at the beginning of the school year, they were basically second graders.

In this classroom, it's a lot less restrictive than my previous practicum. The kids are a little more mature than the third graders who I was working with in the other classroom so we have a lot more rules and regulations and I have to be a lot more aware of those kinds of things than in the third grade classrooms last semester, so . . .

Matt: So how did you resolve working with the third graders?

Sharon: Well, I don't know if I ever did. I think I just kind of got through that practicum. I kept forgetting things. I remember teaching a lesson about writing a letter and I told them where to write the date and the return address and they had all kinds of trouble putting it on the upper right-hand corner . . .

Matt: They got it too close to the edge of the paper or too far away?

Sharon: Right. I should have made them fold their page in half and then use the fold as a guide. Just because I didn't do that one simple thing, they just had their addresses all over the place—I just couldn't believe how much guidance they needed for everything!

Matt: So how did you come up with the idea of folding the page in half?

Sharon: Oh, my supervising teacher suggested it. If I had sat and thought about it for two seconds I would have come up with that on my own. I guess I just didn't realize how much guidance they need for every little step. It's the same when I would tell them to raise their hands—they'll sit there with hands raised forever until I told them that they could put their hands down.

Matt: It sounds as if you were assuming too much.

Sharon: I guess . . .

Matt: What about managing behavior?

Sharon: Well, in the third grade class, there was a boy who was chronically misbehaved. He and I had zero rapport. It was really hard for me to deal with him, and he acted out very severely one day when the teacher was gone for about an hour and half.

Matt: What did he do?

Sharon: He kept interrupting the lesson. He wouldn't raise his hand, got out of his seat, threw pieces of paper at the wastebasket like he was taking basketball shots, and he finally started climbing over the furniture. By that time, I had lost control. He didn't listen to a word I said so I just let him do whatever he wanted, but that completely disrupted the whole class. It was a horrible,

horrible day. My supervising teacher had a system of behavior modification set up but it didn't work for me with this kid. He didn't take me seriously. I just didn't have the same kind of sureness or confidence that the classroom teacher had.

Matt: Well, was there anything in that third grade placement that was successful? Surely it couldn't have all been that bad . . . ?

Sharon: There was a math lesson where everything was fused together and harmonious.

Matt: What was different about that lesson?

Sharon: I'd have to attribute that to my planning. My planning was great. I had every detail thought through, and I had a lot of fun writing it up and thinking of the ideas to make it work. They loved it, and I had a lot of fun. It just all flowed really well. That's happened in this fifth grade a couple of times, again in math. I think I really enjoy teaching math because it's concrete—there's a right answer and there's a wrong answer.

Matt: You don't have to worry about folding pages, right?

Sharon: That's right. It was because I wrote out everything beforehand and I had it all very clear in my mind. That's one thing that I think interferes with my teaching pretty severely. If I don't understand the content exactly I have to keep referring to my notes so I can't just let my teaching flow. If I get a handle on things ahead of time, I'm freed up to look out there into the class and see what's going on. That doesn't always happen, though. Just today Eileen told me that I didn't see one girl in the back of the class cleaning out her desk. I didn't even notice because I was kind of fumbling around with my notes. I was really embarrassed about that.

Matt: There seem to be a lot of problems. What do you think is the most difficult one to solve?

Sharon: It's probably being second in command—I don't know the whole framework of how the classroom operates. I never figured it all out in the third grade placement. I was in there for seven weeks and I never got the whole picture because it wasn't mine. I didn't conceive it, so I didn't have all these little details in my mind. Also, that the kids behave differently with me than they do with the classroom teacher. They tend to act out more. I also worry that it's in my character to let them get away with more because I tend to be pretty lenient with them.

Matt: How are you going to resolve this?

Sharon: Well, I don't know. It's a big issue. I have a feeling I'm just going to have to kind of find my way through it when I have my own classroom, but that seemed to be a concern of my university supervisor and my third grade placement teacher last semester. They didn't think that I thought of myself as an authority figure—I don't—I've never been an authority figure in any situation so I think that's going to be the biggest adjustment for me.

Matt: Just how discouraged are you?

Sharon: Well, I've found it a little hard to feel 100 percent motivated all the time because I'm paying to do this—I'm paying to do this job and I'm not being paid for my work. I mean I know I'm supposed to be taking full advantage and just working hard right now but I don't think I am. The third grade was really very difficult—tons of kids with behavior problems, many who couldn't read, just everything all mixed together.

It's really scary to think about how important the teacher is to establishing the climate in the classroom. I find that a big responsibility because the kids are constantly watching me. You have to be motivated yourself to motivate your kids. I'm also worried about being able to maintain a real even keel and not letting on how scared I am. Your mind has to be on constantly. You can't shut it off. When I was in the business world, when I felt stressed out, I could put my head down on my desk for five minutes. When you're teaching you can't—that's a big responsibility.

Matt: Where have you turned for help, Sharon, aside from talking to me?

Sharon: Well, that's part of the problem, Matt. I really think nobody can help . . .

Jessica's Wrath

Chief Protagonists
JESSICA OWENS, teacher
MIKE OLSEN, principal

Jessica Owens had worked as a teacher at Grove Hill High School for the past three years. Her specialty was working with students with emotional and behavioral problems. Grove Hill's principal, Mike Olsen, knew her to be patient, cooperative, and energetic. As far as Mike knew, any problems that Jessica encountered were dealt with effectively and without the need for his intervention. Late in the winter, Mike was surprised when Jessica suddenly appeared at his office door in the middle of the school day:

Mike: Oh, hi, Jessica, how are you? I've been so busy that I haven't had a chance to see any teachers lately.

Jessica: Well, I've just about had enough of all this, Mike, and I need to see you right after school today!

 Mike was puzzled. This was not the Jessica he had come to know.

Mike: Sure, Jessica, I can see you at 3:30. Is there anything I need to know before you get here?

Jessica: No—just be here at 3:30.

Jessica left as swiftly as she had appeared. Promptly at 3:30, Jessica collapsed into the chair across from Mike's desk.

Mike: Jessica, I was quite concerned about what happened this morning. What on earth is wrong?

Jessica: I've just had enough, Mike, and this can't go on any longer. I'm ready to resign.

Mike: Resign? I didn't know you had anything that serious going on to be thinking about . . .

Jessica: Well, I have, and, quite frankly, I don't expect you to fix it. I just want you to know about this nonsense so if I quit, it'll make sense.

Mike resisted the urge to tell Jessica that she was probably overreacting. He made a conscious effort to settle back in his chair. He decided to listen.

Mike: Tell me what's going on, Jessica, we need to get to the bottom of whatever is upsetting you so.

Jessica: Well, Mike, you know I don't cause trouble around here. I come to work, I do my job, I go home. That's it. I don't get into all the juvenile gossip of the faculty lounge, I keep my nose out of all the puerile shenanigans that seem to keep so many people on this staff motivated, and I work harder than most . . .

Mike: That's pretty much the way I see you, Jessica. I think you're an asset to our school and our kids. Tell me a little more—try to be as specific as you can.

Jessica: It's difficult to know where to begin. For a start, I'm sick and tired of just about all the teachers in charge of the enrichment activities. You'd think that people involved in teaching art, music, life skills, and "things aesthetic" would have a sense of awareness that would help them deal with problem kids. Apparently not!! They haven't a clue about what to do with my kids, and, as far as I can tell, they don't seem to be willing to learn. It's truly pathetic.

They continually complain: "Jody's manners are atrocious," "Gene's the rudest boy I've ever met," "Alan's temper will get him in jail before long, you wait and see." Please—what do these people expect? I'll bet they've never looked into the many reasons *why* some of these kids are the way they are—they've certainly never asked me! They seem to have an extremely hard time with discipline, and what really angers me is that they still seem to think that when one of my kids has a problem in their classes, *it's my fault!!* Now,

Mike, just in case you think I'm taking this too personally, you need to know that three weeks ago Jean Ivey in the library, Matt Solon in music, and Andrea Watts in physical education asked to meet with me about my kids' behavior in their class. When I asked them what the meeting was about, all they would say was: "We need to talk to you about your kids' behavior in our classes." I didn't know what to expect!

Mike: What happened?

Jessica: Well, their bottom line was that they could not possibly teach my students in their classes. Gee, so much for being competent professionals! It's the same old complaints about the same old things every year. Apparently, they had also spoken to Sally in their departmental meeting prior to meeting with me. Sally, as usual, played her head-of-department-role to the hilt and reminded them that if my kids got too disruptive, they should be sent back to my classroom for the rest of the period. I think it's terribly unfair that these teachers have the support from Sally to send these kids back to me when they act out—what happens with other teachers' kids when they act out? Do they get sent anywhere? Well, of course they don't!! I don't see why I should end up babysitting kids because other teachers can't control them. They're so concerned that my kids will disrupt their classes that they think nothing of just sending them back to me. This means no planning period for me and another day without a break! To make a long story short, nothing was accomplished in the meeting aside from the general whine session about my kids. I tried to offer solutions, make suggestions, be supportive, but nothing helped. They were simply determined to dump it all on me.

Mike: OK . . .

Jessica: Speaking of the enrichment activity teachers, I'm completely exasperated with Meryl Valli, the new art teacher. She sent me a pretty angry note demanding some solution for controlling one of my female juniors. It always amazes me that these teachers come to me for solution *before* they try anything. What did she learn in college? It seems to me that behavior management is a basic teaching skill.

Mike: So you . . .

Jessica: It's not only the enrichment activity teachers. I've about had it with Shelli Simpson, the school psychologist. Last year she instituted lunch with me once a week. I thought it was a waste of time. She insisted on doing it again this year. While she was droning on in her characteristic psychobabble, my aide was having a terrible time trying to control the kids at lunch. My lunch was wasted and the kids were awful. I'm not going to do it again—Shelli can find some other trivial activity to justify her inflated salary! Let me give you another example. Shelli approached me a while ago about meeting with her next week to set up times for her to see my kids on a regular basis. What a joke! Shelli's spent an eternity getting ready to get ready, and is still "working on her schedule!" I suggested she let me know when she'd gotten that challenging task done and then we'd talk about trying to help kids!

Shelli's equally inept in dealing with parents. I went with her to visit a sophomore's mother. The mother had called in response to our inquiries about rumors about the sophomore's unflattering activity after a community youth dance. Apparently the kid had gotten drunk and then gotten arrested for being drunk in public and public indecency. Shelli decided that she wanted to run the meeting but got completely sidetracked by mom. Shelli was so befuddled that she did not ask about the rumors, which was why we had set up the meeting in the first place! I'm sorry, but it's probably clear I have little use for school psychologists. I haven't found one yet who can truly justify their existence on the payroll. Shelli certainly lives up to my belief.

Mike: Well, what did . . .

Jessica: It's not only the enrichment activity teachers and the school psychologists. Last Thursday I sent one of my students to the office on a discipline referral. I thought Fran was a better assistant principal than what she turned out to be. Fran decided to keep my student in the office the remainder of the day. I sent the kid's classwork to the office and explained to Fran that I thought the student should not be allowed back in class until her mother came in for a conference. On Friday morning, the student came to class smiling and telling everyone that she was back and nothing had happened to her in the office! I promptly went to find Fran to find out why the student had returned to class. I explained to Fran that she had just succeeded in undermining me by showing the student and the rest of the class that discipline referrals seem to have no consequences. Fran changed her tune and decided to put the student in ISS (in-school suspension) for the remainder of Friday. I feel very strongly, Mike, that unless I use up precious energy pressing these issues I get no backup from the office.

Mike: Well, let me . . .

Jessica: I'm really steamed at the special education referral process as well. I got a note Tuesday from Fran that I would be getting a new student. That's fine. However, when I read the student's cumulative file, it was clear that she was mentally retarded and *not* emotionally or behaviorally disordered! When I questioned Fran as to why this kid was being placed in my class, she told me that all MR classes were full, and my room was the only class with space. At this point *I LOST IT!!!* I couldn't believe it—the more I questioned the decision, the more Fran tried to justify her decision. It was truly silly. She didn't have a leg to stand on! I was furious for the rest of the day. Fran later asked me when I wanted the student to turn up in my class. I asked her what she was talking about, and she said that *I* would be the one to inform the family when the child should come to school! I let her know that this was the first I had heard of this stupid policy.

Mike: So what shall we . . .

Jessica: There's more. I have a really difficult tenth grader—Daneen Jones. Her mom is a disaster—she's on the streets again and "using." Daneen hasn't been to school in a while. During spring break Daneen became so uncontrollable that she ended up in county juvenile detention. Finally, Shelli set up a meeting of all Daneen's support people so that "everyone could get feedback on what everyone else was doing" with Daneen and how we should proceed. The health nurse was there, as was Daneen's social worker, Daneen's mother, me, Shelli, another psychologist who had dealt with Daneen at her previous school, the juvenile system liaison, and another special education services person. What bothered me the most was the amount of bull that these social services people provide as they dance around the real issues. When Shelli asked if anyone had talked to Daneen about birth control (both Shelli and I are almost sure that she's sexually active), the nurse and the social worker disagreed with us, saying that they had asked Daneen this very question and Daneen had vehemently denied it! Right!! Daneen is one of the most manipulative kids I've met, and her truth-telling ability is, shall we say, "impaired." I decided to cut right across the bull and questioned whether Daneen was telling the truth. I suddenly became the meeting "heavy," but it seems to me I was the only one facing the truth.

   I've had it, Mike. Enough is enough. Either they and you want me here to do the job, or not. It's time for everyone to fish or cut bait . . .

Caught in the Middle

Chief Protagonists
LOUISE JONES, teacher
JULIA BELL, Louise's aide
SHAUN HALEY, principal
LEANN GROSSLEY, substitute teacher

Louise Jones's sixth grade class seemed to take longer than usual to come in and settle down after their morning break. With the warm sunny weather and the playground right outside the classroom window, they were reluctant to resume the joys of math.

This was my second year as a substitute teacher in the Geneva City school system. Being a substitute teacher gave me valuable learning experiences in a wide variety of classes and schools while I attended East State University where I was working on my master's degree in education. I had been in the system long enough that most of the principals knew me by name and often called me when a teacher or aide was absent.

As the children filed in, I recalled the first time that I had worked with this class three weeks earlier. Shaun Haley, the principal of Church Street Elementary, had called to get me to fill in for Julia Bell, Louise's classroom aide. I remembered leaving Louise's class that day with a renewed excitement about my chosen profession. When Shaun called again, this time to substitute for Louise, I looked forward to working with the sixth graders again. I recalled that while the class was not that large—eighteen students—they were a lively bunch whose enthusiasm knew no bounds. They were curious, funny, and motivated.

On this second visit, I arrived a little early to get the "feel" of the classroom. I had learned long ago that most teachers who knew they would be absent would leave instructions and materials in plain view on their desks. I checked Louise's desk. Sure enough, there were several pages of detailed notes and directions. As I carefully read Louise's messages, I made a mental note of what I needed to do and jotted down several reminders on a pad. Deep in concentration, I became somewhat puzzled by several inserts in the morning activities where Louise had added post-it notes all saying the same thing: "Check with Julia for details of what to do here." I felt a little uncomfortable with these mysterious directives—eleven in all. I liked to know *exactly* the way the morning would go. I had had enough unpleasant experiences desperately trying to improvise with children to whom I was a relative stranger!!

Activity in the hallways increased, and I made a quick trip to the staff lounge for a fresh cup of coffee before the day began. On the way, I pondered my situation: I was acutely aware that the introduction of a substitute teacher was, at best, unsettling for the students, who almost always perceived that I was "not their real teacher." I had always managed to overcome these perceptions by being well prepared by the start of the day. At least I had worked with this class once before. Louise's little notes meant that I couldn't possibly be as prepared as I wanted to be. Another nagging thought arose: was I to be the aide to Julia or a replacement teacher for Louise, with Julia acting as my aide? By the time I returned to the classroom, Julia was already there.

Louise had told me that Julia was a competent aide. She had had no prior teacher training except an in-service that the city schools required of all aides working in elementary classrooms. She had been an aide since the in-service several months earlier. A rather large, imposing figure, Julia's long, straggly hair framed her pale face. She wore very thick, smudged spectacles that enlarged her dark brown eyes. She seemed to move quite slowly but with great deliberation. My initial impression was that she appeared very cautious and very tentative.

Me: Hi, I'm Leann Grossley. Shaun Haley asked me to substitute for Louise. You must be Julia Bell?

Julia: Good morning, Leann. Nice to meet you . . .

Me: I've already looked over Louise's instructions, so . . .

Julia: Yes, I know. I'll get things started as soon as the bell rings. In the meantime, would you mind checking over these math sheets? The answer key is right here.

Julia, it appeared, liked to be in charge, and I didn't feel like arguing. I moved to Louise's desk and began grading the sheets.

Class began at 8:00 sharp. The tardy bell rang at 8:05 and was followed by a series of school announcements over the public address system. A bell signalling the beginning of the academic day rang at 8:10. Julia's teaching style became quickly apparent. She delivered instructions in a booming voice, her ample arms flailing the air to emphasize her point. Her directions were constantly punctured by admonitions to various students who were not complying with her wishes:

Julia: Now, we're going to begin—Phil, get a move on!! We're going to begin our math—Mary, what's the matter with you? Can't you sit still even for a few minutes? Let's begin by opening our math books to page—Manuel, are you quite finished with your little private conversation now? Thank you *so* much. Turn to page 231. Quickly now!!

After several more minutes, Julia finally succeeded in getting the class focused. Several students looked somewhat anxious. It was clear that Julia was revelling in her role of "teacher for a day." The math lesson swiftly became a macabre game of Julia doing her level best to catch students in wrong answers. When she did, her punishment was a diatribe that left the offending student mortified:

Julia: Conchita, what's the answer to number seven?

Conchita: Thirteen . . . um, no, twelve, . . . wait . . .

Julia: Can't you make up your mind? If you'd been listening to what we did in class yesterday, you'd know! Are you sure you're supposed to be in this class? Doesn't seem like you should be from what you're saying—that's the easiest math problem in the whole exercise!!

Conchita turned bright red and remained silent for the rest of the lesson. Julia was relentless, but not everyone got the same treatment.

Julia: Jonathan, number eight.

Jonathan: Thirty-seven.

Julia: Exactly! Jonathan, it's so *nice* to have people in this class who have brains—and use them. Why don't you try number nine as well?

Jonathan: Sixteen.

Julia: Of course! Conchita, are you getting the picture now?

I felt so sorry for Conchita and several others who failed to escape Julia's wrath, and who never had a chance, it seemed, to redeem themselves. As the unswerving barrage continued, I became increasingly angry. What had children like Conchita done to deserve this? It was clear that they didn't understand the work, but Julia's little game did not involve teaching. Julia changed her focus to Chris, a reedy, sandy-haired boy who, it seemed to me, wore a permanently baffled look. I had noticed that look the last time I had worked with the class. I also remembered that Chris appeared to be one of the weakest students in the class. When Julia called his name, I knew things would go from bad to worse.

Julia: Chris, number fifteen, now!

Chris was visibly startled. His brow deeply furrowed, he stared at his book. The room was absolutely silent. By this point, nobody was looking up from their books. It seemed that the other students were simply glad that Chris had been chosen and not themselves. Their bowed heads betrayed their wish to hide as much as was possible while sitting in a desk facing Julia's stony gaze. Chris began to squirm in his seat, his left leg trembling slightly.

Chris: Number fifteen?

Chris was playing for time, hoping to delay the inevitable.

Julia: What's the matter with you? Are you deaf? If you're deaf, you shouldn't be in here!! Deaf people don't belong here—we move too fast! Chris, are you *really* deaf, or as *usual,* just not paying attention? You should, you know, your grades are the worst in this class!!

Chris: I'm sorry, I thought you said . . .

Julia: Number *fifteen.* What's the answer?

Chris: Twenty-three?

Julia: Twenty-three? How on earth did you get twenty-three? Are you on the planet here with us? Twenty-three? *Twenty-three? Puhlease!!*

Chris looked like a stunned animal. As Julia turned her gaze to another victim, I couldn't stand it any more. I got up and went over to Chris's desk. As I crouched down beside him to help him find his place, Julia turned on me.

Julia: Ms. Grossley, I'd appreciate your waiting to help Chris until I've finished the exercise. He'd do a lot better if he'd listen and get his homework done. It's really not your problem.

Against my better judgment, I retreated to my seat, just as humiliated as some of the students had been. I felt my cheeks getting hot, and my knuckles were white in my clenched fists. Several students, risking Julia's unwanted attention, looked sympathetically in my direction. By the time the midmorning break arrived, I was more than ready to escape the oppressive atmosphere.

The children straggled reluctantly in from their break. Julia positioned herself at the classroom door, and, as usual, was yelling at the kids.

Julia: Move it, we don't have all day you know. Josh, sit down *NOW!!* Felicity, what's your problem? Do you need me to come over there and solve it for you? You'll be really sorry!! If you people won't settle down, I'll begin writing down names!! You know what that means—name down, then the office!! I'll bet you don't want that to happen!!

Everyone quickly settled down and looked at Julia. Everyone, that is, except Chris, who had his head down on his desk.

Julia: Chris, get your head up this minute!! What do you think this is—your bedroom?

Chris didn't respond. But Jonathan did.

Jonathan: Ms. Bell, I think Chris is sick. I think he threw up on the playground . . .

Julia: Nonsense—he was fine before the break, he should be fine now. Chris—up, *NOW!!*

Chris didn't respond. Julia was furious.

Julia: Get your head up *NOW*, get with the program, or you can get out and go to the office!

Chris had had enough. Looking up for the first time since entering the class, he gave as good as he had gotten.

Chris: I will do anything I want to and *YOU* can't make me do anything!

Julia: I *CAN* send you to the office!

Chris: SO?

The entire class was watching, blow by blow. Julia was trembling as she walked over to Chris's desk.

Julia: How *DARE YOU???*

Without warning, Julia turned to me. She turned so swiftly that I jumped.

Julia: It's either Chris leaves or me. *YOU* take him to the office and write the referral when you get there.

Reluctantly, I walked to the door, opened it, and waited for Chris to join me. Slowly, he pulled himself up out of his seat, tears streaming down his cheeks. Every pair of eyes tracked us through the door on our way to the office.

There was so much I wanted to say to Chris. I wanted to tell him that it wasn't all his fault. Julia had been awful. It had all happened so fast. One minute we were coming in from break, and the next minute there was this ugly confrontation.

There I was caught between Julia and Chris. I very much wanted to side with Chris, and yet, what example would I be setting for Chris or the other students by taking one side against the other? After all, Julia worked with these students every day and Louise had given no hint to what I had just witnessed. As we slowly walked to the office, I agonized over what Chris must have been feeling.

I filled out the referral to Shaun with a heavy heart. Chris, seated in the office, looked so dejected. He was pale, sweaty, and breathing rapidly. I sent him to the nurse.

As I turned to leave, I made a decision. Returning to the office counter, I attached a note to the referral:

Mr. Haley:
I really must talk to you about this referral. If you don't get this before I leave at the end of the day, please give me a call at home.

Teaching for me would never be the same.

Thematic Index

General Index

271